# COMPETITION CAR
# COMPOSITES

*Other books by this author:*

COMPETITION CAR DOWNFORCE
COMPETITION CAR PREPARATION
COMPETITION CAR DATA LOGGING

# COMPETITION CAR
# COMPOSITES
## A PRACTICAL HANDBOOK

## Simon McBeath
### Foreword by Brian O'Rourke

**Haynes Publishing**

First published February 2000
Reprinted December 2002 and April 2004

A catalogue record for this book is available from the British Library

Published by Haynes Publishing,
Sparkford, Yeovil, Somerset BA22 7JJ, UK

Tel: 01963 442030 Fax: 01963 440001
Int. tel: +44 1963 442030 Fax: +44 1963 440001

E-mail: sales@haynes.co.uk
Web site: www.haynes.co.uk

ISBN 1 85960 624 5

Library of Congress catalog card no. 99-75576

Haynes North America, Inc.
861 Lawrence Drive, Newbury Park, California 91320, USA

Designed and typeset by G&M, Raunds, Northamptonshire
Printed and bound in Great Britain by J.H. Haynes & Co. Ltd, Sparkford

**Jurisdictions which have strict emission control laws may consider any modification to a vehicle to be an infringement of those laws. You are advised to check with the appropriate body or authority whether your proposed modification complies fully with the law. The publishers accept no liability in this regard.**

**While every effort is taken to ensure the accuracy of the information given in this book, no liability can be accepted by the author or publishers for any loss, damage or injury caused by misuse of, errors in, or omissions from, the information given.**

# Contents

# Foreword

## by Brian O'Rourke,
## Chief Composites Engineer,
## Williams Grand Prix Engineering Ltd

MY FIRST THOUGHTS, when I learnt that Simon McBeath was putting together a book on the subject of composite materials and their application to practical racing car production, were that, most immediately, he was extremely brave to tackle such a difficult subject; and, more importantly, that if he succeeded, there would most definitely be a ready market for it.

I first became interested in structural composites through my job as a stress engineer in the aerospace industry in the mid-1970s, and very soon found that, whilst the fundamentals of the manufacturing process were easy to pick up, the number of books available to help me understand their behaviour amounted to one. Whilst the introductory five pages provided an appetite-whetting explanation of the basics, page six made me wish that I had studied Greek rather than engineering, and 50 per cent of the remaining pages were liberally coated with matrix algebra. Though my education had equipped me to cope with this, it was sometimes an effort to keep uppermost in my mind what exactly a design engineer was wanting to achieve by using these materials; they were, after all, only sophisticated rags and glue.

Since then I have collected numerous books on the subject of composites and have found – with the exception of the chapters dealing with laminate analysis, which look suspiciously like those in the original book (the laws of physics do not change, I suppose) – that there has been a steady improvement in the presentation of information, so that a professional engineer with a broad mind can now find his or her way into the subject with reasonable confidence. Definitions, however, are still not usually put across in a conversational manner – for example, Q: What is a composite? A: 'A macroscopic combination of two or more materials having a recognisable interface between them…' Whilst those working with composites on a Formula 1 car should be expected to manage at this level, quite how someone approaching the subject from a 'hands-on' direction, and without an engineering background, would fare is not obvious to me.

Somehow, Simon McBeath has managed to make this step, and to the point where his knowledge of the subject is extensive. More remarkable still is that he has also been able to write this book, which sets out the whole subject in a thoroughly readable form so that others will understand it too. This, in my opinion, makes *Competition Car Composites* unique. It will prove invaluable not only to those actively involved in motorsport, who wish to be more adventurous (and he gives you fair warning when you are heading into potentially risky areas) in their own car construction, but also to those who have discovered composite materials and want to understand the subject for its own sake.

# Author's preface

THE WORD 'COMPOSITE' seems to mean different things to different people, but a useful definition could be: 'made up of two or more parts or elements, and having better mechanical properties than the individual constituents'. Composites are not new – ancient civilisations made straw and clay bricks, wattle and daub walls, and linen and plaster mummy cases. The common factor is the combination of materials – a matrix and a reinforcement – to produce a composite with properties better than those of its components.

There is a general tendency within motorsport to use the term 'composite' to refer only to those components utilising carbon or aramid fibres. However, for the purposes of this book it is going to be interpreted as indicating all such strengthened materials as are used in motorsport, from good old glass fibre reinforced plastic (GFRP) through to the increasingly pervasive carbon fibre reinforced plastic (CFRP), as well as all the so-called 'sandwich structures' in which each can be employed.

There are two reasons for adopting this wider definition. Firstly, GFRP is a composite material, being composed of two primary elements; and secondly, in order to be able to take advantage of the more 'advanced' materials using some of the methods described, it will be necessary to start off with GFRP techniques before progressing to more sophisticated materials and associated techniques.

The primary purpose of this book is to provide a practical guide on composite materials and techniques that can be exploited by the 'do it yourself' competitor, preparer or constructor in a home workshop, without involving them in the purchase of expensive plant or equipment. Covering everything from basic 'wet lay-up' GFRP through to elevated temperature cure 'pre-preg' carbon fibre, it will facilitate the manufacture of such components as body panels, spoilers, aerofoils, ducting, and dashboards.

# Acknowledgements

SPECIAL THANKS MUST go to Vic Claydon for his creative input, as well as for checking my efforts and keeping me on my toes during the writing of this book; and to Brian O'Rourke for taking the time out of a hectic schedule to write the Foreword.

My thanks also go to the following: Martin Armstrong, Structural Polymer Systems; Helen Belcher, Instron; Cellbond Composites Ltd; John Damon, GKN Westland Helicopters; Colin Evans, Amber Composites Ltd; Hexel Composites; David Hudson, Mitsubishi Ralliart Europe; Penske Cars Ltd; Dell Quigley, DJ Racecars; Keith Read, MIRA; Phil Sharp, DPS Composites; Eric Taylor, Carr Reinforcements; Martin Taylor-Wilde, Multi-Sport Composites; Chris Tucker and Christine Riddle, Scott Bader Co Ltd; and Joan Villadelprat, Benetton Formula Ltd.

I am grateful, too, to the many fellow enthusiasts, competitors and constructors to whom I've chatted over the years regarding composites on competition cars; and especially the ones who bought components from me – there were times when I may not have been able to eat without you.

And, as always, to Tracey, for ceaseless encouragement, support and constructive criticism.

# Chapter 1

# Materials

## Introduction

Materials in fibrous form are known to have some of the best mechanical properties of all available structural materials; yet their ability to cope on their own with bending and compression loads is very low. However, by embedding them in a matrix, such as a cured resin, it is possible to take full advantage of the outstanding strength and stiffness that become available. This is the world of fibre reinforced plastics, or FRPs.

FRPs have been widely adopted in the motorsport industry for various reasons, but perhaps first and foremost because they can be moulded into a virtually limitless range of shapes relatively easily. Complex bodywork curvature that previously required the well-honed skills of a master metalworker can be achieved more readily, at less cost, and – in the early days at least – with less specialised equipment. That's not to denigrate the expertise of the moulders, trimmers and, especially, the highly skilled pattern makers responsible for creating the shapes which are to be moulded from, since – as we shall see later – this is the most important part of the process. But once a mould has been made from the master pattern, it is then easier to produce numerous identical replicas than it was to manufacture the original. And whilst the moulding techniques do not lend themselves to mass production, being fairly labour intensive, the so called 'tooling costs' (that is, the cost of making

the patterns and the moulds in the first place) are quite low, and make small volume production commercially viable. (Compare this to injection moulding, where tooling costs are very high and unit costs very low, rendering it more suitable to the mass production of certain plastic components in some applications, such as those found in and on a production car.) Fibre reinforced plastic moulding methods therefore lend themselves ideally to motorsport, where the quantities needed of individual components are generally small, and where designs, and hence tooling requirements, change frequently.

The basis for a fibre reinforced plastic (FRP) composite material is, as the term suggests, a mass of reinforcing fibres combined with a 'plastic' resin matrix, which binds and holds them. The properties of the resulting material depend on the properties of the fibre, the properties of the resin, and the manner in which the two are combined. The physical processes involved in FRP moulding are not particularly complex (even if the chemical ones are), but there is a very real and exciting magic about the application of a liquid resin mixture to a textile fabric which, once the resin matrix has 'cured', produces a strong, stiff and durable component. This in part is what makes the whole subject so fascinating. There is still, too, despite what some people might have you believe, an element of the black arts about making composite components and structures, and the phrase 'empirical design methods' still gets employed, even by Formula 1 car designers when discussing subjects like chassis construction.

In order to put a clearer perspective on the more practical subsequent chapters, this first chapter will look at the background of the materials involved. There's quite a bit to digest here, but it's arranged into sections in such a way that the aspects of most interest to a reader should be easy to find. So let's start off by looking at the various fibre reinforcements that can be used and the fabrics made from them, and then go on to examine the resins that hold them together. Using this approach will help to highlight the different mechanical properties of the materials that can be exploited, and enable us to begin to categorise composites according to their suitability in various applications. We'll begin where fibre reinforcement on competition cars began – with glass fibre.

## Reinforcing fibres
### Glass fibre
Most people reading this book will be familiar with glass fibre reinforced plastic, otherwise known as GFRP, or just glass fibre (or fibreglass). This material has been around for years, since just after the end of the Second World War, in fact, when the builders of navy vessels started to take advantage of its properties. It wasn't long before it found its way into the automotive industry, and then the motorsport industry discovered it to be eminently suitable for making bodywork, being pretty simple to use and relatively inexpensive. Famous American constructor and team owner Jim Hall even built the chassis of one of his Chaparral series of sports racing cars out of GFRP during the 1960s, though he reverted to aluminium thereafter. Glass fibre's main use in motorsport is still in the construction of bodywork, its longevity in this application demonstrating just how useful it is, many components even from professional manufacturers still being made from GFRP. Its advantages, along with its cheapness, result from its useful strength to weight ratio and ready availability. Even if you've never made anything out of GFRP yourself, you will almost certainly have come across something made

*'Chopped strand mat' glass fibre fabric.*

from it, and possibly even carried out some repairs to it!

In its everyday bulk form, glass would not immediately come to mind as a useful material for making competition car components. It breaks all too easily, and does so because it suffers from random surface flaws which, when a piece of glass is stressed, propagate through the material very easily, so that the glass cracks and breaks. But when the mineral ingredients to make glass are melted down at around 1600°C, then drawn through tiny holes whilst cooling, to transform them into small diameter filaments (5 to 25 microns, or about 0.0002 to 0.001 inches), though there may still be the same number of surface flaws in a given mass of the material the proportion of the fibres thus affected is small, which means that most of the fibres remain very strong. So in a bundle of fibres, the actual strength exhibited is much closer to the theoretical 'flawless' material's strength. Consequently, bundles of glass fibres possess good stiffness and appreciable tensile strength – that is, resistance to breaking when subjected to tension along their own length.

These properties allow the fibres to be produced in long filaments and wound onto reels. From here the next step is either to produce glass fibre yarns, which are bundles of close, twisted filaments; or glass fibre rovings, which are loose bundles of filaments. Yarns and rovings are classified according to their weight. In metric terms, yarns have what is called a 'tex' value, which is the weight in grams of 1,000 metres of yarn. In imperial terms they have a 'denier' value instead, consisting of the weight in pounds of 10,000 yards. Glass yarns are generally in the range 5 to 400 tex, while rovings are in the range 300 to 4,800 tex. The next stage in the process is for the yarns or rovings to be processed into one or other form of fabric, as we shall see later on in this chapter.

Glass fibre comes basically in four fibre types: E, R, S and T. E-glass, made from alumina borosilicate, is by far the most commonly used, and, not coincidentally, the cheapest. But it also has the lowest mechanical properties. Nevertheless, it does produce GFRP laminates with good stiffness and strength, and is perfectly satisfactory in a lot of applications. S-glass was originally produced for aerospace and military applications. Chemically it has a higher silica content and no boron, and is a lot more expensive than E-glass. The commercial grade, actually called S2 but often referred to simply as S-glass, is made with fibre diameters 50 per cent smaller than E-glass, which furnishes them with more intrinsic strength (as a result of a lower proportion of flaws), and also increases the surface area available for bonding to the resin matrix, giving a stronger laminate. S-glass is also more water resistant, though this tends to be of more interest to boat builders than competition car constructors. R-glass is chemically and mechanically the same as S-glass, but is made in Europe rather than the USA, whilst T-glass is a Japanese-made equivalent.

### Aramid fibre

Aramid fibres – or aromatic polyamide fibres to be more precise – are related to nylon, but by virtue of their slightly different chemical composition, they possess different, and quite extraordinary physical and mechanical properties. Better known by their trade names of Twaron and, most widely available, Kevlar, aramids first became available in around 1972, being used initially to replace the steel wires in commercial tyres. Versions of aramid are used in so-called ballistic clothing and body armour because of the material's very high impact and penetration resistance. Produced by drawing filaments direct from a chemical brew, its full chemical name is polyparaphenylene terephthalamide.

In the world of FRPs, the advantageous properties of aramids are their high tensile strength, reasonably high stiffness,

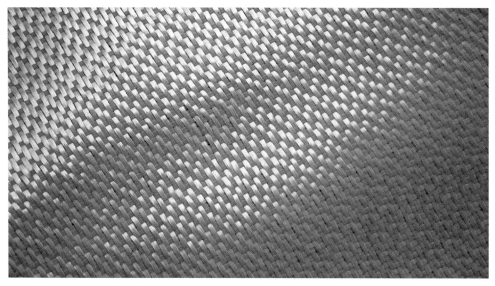

*Aramid cloth, known by the trade names of 'Kevlar' and 'Twaron'.*

relatively low density, and a toughness and resistance to abrasion that have to be seen to be believed. In fact these very properties contribute to one of aramid's few drawbacks – its unwillingness to be cut by anything other than special (expensive) shears. It *can* be cut – albeit not very neatly – with certain types of snips, but patience is needed.

The other principal disadvantage of aramid fibres is that they have low compressive strength, that is, strength in compression along the length of the fibre. This is thought to be caused by the make up of the fibres themselves from smaller, almost microscopic diameter fibrils, which tend to buckle under compressive loads. This has an unfortunate consequence in a laminate, creating a propensity for what is known as inter-laminar shear, or separation of the layers within a laminate when under compressive load. For this reason aramids tend not to be used where appreciable bending loads can occur. They are at their most effective in bodywork – where their low density and strength can create stronger and lighter panels than glass fibre – and in structural applications that make use of the material's high tensile strength and

impact resistance. They are frequently employed as a 'fail-safe' back-up to stiffer, more brittle fibres such as carbon fibre, which we will look at next. Aramids are typically made up into rovings in the range 20 to 800 tex.

### Carbon fibre

Carbon fibre was originally produced and used commercially in the late 19th century by Swan and Edison, to provide the filament material in the first electric light bulbs, but it wasn't until 1963 that structurally useful carbon fibres were produced at the Royal Aircraft Establishment at Farnborough in the United Kingdom. At that time it was an extremely expensive material, and you needed an aerospace programme research budget to even contemplate its use. However, it has been in regular use in motorsport since the early 1970s, and happily the cost has come down markedly. Carbon fibre is now within the budget of most motorsport competitors and constructors, especially if used in DIY projects such as those highlighted within this book.

Raw carbon fibres are produced by the controlled thermal treatment of organic (ie carbon containing) precursor fibres.

The most widespread precursor is poly-acrilonitrile, or PAN, though cellulose and fibres produced from coal tar pitch are also used. The heat treatment involves carbonisation of the precursor fibres to burn away non-carbonaceous matter, followed by the so-called 'graphitisation' of the fibres at temperatures in the range 2,600 to 3,000°C. This process, and the deliberate prevention of shrinkage, serves to arrange the carbon atoms into an ordered, graphitic crystalline structure along the length of the filaments. It is this aligned structure that gives the fibres their useful mechanical properties, namely high strength and stiffness.

In particular, carbon fibres have the highest specific stiffness (that is, stiffness relative to density) of any currently commercially available fibre, in addition to high tensile and compressive strength, and good resistance to corrosion and fatigue. There is a downside though – the impact strength of carbon fibres is lower than glass or aramid fibres, and the high modulus variants of carbon fibre are especially brittle in nature.

By varying the temperature of graphitisation the manufacturers of carbon fibre are able to modify the end-product's properties. So, fibres heated to around 2,600°C end up as 'standard modulus' fibres, also known as high strength or HS carbon, whilst those heated to 3,000°C are known as 'high modulus' or even 'ultra high modulus' fibres. An intermediate grade is known, unsurprisingly, as 'intermediate modulus'. The tensile modulus values (see definitions in the next section) for the different carbon fibre types are shown in the table below.

We'll break off now, if you'll pardon the pun, and consider some of the struc-tural terms and definitions that are likely to crop up now and again.

## Structural terms and definitions

You will often see terms like 'tensile modulus' and 'specific strength' cropping up in any discussion on structural materials, and although this book is not an engineering text by any stretch of the imagination, it will pay us to get a few definitions straight at this point. It won't take long, so stick with it, and then we'll all know what's being referred to. I promise I'll try to keep the gobbledegook to a minimum.

Firstly, the term 'strength' is not what it may seem. For example, the 'ultimate tensile strength' – the value of load at which a material fails – that you may see quoted for a material is, in fact, the ultimate tensile *stress* value, often denoted by the Greek letter $\sigma$ (sigma). Stress is defined as force or load divided by the area of a material over which that force or load is applied, and the units are thus in pounds per square inch or Newtons per square metre (also known as Pascals). This is sensible if you think about it, because in order to determine the ultimate tensile strength of a material, you need to test a real, three-dimensional piece of it, which therefore has a cross sectional area. And again it will be evident that a piece of the material twice as thick in one direction as another piece will require twice the load to break it, though the ultimate tensile stress value will be the same.

Tensile strength, or stress, describes a material's behaviour under tension. Thus, the tensile strength of a carbon fibre is its strength when being pulled along the axis of the fibre. Compressive strength is the exact opposite – that is, the behav-

## Table 1–1 The categories of carbon fibre

| Type of carbon fibre | Tensile modulus, GPa | Tensile modulus, psi |
| --- | --- | --- |
| Standard modulus, HS | 160 to 270 | 2.32 to $3.92 \times 10^{11}$ |
| Intermediate modulus (IM) | 270 to 325 | 3.92 to $4.71 \times 10^{11}$ |
| High modulus (HM) | 325 to 440 | 4.71 to $6.38 \times 10^{11}$ |
| Ultra high modulus (UHM) | over 440 | over $6.38 \times 10^{11}$ |

iour when the fibre is being compressed along the axis of the fibre.

Strain, usually denoted by the Greek letter $\epsilon$ (epsilon), is defined as the percentage elongation a material undergoes when subjected to load, and describes how that material deforms under a particular type of load. All materials deform when loaded, to some extent or other.

Dividing the stress by the strain values for a particular material produces a figure known as the 'Young's Modulus'. This value gives an idea of the material's 'elastic behaviour', or how much it deforms under a given load over a given area. It is also seen as a measure of a material's stiffness in bending, which after all is just a combination of tension and compression. By expressing the modulus as a function of tensile stress the tensile modulus can be determined, which was the parameter quoted in the table above for the different varieties of carbon fibres. It is now apparent that the high modulus fibres can be thought of as high stiffness fibres.

One other concept that it's worth covering here is incorporating the density values of each material to demonstrate their specific performance for a given weight. This allows a better comparison between different materials in some instances. For example, the specific tensile strength of a fibre is its tensile strength divided by its density, whilst the specific tensile modulus is the tensile modulus divided by the density.

Finally, a quality which is very important is 'toughness'. Not to be confused with strength, toughness is the measure of a material's resistance to fracture by crack propagation. We mentioned this quality in passing when discussing the propensity of glass (as opposed to glass fibres) to fracture easily – it offers very low resistance to the propagation of cracks when put under stress. The table below illustrates 'toughness' values for some well-known materials, which helps put this attribute into perspective. Notice that the units of toughness are in amounts of energy (kilojoules, or kJ) per square metre. This reflects the fact that toughness is assessed as the amount of work (energy) that has to be applied to propagate an area of crack.

### Table 1–2 Comparison of 'toughness' of some materials

| Material | Toughness, kJ/sq m |
| --- | --- |
| Pure copper | 1,000 |
| GFRP aligned with fibres | 100 |
| Epoxy | 0.3 |
| Polyester | 0.1 |
| Glass | 0.001–0.01 |

Clearly GFRP when stressed along the fibres is a tough material, whilst the resins that we shall talk about shortly are not at all tough – they are quite brittle in fact. The lack of conversion to imperial units here is only partly laziness, because the values are offered as comparative examples only.

### Fibre properties

We can now look at the more interesting structural properties of the main fibre types so far examined, and it's simplest if we chart and graph them so that they can be compared to each other more easily. The properties for which values have been obtained are: density (denoted by the Greek letter $\rho$, rho), tensile strength ($\sigma_{TS}$), specific tensile strength ($\sigma_{TS}/\rho$), tensile modulus (E) and specific tensile modulus ($E/\rho$). Because there's a range of values available for each fibre type, various references tend to quote different values. Therefore I have calculated simple averages from a number of references for the purpose of giving what might be termed 'typical values' (see Table 1–3). For clarity, units have been omitted from the table, but are kg/m$^3$ for density, GPa for both tensile strength and tensile modulus, and, very confusingly, MNmkg$^{-1}$ (mega Newton metres per kilogram) for specific tensile strength and specific tensile modulus. Don't worry about the units – they could just as easily

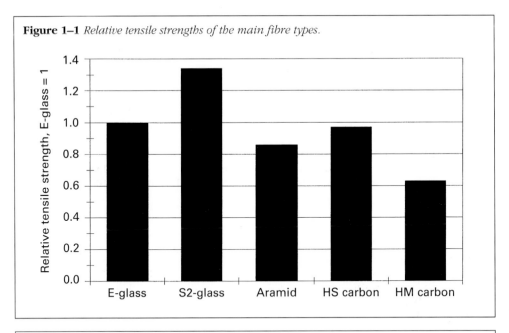

**Figure 1–1** *Relative tensile strengths of the main fibre types.*

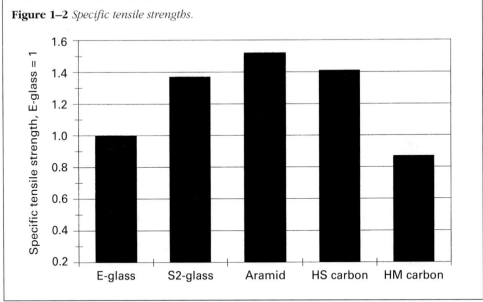

**Figure 1–2** *Specific tensile strengths.*

be mega falsehoods per general election. The real value for us is to compare them fibre for fibre, which is what the graphs in Figures 1–1 to 1–4 do, relative to E-glass.

A number of interesting points emerge from these figures. The first is that E-glass actually has quite a high tensile strength, while S2-glass has the highest tensile strength of all these fibres. However, when looked at on a strength per unit density basis, aramid's low density and moderate tensile strength bring it to the fore on a specific strength basis.

When it comes to stiffness, though, the modulus and specific modulus values illustrate, firstly, how Kevlar can be a

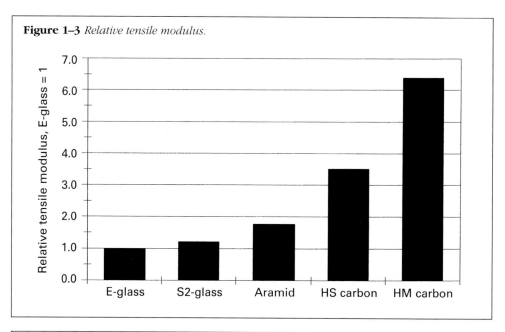

**Figure 1–3** *Relative tensile modulus.*

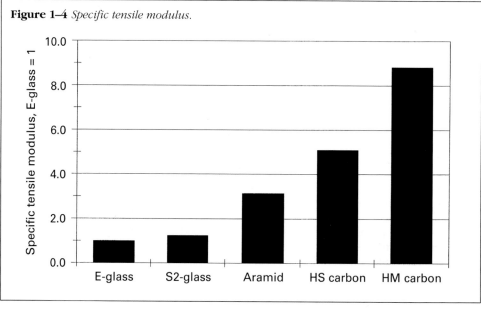

**Figure 1–4** *Specific tensile modulus.*

## Table 1–3 The principal fibres and some of their physical properties

| Property | E-glass | S2-glass | Aramid | HS carbon | HM carbon |
|---|---|---|---|---|---|
| Density | 2,550 | 2,490 | 1,440 | 1,760 | 1,850 |
| Tensile strength | 3.5 | 4.7 | 3.0 | 3.4 | 2.2 |
| Specific tensile strength | 1.37 | 1.88 | 2.08 | 1.93 | 1.19 |
| Tensile modulus | 72.0 | 87.0 | 127.0 | 252.5 | 460.0 |
| Specific tensile modulus | 28.2 | 34.9 | 88.2 | 143.5 | 248.6 |

major step up from glass, but secondly, how moving to carbon brings large gains in fibre stiffness, especially – as you would expect – the high modulus variety.

## Other fibres

There are other, less commonly used fibre types available, which will be dealt with only briefly here since they are not really practical for home workshop use in competition car components.

The first fibres employed in composites were natural. Jute and sisal were widely utilised, and during the Second World War, when it looked as if there might be a shortage of aluminium, a Spitfire aircraft fuselage was made from a composite called 'Gordon Aerolite', which consisted of flax (linen) fibres embedded in a phenolic resin matrix. The airframe apparently met the static performance requirements of the day, though in the end the supply of aluminium was maintained and Gordon Aerolite wasn't needed.

Polyester fibres are utilised in canoe and dinghy construction, offering low density, good impact resistance, and a smooth finish, but low stiffness. A high molecular weight form of polyethylene fibre can be produced which has a high tensile strength and low density, producing the highest specific strength of any currently available commercial reinforcement fibre. But low tensile modulus mitigates against its use. Quartz, or pure silica fibres, can be made which have good mechanical properties and very good temperature resistance, but cost is currently very high. Boron is also very costly, but mixed with carbon can give very strong, very stiff hybrid fibres. Ceramic fibres have also been used, but generally only to reinforce non-polymer matrices such as metal alloys.

In addition to the criteria discussed above, others such as compressive strength, fatigue resistance, fire resistance and cost may all come into play in the ultimate selection of fibre. But, as stated earlier in this chapter, the performance of a composite depends only partly on the fibre properties – the resin matrix has a large role to play too, and the way in which the fibres and the resin are brought together is also crucial. However, before moving on to resins we'll take a tour around fabric production to see the different methods by which reinforcing fibres are put together to make for easy handling, and how these different make-ups influence the properties of the end-product.

## Fabrics

There is nowadays a bewildering variety of reinforcement fabrics available, made from the fibres highlighted in the previous section. In essence, though, they can be regarded as falling into three categories: non-woven, woven, and uni-directional. The non-woven group is fairly simple, and usually only utilises glass fibres. The woven group includes many different weave types and incorporates all the main reinforcement fibres. The uni-directional group also incorporates myriad styles, and all the main fibre types crop up here too. As we look at each type, a few terms pertaining to the textile industry will crop up. Definitions will be provided along the way, and will also be found in the glossary.

### *Non-woven reinforcement fabrics*

The main fabric to fall under this heading is what used to be known simply as 'glass fibre mat', but is now called 'chopped strand mat', or CSM for short. The latter descriptive name indicates in part how the fabric is made – it comprises chopped strands of glass fibres, usually in the range 0.75–1.5in (approximately 20–40mm) long, randomly laid in thin, flat sheet form. The fibres are held by a chemical binder to give a slightly stiff, but easy to handle fabric which can be bought on a bulk roll, or in smaller lengths, or even in small quantities folded up in a packet. CSM is typically supplied to a width of just under a metre (about a yard). In general, the bigger the quantity you buy, the cheaper per square metre or per kilo (it is sold in both measures) it becomes, and you can sometimes buy boxes of offcuts for even less than the price of a bulk purchase.

It should perhaps be mentioned in passing that it is also possible to buy loose chopped strands by the kilo rather than in fabric form. This can then be mixed with resin and sprayed on, a process which requires specialist equipment and thus falls outside the scope of this book. However, it is also feasible to utilise chopped strands 'manually', to make a fibre reinforced 'paste' which can be used, for example, to plug deep recesses into which fabric cannot easily be persuaded to go.

In common with all fabrics, CSM is sold in different weight grades. These are pretty well universally referred to nowadays in metric units, which is to say grams per square metre (gsm) of dry fabric; but traditional ounces per square foot or square yard are still used in some quarters. For some reason, and just to confuse things further, ounces per square foot (oz/sq ft) – generally abbreviated to just ounces – used to be the reference for CSM, whilst woven glass fabrics were graded in ounces per square yard. There can be no better reason for sticking consistently to the metric units than to avoid this confusion, but conversions will be made along the way for the reader's convenience.

CSM can be bought in weights ranging from 225gsm (approximately 0.75oz/sq ft), through 300gsm (1oz), 450gsm (1.5oz) and 600gsm (2oz) to 900gsm (3oz). It is the cheapest reinforcement fabric you can buy, probably the simplest to use overall, is easily 'wetted out' by resins (more on this later), and is relatively bulky, so that the required stiffness and strength in a product can be readily built up. It is also, theoretically, isotropic, which means that it has virtually identical properties in all directions across the fabric. This means that it matters little how you orientate it in the product, because it will have the same strength and stiffness in all directions. When wetted out with resin, CSM can also be made to conform to most compound curves fairly easily. One disadvantage of CSM, though, is that it has a higher resin consumption, weight for weight, than woven fabrics, which, as we shall see in more detail later, is one of the reasons that the mechanical properties of a laminate made from CSM are not as good as those of a woven fabric-based laminate.

Another non-woven form of glass fibre fabric is 'surface tissue', which is really just a finer, lighter-weight version of CSM. Composed of individual fibres rather than strands of twisted fibres, and typically weighing around 30gsm (0.1oz/sq ft), such tissue is used to give a smoother finish to the surface away from the mould – that is, on the back – than is possible with CSM. It also acts as a barrier to prevent fibres of CSM penetrating through the 'gel coat' (more on this later too) to reach the outer surface.

### Woven fabrics

Whereas non-woven fabrics are made up of randomly orientated fibres, in woven fabrics the fibres are aligned in specific orientations. By virtue of the flexibility of weave styles available, and the variations in tex count and 'thread count' (the number of threads per unit distance across or along a woven fabric) that are possible, a wide range of weights and styles of woven reinforcing fabrics is available.

There are a number of pros and cons to using woven fabrics in place of non-woven CSM, whatever fibre type is utilised. A woven fabric is likely to contain more fibres in a given volume than CSM, which leads to better mechanical properties in the finished laminate (more details on why this is so later on in the chapter). This in turn leads to the option of a lighter, thinner laminate for a given strength or a stronger laminate for a given weight. Woven fabrics need less resin to wet them out fully, and this produces a higher fibre:resin ratio, or 'fibre volume fraction'. This again leads to better laminate mechanical properties. In addition the clear and obvious fibre orientation defined by the weave pattern makes it feasible to engineer a composite in which the fibres are aligned with expected load paths in a structural component. In other words, the strength and stiffness can be aligned in the direction in which they are most needed.

There is normally a penalty, of course, which is cost, but the extra expense of a similar weight woven glass fibre fabric over CSM is not particularly great; indeed, from shopping around through various price lists it is apparent that some suppliers sell CSM for a higher price than others charge for woven glass fabrics.

Before we get onto the different styles of woven fabrics, there are a few definitions to cover. Woven fabrics are produced on looms by combining two sets of yarns or rovings, henceforth referred to for simplicity, in this brief discussion, as threads. The set of threads running the length of the fabric are called the 'warp' threads, whilst those running across the fabric are known as the 'weft' threads. All weave styles produce a regular pattern of intertwining of warp and weft threads,

but there are some common styles that it is necessary to know about because they have an influence on the way the fabrics handle and on the properties of the final laminate.

The simplest and probably the most commonly encountered weave style is known as 'plain weave'. In this, each warp thread passes over and under each weft thread, and vice versa, producing a very stable fabric to handle, and one which is quite difficult to distort. The downside to this, though, is a fabric with relatively poor 'drape', which means it is reluctant to conform to complex curvature. The nature of plain weave makes it easy to 'wet out' with resin, and this, combined with its stability, accounts – partly at least – for its popularity. It is also one of the cheapest weave styles, which naturally also has a bearing on its popularity. However, it may be worth bearing in mind that the sinuous path that each thread takes through the fabric means that plain weave does not produce the best mechanical properties of woven reinforcements in the finished laminate.

A 'twill weave' sees one or more warp threads alternately woven over and under two or more weft threads in a repeating pattern. There are a number of variations

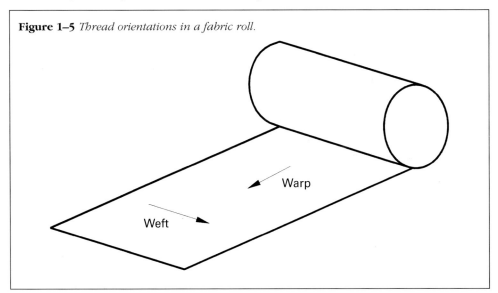

**Figure 1–5** *Thread orientations in a fabric roll.*

Warp

Weft

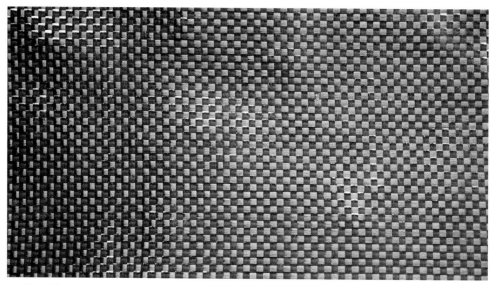

*Carbon fibre fabric – this is a 'plain weave'.*

on this theme, but perhaps the commonest twill weave is '2 × 2', in which each warp thread passes alternately over and under two weft threads, and the weft threads pass over and under two warp threads. Another common variant is '3 × 1' twill, where each warp thread passes over three and then under one weft thread, and vice versa. Others, such as '4 × 4', are available, but whatever the precise construction, twill weave always creates a characteristic straight or broken 'herring bone' diagonal pattern. (A common everyday twill weave fabric with which most people are familiar is denim.) Twill weave in reinforcement fabrics produces a more drapeable material capable of adopting more complex curvature than plain weave, but which is at the same time somewhat less stable and more prone to distortion during handling. It also wets out with resin more easily, and, by virtue of its somewhat longer straight thread runs, it produces slightly better mechanical properties in the finished laminate.

A 'satin weave' is a form of twill weave modified to decrease the number of thread intersections, and is designated by a 'harness' or 'h' number – generally 4, 5 or 8 – which specifies the number of threads a warp or weft thread passes over or under before weaving under or over a single thread, and so on in a repeating fashion (actually, the number of threads passed over or under is the 'h' number minus one). This produces characteristically flat, smooth fabrics with very good drape and conformability, but also instability in handling. Because of the relatively long thread runs, the mechanical properties of laminates utilising satin weaves are again slightly improved. However, one point needs watching, which is that because satin weave creates a fabric in which warp threads predominate on one face and weft threads on the other, the fabric is 'unbalanced'. This can create distortion during resin curing unless half the number of plies in the laminate are symmetrically inverted in the lay up either side of the middle layer. Again, more on this later.

Other reasonably common weave types that you may encounter are 'crowsfoot', which is a form of satin weave, and 'basket weave', which is similar to plain weave except that two or more warp threads cross over two or more weft threads side by side. But plain, twill and

*Carbon fibre fabric – this is 'twill weave' with the characteristic diagonal herringbone pattern.*

satin are the most prevalent types of weave. Your decision regarding which to use will depend on the nature of the item you are going to make, and the best compromise you can obtain in handling and finish. The chart below may help with selection.

## Table 1–4 The pros and cons of various weave types

| Property | Plain | Twill | Satin |
|---|---|---|---|
| Stability | Good | Moderate | Poor |
| Drape | Poor | Good | Excellent |
| Smoothness | Poor | Moderate | Excellent |
| Balance | Good | Good | Poor |

Another decision to be made with glass fibre fabrics is whether to use yarns or rovings for the threads. In essence, twisted yarns are used in finer, lighter weight fabrics (typically 20 to 300gsm, or 0.6 to 8.9oz/sq yd), and offer higher strength per unit weight. They are thus best suited to thin laminates. Rovings, on the other hand, are less expensive and easier to wet out by virtue of the looser thread formation, but are made to heavier tex values and woven into medium to heavy fabrics (typically 300 to 800gsm, or

8.9 to 23.6oz/sq yd). Rovings are therefore better suited to thicker laminates.

We have only looked at fabrics constructed from warp and weft threads at 90° to each other, and indeed you will often see these materials referred to as 0/90° fabrics, where the warp is designated as the 0 direction. Clearly these will provide strength and stiffness in the two fibre directions, and if these mechanical properties are required in any other direction, then it may be that plies of fabric must be co-laminated in such a way that fibres lie at angles other than 0 and 90°. Alternatively, 'multi-axial' fabrics are available, which have plies with fibres orientated at angles in addition to 0/90°, for example at +/–45°. These multi-axial fabrics are sometimes stitched together to produce this effect, or they can be woven to give two sets of threads at 45°. Where particular reinforcement along a certain direction or path is required, however, or perhaps where only local directional reinforcement is necessary, then uni-directional fabrics can be utilised.

### Uni-directional fabrics
Uni-directional fabrics, or UDs, are made up of fibres running wholly, or almost

wholly, in a single direction, usually the warp (0° fabrics). They are available in glass (E, R or S2), aramid and carbon. The single most important aspect of UDs is that they offer the ability to align reinforcing fibres exactly as required, and in the optimum quantity – that is, without potentially non-essential weft threads, which add weight but possibly nothing of structural value in certain applications. This is not to say that weft threads, and therefore woven fabrics, are inherently wasteful and unnecessary, but rather that in certain instances they may be.

UD fibres are held in position either by small quantities of other threads stitched or woven in place, or by some form of binder. However, the latter form is generally not compatible with ambient temperature cure resin systems. In the case of pre-impregnated fabrics (or 'pre-pregs', for which see Chapter 8), the resin impregnated into the fabric holds the fibres in position, and no other threads or binder are necessary.

Because of the predominance of the reinforcing fibres in a UD fabric, and the small amount of fibre distortion that even woven UDs require to hold them together, the fibres are straighter than in any other reinforcing fabric. Consequently the structural properties of laminates made from UD fabric are at their best, at least in the direction of the fibres.

### Hybrid fabrics

It is possible to combine the properties of reinforcing fibres by mixing them in woven fabrics. Usually this involves using one fibre type for the warp threads, and a different type for the weft threads. In this way the advantages of one fibre can be used to offset the disadvantages of another, or the combined advantages of different fibres may enhance the product overall.

Carbon/aramid hybrids benefit from the high compressive and tensile strength and high stiffness of carbon as well as the high impact and tensile strength of aramid. Both fibres are expensive, so there is no cost advantage. Aramid/glass hybrids benefit from the low density, high impact resistance and high tensile strength of aramid, and the good compressive and tensile strength and overall cost reduction of glass. Similarly, carbon/glass hybrids gain from the low density, high tensile and compressive strength and high stiffness of carbon together with the low cost of glass.

Hybrid fabrics can be produced in the usual range of weave styles, with the intrinsic properties that each of these offer, and can be incorporated into laminates in the same ways as other fabrics.

### Fibre applicability

We can now summarise the pros and cons of the different readily available fibres.

Glass provides the cheapest reinforcement, especially if chopped strand mat is used. CSM is suited to applications where low cost is at a premium, and where structural demands are relatively low. Nevertheless, with thought and care, reasonably light, tough, stiff and strong components can be made from CSM. Woven glass provides very good strength and stiffness at a reasonable cost.

Aramid fibres possess good tensile strength, good impact resistance and low density, but their high cost is a disadvantage, as is their poor compressive strength, their propensity to degrade under ultraviolet light (which is a natural constituent of sunlight), and the need for special shears to cut the stuff! But lighter, stiffer, stronger components can be made from aramid than from glass.

Carbon offers high tensile strength, high compressive strength, high stiffness, low weight and good fatigue resistance, but is again costly. It also suffers from poor impact strength. However, strong, very stiff, lightweight components can be made using carbon. And let's not dismiss the aesthetic value of carbon fibre either. Structural composite engineers will no doubt heap scorn on the idea, but the fact is that 'the carbon look' is so appealing that people now make self adhesive rolls of 'carbon look' plastic. But why waste money on a tacky (in both senses) imitation when you can waste money on the real thing? You may not actually *need* carbon in a given application, on a structural-properties-versus-cost-justification basis. But you can make a lighter, stiffer component with carbon that also looks appealing, and I see nothing wrong in that.

## Resin systems

There are two generic forms of resin used in composite manufacture, defined as thermoplastic resins and thermosetting resins, the latter term often being abbreviated to 'thermosets'. Thermoplastics include polyamide (nylon), polypropylene, polycarbonate and a remarkable one called polyetheretherketone, or PEEK, which the aerospace industry is especially excited about. Thermoplastics have the ability to be heated and melted into liquid form and cooled until they are solid, and the process is reversible. The 'cure time' – that is, the time required for the resin to harden to the point at which the composite material achieves its desired structural properties – is also quite short. Thermosets, on the other hand, start out as liquids but are turned irreversibly solid by the application of heat. Their curing cycle, even when accelerated by additional external heat, is relatively slow; however, specialist equipment is not necessarily required for their effective use.

In practical terms, the home workshop laminator is unlikely to be able to use thermoplastic resins because of the specialist equipment that would be needed to melt the material and to apply it, so thermosets are the solution. Again, there are several such resins that can be used in composite manufacture, but practicality and availability cut the choice down to just two – polyester and epoxy resins. Others include vinylester, phenolic, silicone and polyimide resins, which are used in different industries and applications.

The job of the resin system is to combine with and bond to the reinforcing fibres so that loads may be supported by the latter, and transmitted through the material from fibre to fibre. It also stabilises the fibres against buckling under compressive loads, and protects them from mechanical and environmental damage. The two commonly used resins perform these tasks with different efficiencies and, naturally, at different costs. So in the same way that there are choices of fibre and fabric to be made which are dependent on budget and the end use to which the product will be put, there are similar choices to be made concerning which resin system to use. Let us look at the two basic options and compare their properties and applicability.

### Polyester resin

Though this type of resin has been around for a long time, ongoing development has ensured that its handling and properties have improved over the years. The typical resin you would buy from a mouldings supplier has the consistency of thin honey at normal room temperature. It is more or less transparent, has a colour that can be anything from greenish to brownish to pinkish, and a sweet smell that actually derives from the organic solvent that makes up a large proportion of the resin, which is styrene. This solvent, in part, dilutes the resin to a manageable 'viscosity' so that it can be brushed or rolled. Polyester resin is actually made from coal and petroleum derivatives, and is essentially a solution of polyester in styrene. There are several other constituent compounds too, which either assist with the handling or curing properties of the resin, or which bestow some specific property to the end product once the resin has cured.

The actual curing process in polyester resin is initiated by two types of compound. One is referred to as the 'accelerator', which enables curing to take place

*Polyester resin, gel coat, and catalyst.*

at room temperature, and is usually mixed in as a constituent of the resin for convenience. The other is the 'catalyst', which is added just prior to the resin's use. The resin will not cure in any practical timescale at room temperature without these components, but once they have been added in more or less the correct quantities, the curing process commences and effectively cannot then be stopped. The phrase 'more or less correct' might sound a little vague, but the only thing that is really altered by varying the amounts of accelerator (usually already fixed for you) or catalyst is the rate at which the resin cures. There are sensible limits within which you need to keep the proportions (more on that later), but it can be useful to know that it isn't critical to get things spot on. However, it does make life easier and more predictable if you keep catalyst proportions consistent. Be warned that liquid catalysts are usually organic peroxides, highly reactive chemicals that demand respect,

and careful reading of the labels and instructions that come with them is essential. Treated properly, they will not cause you any problems. So don't be put off – if you're brave enough to cross a busy road, you already take much greater risks than are involved in the proper handling of chemicals or the correct performance of the procedures that are mentioned in this book.

The addition of the catalyst triggers a chemical reaction in the resin which causes the styrene molecules to form what are known as 'cross-links' between the long chain molecules of polyester. This eventually forms a complex three-dimensional network of linked molecules which sets solid once cure is complete. The curing reaction is exothermic – that is, it creates its own heat in a self-perpetuating reaction that continues until all the reactants in the mix are used up. Remember the definition of thermosetting resins, given above? Now you can see why polyester resin is a thermoset. The actual temperature generated depends on whether the catalysed resin is spread out over a wide area in a laminate, in which case the heat is dissipated rapidly; poured into (or left in) a confined area such as a three-dimensional casting mould; or is left rather too long in its mixing pot. In the latter two situations the temperature can get very high indeed, over 150°C. If it is appropriate, you can pour resin that gets this hot into a bigger vessel, such as a metal tray, to help cool it, or to delay its curing time slightly.

There are three distinct phases in the cure reaction. The first is the 'gel time', which is also more practically known as the 'pot life'. This is the time it takes for the resin to turn from a runny liquid that can be applied by brush to a soft, sticky gel that cannot. The gel time, or pot life, is therefore a measure of how long you've got to use the batch of resin you've mixed. Then there is the 'hardening time', which is more or less self-explanatory, and is the time it takes for the resin to harden sufficiently so that the moulding or laminate may be prised out of its mould. And finally there is the 'maturing time', which can be anything up to a few weeks, depending on the resin system you use and the temperatures in which the laminate is cured and stored. This is the time taken for the resin to reach its full hardness and stability.

A number of factors influence the pot life and hardening times of polyester resin. Firstly, as already mentioned, the catalyst content speeds up the pot life, more catalyst giving a shorter pot life. More catalyst also speeds up the hardening time, though interestingly the time to full hardness may not vary significantly with catalyst content, as shown by the graph in Figure 1–6.

Then there is the reactivity of the catalyst used. Most suppliers will offer low, medium and rapid gelling catalysts, which behave as you might expect from their names, and as the example in Figure 1–7 demonstrates.

Ambient temperature has a big influence on pot life, which is markedly shortened by warmer conditions, as shown in Figure 1–8. Hardening and maturing

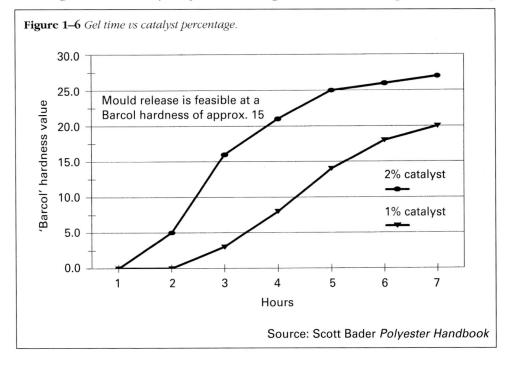

**Figure 1–6** *Gel time vs catalyst percentage.*

Mould release is feasible at a Barcol hardness of approx. 15

2% catalyst

1% catalyst

'Barcol' hardness value

Hours

Source: Scott Bader *Polyester Handbook*

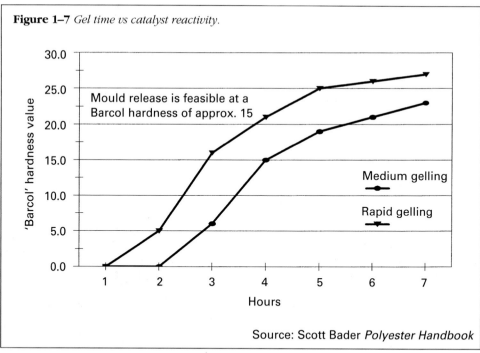

**Figure 1–7** *Gel time vs catalyst reactivity.*

Mould release is feasible at a Barcol hardness of approx. 15

Medium gelling

Rapid gelling

Source: Scott Bader *Polyester Handbook*

times will also both be shorter at higher ambient temperatures. In preferred circumstances, so called 'cold curing' or ambient temperature curing of polyester resin should be done at no less than 15°C. Maturing times can be considerably

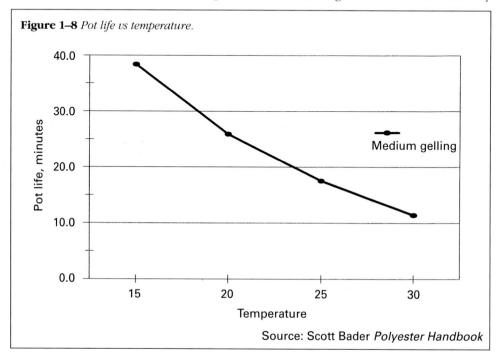

**Figure 1–8** *Pot life vs temperature.*

Medium gelling

Source: Scott Bader *Polyester Handbook*

shortened with elevated temperature 'post-curing', and you can reckon on every 10°C increase in temperature roughly halving the maturing time. So if a laminate was fully hard after 30 hours at 40°C, it will only take about 15 hours at 50°C. Post-curing at 80°C reduces time to maturity down to around three hours.

As already discussed, the volume of resin being used also influences pot life by virtue of the exothermic heat generated. This can mean that a beaker full of resin will have a shorter pot life than the same resin poured into a wide, shallow tray.

All of these factors will be discussed in a practical context when we get on to the subject of making sample laminates in the next chapter.

When you come to look at suppliers' product and price lists you will find that various types and grades of polyester resin are available, including 'general purpose lay-up resin', which is eminently suitable for most non-critical jobs on competition cars. Others are water resistant, chemical resistant, and even fire retardant. Take the suppliers' advice if you think you may need one of the more specialised types of polyester resin.

### Epoxy resins

Introduced in the 1960s initially as adhesives, epoxy resins – which derive from chemicals produced by the petroleum industry – are now available with a wide range of properties, both pre- and post-cure, to suit most requirements. In pre-cured form they can be obtained as clear to amber coloured low viscosity fluids suitable for application with a brush and ambient temperature cure; as pastes that are more suited for use as adhesives; and what we might call 'low-tack' solids that have been pre-impregnated into a fabric and require additional heat to cure them (see Chapter 8). In a cured state, properties can range from tough and highly flexible to very strong and hard.

So whatever technology you intend to employ to make your composites, be it

*Epoxy resin and hardener.*

good old-fashioned 'wet lay-up' or more sophisticated methods, there will be at least one epoxy resin that will fulfil your requirements. In fact the choice is pretty bewildering, and selecting what is most suitable is best done with the assistance of the suppliers' technical services departments, which are always keen to help.

Like polyester resins, epoxies are 'thermosets', but the curing process is quite different, and is initiated by the mixing of two components, usually designated 'resin' and 'hardener'. The proportions in which resin and hardener need to be mixed will depend on the specific product you use. For example, some epoxies are mixed (usually by weight) on a ratio of 1:1 – that is, equal weights of resin and hardener – whilst others might be mixed at 4:1, meaning four parts resin to one part hardener. But whatever ratio is specified for a given product, it is imperative that you keep to it as accurately as you can. This is because, whereas with polyester resin the reactants are already mixed for you and the addition of the catalyst simply initiates the cure, with epoxies the resin and the hardener *are* the reactants, and if they are not mixed in the right proportions there will be a surplus of one or the other, which will impede the curing process and lead to a much inferior end product.

Whereas polyester resin cure is brought about by the 'cross-linking' of molecules to produce a solid, with the polyester molecules joined at their middles by styrene molecules, epoxy resin cures by the bonding of the ends of the constituent molecules, which produces an inherently stronger, 'stiffer' solid. As an analogy, think of a tubular spaceframe racecar chassis: joints are located at the ends of tubes rather than along their unsupported lengths, because that produces a stronger and stiffer chassis. So it is with epoxy resin, and this partly explains why epoxy is superior to polyester.

The handling of ambient temperature cure epoxy once it has been mixed is not dissimilar to polyester. The curing process is exothermic, which is what drives the reaction, so there is a limited pot life, and specific periods of time are required for it to harden and mature. However, the manufacturers tend to use different terminology to describe some of these processes, such as the slightly more meaningful 'demould time' instead of 'hardening time' to cite but one example. As the resin and hardener are mixed, the heat generated accelerates the cure rate, and at the same time causes a reduction in viscosity. But then the viscosity increases (not something you notice with polyester), slowly at first and then more rapidly as you approach the gel point. As with polyester, pouring curing resin into a shallow tray helps to dissipate the heat of reaction, and extend the useful pot life.

Ambient temperature also has just as significant an influence on epoxy resin pot life and cure times as it does with polyester, with higher temperatures leading to a shorter pot life and more rapid

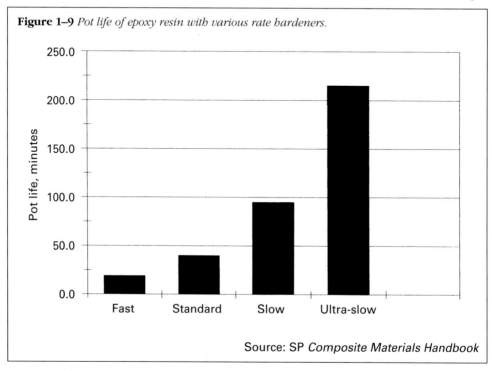

**Figure 1–9** *Pot life of epoxy resin with various rate hardeners.*

Source: SP *Composite Materials Handbook*

curing. Varying the quantity of catalyst in a polyester system can provide some control of pot life and cure time, but that option is not available with epoxies because of the criticality of the mix proportions. However, analogous to varying reactivity catalysts, different reactivity hardeners are available which enable the pot life and cure times of epoxies to be varied. They are usually referred to as fast, standard, slow and ultra slow hardeners, and the influence on pot life is shown in Figure 1–9.

Epoxies also benefit considerably from elevated temperature post-cure. For example, one supplier's data sheets suggested that compared to a 28-day cure at 21°C, a 24-hour cure at 21°C followed by 16 hours at 50°C produced an almost ten per cent increase in the resin tensile strength and a more than 20 per cent increase in the inter-laminar shear strength of a glass fibre laminate bound by the resin. These types of factor can be important in structural applications.

### Resin pros and cons

We can summarise the good and not so good points of the two main resin types under consideration here as follows:

### Table 1–5 The good points

| Polyester | Epoxy |
| --- | --- |
| Cheap | High strength |
| Easy to use | Strong adhesion to |
| Adequate properties | fibres (and other |
| for general purposes | materials) |
| and non-critical | Good chemical |
| components | resistance |
| Rapid curing | Good temperature |
| | resistance |
| | Good long |
| | term stability |

### Table 1–6 The not so good points

| Polyester | Epoxy |
| --- | --- |
| Lower mechanical | Expensive |
| properties | Curing times can be |
| Smelly | longer |
| Poorer long-term | Liquid resin and |
| stability | hardener have |
| Doesn't bond well to | greater health |
| aramid fibres | hazard |
| | Critical mixing |
| | proportions |

### Laminate properties

Having examined fibres, fabrics and resins in some detail and looked at their respective properties, what really matters are the properties you can expect from a given fibre and fabric in a given resin when combined in a finished laminate. This section will put together some direct comparisons, to help you select the most suitable materials for your own composite projects.

The performance of a composite, resin impregnated fabric is a function of the mechanical properties of the fibres in the fabric, the mechanical properties of the resin itself, the strength of the bond between the fibre and resin at their interface, the proportion of fibre to resin in the composite (also known as the fibre fraction) by weight or volume, and the orientation of the fibres within the composite. Figure 1–10 illustrates generically a set of typical stress-strain curves of a fibre, a resin and a cured FRP composite. This shows clearly how the composite's properties fall in between those of the fibre and the resin. It would seem, then, that in order to maximise the performance of a composite laminate the aim would be to get as high a proportion of fibre relative to resin as possible. This is absolutely true, but only up to a point. Clearly, if the fibre fraction was 100 per cent there would be no resin to bond the fibres together, and the material would not be much use in any situation, especially one involving even slight compressive loading. The best properties are usually obtained at around 60 to 70 per cent fibre fraction. As we will see in later chapters, with some laminating methods these ratios are achievable, but with others they are not, so this is yet another

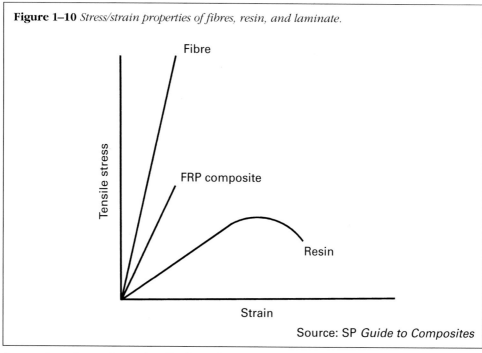

**Figure 1–10** *Stress/strain properties of fibres, resin, and laminate.*

Source: SP *Guide to Composites*

factor that determines the final performance of a laminate.

An important factor to consider before buying a reinforcing fabric is the 'finish' applied to it during manufacture. Surface finishes are applied for two reasons: firstly to help protect the fibres from damage during the conversion from fibre to fabric, which involves some fairly robust mechanical procedures; and secondly to give a resin-compatible surface to the fibres that boosts the bond strength between fibre and resin. So check that the finish applied to the fabric you want to buy is compatible with the resin system you want to use.

Table 1–7 shows some physical prop-erties of glass laminates, with different forms of glass fabric reinforcing a polyester matrix.

A number of points are worth emphasising from this table. First, look at how the tensile and flexural strengths of the resin are enhanced by the presence of a reinforcing fabric, but also note that the resin contributes significantly to compressive strength. Then look at the two columns referring to CSM, and notice the effect on the mechanical properties of increasing the fibre volume fraction from 30 per cent to 50 per cent. Most notably, the tensile strength has increased dramatically. Also, compare each property in turn between each fabric type, and notice

**Table 1–7 Properties of different fabric forms of E-glass in a polyester (PE) resin matrix** (Source: *Engineered Materials Handbook, Vol.1: Composites*)

|                          | PE resin | CSM  | CSM  | Woven rovings | Woven fabric |
|--------------------------|----------|------|------|---------------|--------------|
| Glass content, wt%       | 0        | 30%  | 50%  | 60%           | 70%          |
| Density, g/cm³           | 1.22     | 1.5  | 1.7  | 1.76          | 1.88         |
| Tensile strength, MPa    | 59       | 117  | 288  | 314           | 331          |
| Compressive strength, MPa| 156      | 147  | 160  | 192           | 280          |
| Flexural strength, MPa   | 88       | 197  | 197  | 317           | 403          |

how the properties improve as the fibre volume fraction increases. It is also evident from the increasing compressive and flexural strengths that the fabric type is improving the composite as you go to the right-hand side of the table.

It has already been pointed out that resin bond strength affects the laminate properties, and a very simple comparison of glass fibre impregnated with polyester and epoxy resins will illustrate this. In the table above, the flexural strength of woven glass in polyester at a fibre volume ratio of 70 per cent is stated as 403MPa. Another reference, in which various epoxy resins were being highlighted, gives the flexural strength of a woven E-glass in epoxy laminate – at the similar fibre volume ratio of 67 per cent – at between 492 and 574MPa, depending on the exact resin being tested. (Note: the cure of these samples was at 110°C for two hours, compared to ambient temperature cure for the polyester-based samples in the table.) There has been a further substantial increase in this particular property by virtue of the improved bonding strength of the epoxy resin compared to the sample in polyester resin.

In general terms it is reasonable to presume that, in a given resin matrix and for a given fabric weight, weave style and fibre volume ratio, the properties of the laminate will reflect the properties of the reinforcing fabric, as laid out in an earlier section of this chapter. There is, however, an exception to this general rule of thumb, which is the apparent reluctance of aramid fibres to fully 'wet out' with polyester resin. This leads, of course, to lower mechanical properties than might have been expected, and should be borne in mind if you decide to combine the two materials.

Another practical point to keep in mind when determining the likely properties of a laminate is how the fibres and resins behave in practice, especially using 'wet lay-up' procedures in which the fibre volume ratio is actually quite difficult to control and particularly hard to make

consistent. But we're getting ahead of ourselves. Generally it should now be getting clearer which combinations of fibres and resins produce the best properties and will look the best, and therefore which are best suited to whatever task you have in mind.

Cost comparisons are also invaluable, and because absolute prices change from year to year perhaps more rapidly than *relative* prices, it is the latter that are offered here for guidance. Epoxy resin, as has already been stated, is more costly than polyester, and is currently in the order of two-and-a-half to three times the price per kilo of polyester resin. To compare the fibre types in a meaningful way, they are listed in the table below on a price per kilo basis, relative to woven E-glass fabric. The actual prices examined in order to calculate these values were for the nearest fabric to a 200gsm plain weave that was listed in available price lists. Prices obviously vary according to actual weight and also according to weave style.

## Table 1–8 Relative prices of different fabric types

| Fabric | UK Price per kg relative to 200gsm woven E-glass |
|---|---|
| CSM | 0.34 |
| Glass rovings | 0.61 |
| E-glass | 1.00 |
| S-glass | 5.07 |
| Aramid | 5.47 |
| Aramid/carbon 2:1 hybrid | 7.33 |
| Carbon | 7.49 |

It was pretty evident when researching this information that carbon and aramid have come down in price relative to glass over the last few years. Whatever the reasons for this might be, it can only be good news for those of us who want to exploit them in our mouldings.

## Gel coats

A gel coat is a tough outer layer which

acts as a protective coating to a mould or a moulding. Amongst other things it prevents fibres of the reinforcing material from reaching the outer surface, where moisture might seep in and cause degradation. It is sometimes possible to use a coat of resin – allowed to cure before further layers of resin and fabric are put down – to act as this protective barrier, but the low viscosity of lay-up resins means that they drain off sloping or vertical surfaces and pool in hollows. To tackle this problem the manufacturers make modified gel coat resins which are thixotropic. This property endows the gel coat resin with a high viscosity when stored in its container, but when it is stirred or agitated, for example with a brush, its viscosity decreases to the point where it can be painted or even, if it has the right formulation, sprayed onto a mould surface. Once applied to the mould, it regains its high viscosity again, and does not even drain off vertical surfaces.

Polyester gel coats can be either clear or pigmented, and can be supplied either already coloured or with a separate pigment which needs to be added prior to use. Epoxy gel coats are generally pigmented as supplied, so if you want a clear finish with epoxy resin you either need to use a cured resin coat as the outer layer, or alternatively obtain a suitable polyurethane clear varnish that can be applied to the product after it has cured and been released from the mould. This gives a tough, weather resistant layer that also filters out ultraviolet light (which can help prevent the gradual degradation of aramid fibres if they're used near the surface).

## Core materials

The stiffness of an FRP laminate panel is a function of the cube of its thickness, which is to say that if you double a laminate's thickness by doubling the number of layers, you will increase its stiffness by a factor of $2^3$ ($2 \times 2 \times 2$), or eight. But doubling the panel's thickness in this way will also double its weight, which will almost certainly not be desirable. However, if you double its thickness by using the same number of plies as previously, divided equally either side of a lightweight 'core' material sandwiched in the middle, you don't quite get the eight times increase in stiffness, but you can expect to get something like a six-and-a-half to seven-fold increase, and for virtually no additional weight. This has got to be a good thing.

But for a core to be really useful it has to possess some of its own mechanical properties. To make a panel stiff, clearly the core must have a measure of stiffness itself. It must also be able to tolerate the different stresses applied to its surfaces when put into bending mode. This puts the surface on the outside of the bend into tension, and the inner surface into compression, which in turn sets up shear forces within the core. So the core must also have good shear strength, and reasonable compressive strength is also necessary to prevent knocks and bumps from prematurely degrading it. Core materials come in three generic types: wood, foam, and honeycomb.

### Wood cores

So-called 'end grain' balsa wood (with the grain running perpendicular to the skins) has been used as a core material for decades. It is reasonably easy to get hold of, can be shaped and cut easily, and has good compressive strength. However, it has a relatively high density as cores go, and it also absorbs resin unless it is first sealed. Other woods, though generally more dense than balsa, can also be used – plywood, for example, is cheap, easily obtained from a DIY store, can be cut to shape, and is useful in reinforcing local, flat areas where good compressive strength is required. It is also inherently stiff, though not especially light.

### Foams

A range of plastic foams is available,

which are well suited – to varying degrees – as core materials. They are mostly of lower density than balsa wood.

PVC, or polyvinyl chloride, closed cell foams can be supplied in sheet form at various thicknesses, or as 'grid-scored' sheet for improved conformability. Two forms are available: 'cross-linked' PVC foam produces stiffer panels, whilst 'uncross-linked' (also known as 'linear') PVC foam is more flexible but tougher. PVC foam can be thermo-formed – that is, shaped by the local application of heat – to make it take up more complex curvatures too. It is basically compatible with polyester and epoxy resins, but needs to be resin sealed prior to imposing an elevated temperature cure on a composite containing the cross-linked variety.

Expanded polystyrene foam can be obtained cheaply and easily from builders' merchants, in sheet form of varying thickness. It is very light and easy to shape, but has very low mechanical properties. Though it can be used with epoxy resin it dissolves in polyester resin, so unless it is well sealed with a PVA adhesive/sealant or epoxy resin it will vanish before your eyes if you try to use it with polyester!

Polyurethane (PU) foam has moderate mechanical properties, and is easily cut or sanded to shape, but has low conformability. It can be bought as sheet, as block, as a two-pack 'pour-into-place' expanding foam, or even in spray cans of expanding foam available from DIY stores (where it is usually sold as 'gap filler'). Be aware that the expansion of, especially, the two-pack variety – which you mix in equal quantities and then dispense rapidly before the expansion starts – creates substantial pressure if not given appropriate escape routes; one hears stories of people ruining days of work by careless use of expanding PU foam, and I've distorted mouldings this way myself!

PU foam is quite good in lightly loaded

*Expanded polystyrene – a useful, low-cost core material, though not compatible with polyester resin.*

sandwich structures such as body panels, or as a support over which FRP formers or stringers are made in order to create stiffening structures. It is compatible with polyester and epoxy resin.

Other foams include polymethyl methacrylamide – said to have the best mechanical and thermal properties currently available – which is used in the aerospace industry but will no doubt find its way into motorsport once the price becomes sensible. Styrene acrylonitrile (SAN) co-polymer foams are now replacing PVC foams in some applications where the improved high temperature capabilities are of benefit.

### Honeycombs

Honeycombs can be either metallic or non-metallic, but in either case they offer the best compressive strength and stiffness for their weight of any of the core materials. They comprise very thin sheets of their constituent material bonded together in strips at specific, offset spac-ings, which are then stretched to open up the adjacent layers and create the typically hexagonal cell structure (though other cell forms are also made). Though there are others, the most common honeycomb materials utilised for motorsport applications are aluminium and aramid paper (the latter being referred to most often by the trade-name Nomex). Sheets of a thickness typically ranging between 3mm ($^1/8$in) and 50mm (2in) are stretched out into large panels.

When honeycomb is skinned with laminate on either face, the resultant sandwich is barely any heavier than the laminate skins themselves, yet the stiffness increases dramatically. Let us extend the example quoted at the beginning of this section on cores; the physical properties of the three panels are shown in the Table 1–9.

These values are for sandwiches relative to the 'solid' laminate material. You can see that the stiffness and the strength increase massively over the 'solid' mater-

*Nomex honeycomb – a high performance core material.*

ial (comprised, in effect, of just the skins from the sandwich panels). The weight gains will depend on the precise core composition, but this example shows how little weight is added by the use of honeycomb.

## Table 1–9 The benefits of using core materials

| | Solid material | Core thickness t | Core thickness 3t |
|---|---|---|---|
| Thickness | t | 2t | 4t |
| Stiffness | 1.0 | 7.0 | 37.0 |
| Flexural strength | 1.0 | 3.5 | 9.2 |
| Weight | 1.0 | 1.03 | 1.06 |

Why do honeycombs offer such high resistance to bending? The analogy often cited is with the structural I-beam. The faces of a honeycomb sandwich panel correspond to the flanges of the I-beam, whilst the honeycomb corresponds to the web of the I-beam. The flanges and the laminate skins resist the compression and tension forces when the I-beam or panel is put into bending, whilst the web or honeycomb resists the inevitable shear forces between the flanges or skins. However, by spreading the support all over the panel, honeycomb significantly

improves on the I-beam. The actual properties endowed by honeycomb depend on the size of the cells, which governs their spacing and frequency, and on the thickness and strength of the web material from which the cells are formed.

Clearly the adhesive bond between the skins and the honeycomb is crucial if the sandwich components are to be joined to become, effectively, one component. Given the very small area that is available to bond the cell material to the facing laminates, top quality adhesive must be used. Consequently honeycomb is usually only used with epoxy resins and adhesives for optimum performance.

Aluminium honeycomb is the cheapest variety, and also has one of the best strength to weight ratios available. The foil thickness, cell size, and panel thickness can all be varied to obtain the desired properties. The 'crumpleability' of aluminium honeycomb works both for and against it, depending on circumstances. The fact that the core does not revert to its original shape after a minor impact can be a problem, and can create apparently undamaged areas where the laminate skins appear fine but where the core has delaminated behind the skins, leaving them with no support and vastly reduced strength and stiffness. On the

**Figure 1–11** *Honeycomb sandwich panel compared to an I-beam.*

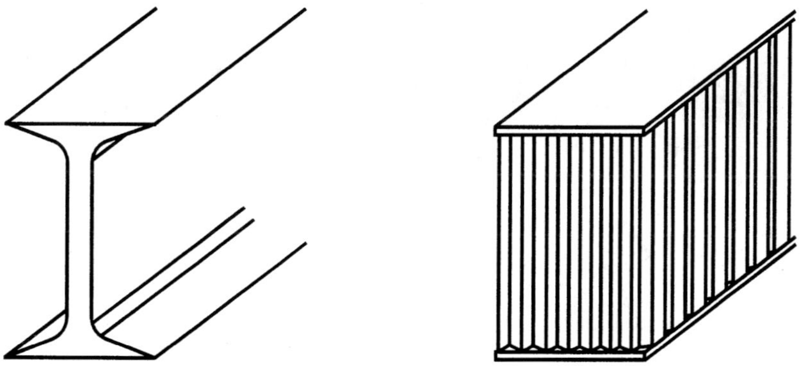

Source: Hexcel Composites

other hand, aluminium honeycomb is an excellent choice for an impact absorption structure, particularly if skinned with aluminium sheet (we digress outside this book's scope only briefly here). Of course, once such a structure has done its job it is disposable.

Aramid paper honeycomb, more usually referred to as Nomex (even though a number of other varieties is actually available), is extremely expensive, but has a better strength to weight ratio than commercial grade aluminium (lower than aerospace grade). It has a low density, possesses good stability, is inherently fire retardant, and has better fatigue resistance. It also possesses what has been described as 'excellent hostile environment resistance', meaning it resists corrosion, high temperatures and so forth. However, it is not as stiff per unit weight as either aluminium grade.

Another interesting honeycomb form is made from woven E-glass coated with cured phenolic resin. It provides the same strength to weight ratio as aerospace aluminium honeycomb, but lower stiffness per unit weight. However, it does have a better stiffness to weight ratio than aramid paper honeycomb. Various carbon fibre honeycombs are also available, coated with various resins; the

mechanical properties of these are very high but, predictably, so is the cost.

### Pre-made sandwich panels

It is possible to buy pre-manufactured flat panels of honeycomb-cored sandwich board, skinned in various materials to various thicknesses. Cores include aluminium honeycomb, aramid paper honeycomb and polyurethane foam, and skins range from glass FRP and aluminium sheet to carbon FRP. They can provide a relatively simple way to build an amazingly strong, stiff and highly effective composite structure, such as a racecar chassis. However, the fabrication techniques required to manufacture such an item lie outside the scope of this particular book.

This has been a rather lengthy chapter, as I intimated at the beginning. But in order to make practical judgements as to why certain materials are suited to particular tasks, albeit without going to the lengths professionals do in making structural calculations, I considered it necessary to provide a reasonably detailed background to the materials that will feature throughout the rest of this book. Hopefully the whys and wherefores of what follows should make better sense as a result.

# Chapter 2

# Equipment and basic techniques

IN THIS CHAPTER we'll cover all the basics you need to get started on the simplest of the FRP moulding techniques, the so-called 'wet lay-up contact moulding' method. The principles of wet lay-up contact moulding will enable you to exploit nearly all of the materials discussed in Chapter 1 without having to purchase or build any expensive specialised equipment. All you need are some simple tools, a few items of protective clothing, the materials and a suitable work area, and you're ready to get moulding. But first, a brief note about health and safety.

## Health and safety
The materials you will be working with pose a potential measure of risk to your health and safety. The suppliers are obliged to inform you of these risks, and what to do about guarding yourself against them, so for the best information on this topic they are the experts to consult. However, as a basic outline of what's involved, you will be dealing in effect with three different types of material – dry fabrics, liquid chemicals, and solid finished products – which each pose different levels and types of risks. These fall broadly into two categories: those which can cause problems by inhalation, and those which can cause problems by coming into contact with the skin or eyes. All of these risks can be minimised by ensuring that you work with adequate and sensibly directed ventilation, and pro-

vide yourself, when necessary, with appropriate protective clothing, including overalls, gloves, boots, goggles, dust masks and respirators. All of these items can be purchased from the materials suppliers, and these days most good DIY stores too. Some of the more specific health and safety points relating to materials, resins and procedures will be mentioned as we go along. But as I said in the previous chapter, don't be put off trying FRP moulding by these warnings. With a bit of applied common sense the actual risks are minimal. However, please note that the author and publisher cannot take any responsibility for your health and safety – that's entirely up to you.

## Tools and equipment
If you have a reasonable kit of general tools for car maintenance and DIY, you'll already possess some of the utensils you need. But here is a list of specific items that will prove either necessary or useful:

- brushes: 1/2in, 1in and 2in (12.5mm, 25mm and 50mm), and maybe wider for larger jobs
- disposable mixing cups or buckets
- mixing sticks
- paddle or washer roller, for laminate consolidation
- weighing scales (eg the kitchen variety) to accurately weigh resins
- syringe, or small graduated beaker (supplied with some liquid medicines), to accurately measure catalyst

– files for finishing trimmed edges on cured laminates
– penknife
– padsaw, hacksaw, to trim cured laminates
– scissors or snips to cut fabrics
– masking tape
– abrasive papers, from coarse to very fine; also the wet and dry varieties
– cutting compound
– paint scraper
– electric drill, with drill bits, grindstones, hole saws
– old newspaper, rags, paper towel
– a flameless heater, preferably with no exposed electrics

*The basic tools and materials for low-cost 'wet lay-up' contact moulding.*

– general tools, including screwdrivers, spanners, and a tape measure
– thermometer (for measuring workshop temperature)

Suitable cheap laminating brushes can be purchased from the resin suppliers. Avoid buying expensive ones, because they generally need to be disposed of after a few uses, and avoid brushes with painted handles – the cleaning solvents you need to use will dissolve this. The suppliers will also sell you the appropriate rollers (for use in consolidating laminates), which you can buy in various widths and diameters. You can also get special disc rollers for working in tight corners. Syringes or small graduated beakers are used for measuring out catalyst volumes, though an alternative is a dedicated graduated catalyst dispenser. If you need heating, flameless heaters are essential – the resins and solvents are highly inflammable, and you shouldn't even smoke in their presence unless you want to get into the local newspaper for quite the wrong reasons. If you use carbon fibre later on, which is electrically conductive in dry form, and which sheds light fibres which waft around in the air, you will appreciate why a heater with no exposed electrics is a good idea. In a reasonably compact workshop, oil-filled radiators are quite a useful source of heat.

### Workspace

A suitable workspace is ideally temperature controlled at between 15°C and 25°C, and is nice and dry (crucial for the storage of reinforcement fabrics). In reality it may well be the space you have available in your garage, workshop or shed. But providing you can arrange for it to be at a minimum temperature of 15°C, and keep it absolutely dry, you will have a useable environment in which to carry out your moulding projects, and to store your materials. The amount of space you need will depend on the size of job you contemplate doing, and in any case, whatever the size of the area you have available, it will probably end up being insufficient – that much seems to be a fact of life. However, you must have good bench space, and ideally you should aim to have one bench (at least) that is wide enough to take the full width of reinforcement fabric you are going to use, with sufficient room to allow you to roll it out for the purposes of cutting and tailoring. Most fabrics come at a metre width or less (roughly 39in), though rolls 1.25m (49in) and even 1.5m (59in) wide can also be purchased. The choice is yours, but a bench measuring just over a metre by, say, a couple of metres will cover most of your cutting needs.

It is always better if you can set up separate areas for cutting fabrics, handling liquid chemicals (resin weighing and mixing), and laminating, and if you've got the space to do that, then that's the way to organise your workshop. But again, you are more likely to be operating in a limited space, which means you will probably have to do your laminating on the same bench as was used for the fabric cutting. This is where all those old newspapers come in handy – you must keep your unused fabrics clean, and away from possible contamination by any of the chemicals you use, or even by the dust created by trimming and finishing mouldings. Regular clean-ups are therefore essential.

However small a space you are working in, though, keep your resin weighing and mixing area away from other work areas, even if you need to set up a dedicated shelf in a corner. That way if you do spill anything – and be assured, at some point you will – then it won't contaminate anything critical. You will also need plenty of shelving to store tools, fabrics, moulds, resins and so forth, and also space to put mouldings that are curing so that you have room to get on with the next job.

Your work area needs to be well ventilated, which, of course, tends to conflict with keeping it warm in wintertime; but that's a compromise you'll have to

resolve. If the weather is suitable you can work outside, but try to avoid direct sunlight on the job when you are laminating, because this can drastically shorten gel times. Once a part is laminated, however, sunlight can be used to speed up cure times quite significantly.

If you are contemplating using your garage as your mouldings workshop, and it is attached to or integral with your house, have a rethink. The styrene vapours from polyester resin in particular can be detected by the average nose in quite low concentrations, and your family will soon complain that your house smells of resin. You can also induce a resin taint in certain foodstuffs if the garage is accessed directly from the kitchen. I have tasted dairy products kept in a refrigerator under such circumstances that not only picked up, but seemingly concentrated the taint of styrene. And not only will the smell get in the house, so too will fibres, not to mention the fine dust that comes from trimming and finishing. None of this will make you popular.

It might therefore make sense to invest in a shed that you can put at the bottom of the garden. A reasonable quality, weatherproof, 10ft by 8ft (3m by 2.4m) shed with a single pitch roof (for adequate headroom), installed electric power and an island workbench, makes a very satisfactory mouldings workshop for the majority of jobs. Sadly, mine is 8ft by 6ft (2.4m by 1.8m) with an L-shaped bench, which is fine for smaller jobs like aerofoils (which I have tended to specialise in anyway), but way too small for anything else. Obviously, if you contemplate working on large mouldings such as sports racer bodywork, not only will you need a larger area but you will also need a large door for entry and egress with the moulds and mouldings. If you are planning a one-off moulding project, and don't feel that the cost of investing in a new shed can be justified, try to find a suitable workshop that you can rent or borrow before resorting to the attached garage again.

## Wet lay-up contact moulding

The basic principle of wet lay-up contact moulding is that a product with only one smooth side is created by simply laminating fibre reinforced resin in contact with a mould. No external pressure is used; nor, typically, is any external applied heat. It is obviously first necessary, therefore, to have a mould with a suitable surface finish resistant to the processes and chemicals used in the creation of the moulding. To obtain a mould in the first place a master pattern, or buck, is normally made, which is a full size, exact replica of the end product. The mould is made on this master pattern, and the moulding is made in the mould.

A release agent has first to be applied to the mould surface, to prevent the moulding from bonding to it. This can take one of various forms, and amongst the more common release agents are specialised silicone-free waxes, and polyvinyl alcohol (PVA). The release agent is left to harden for at least a couple of hours, and preferably overnight (if it's a wax), or until it is absolutely dry (if it's a liquid PVA type). Next, a gel coat resin layer is applied, and is allowed to reach a 'tacky' cure before the layers of reinforcing fabric and resin are laminated onto the back of the gel coat. The right degree of tack has been reached if your finger leaves an imprint but no gel is left on your finger. The whole moulding is then allowed to harden in the mould until it reaches a point where it can be removed as a solid, cured component. The moulding is then trimmed and finished as required, hopefully without recourse to repairs of any kind.

This, then, is the essence of contact moulding. But there are a lot of specifics that need to be covered, and the best way to deal with them is to work through a step-by-step moulding exercise. Many of the details of the exercise that follows shortly, which will be done using polyester resins, will be applicable – either directly or in principle – to a large proportion of the techniques that follow in subsequent chapters. First, however, and not just for those readers who are new to composite moulding techniques, it will be useful to spend some time on a few experiments involving weighing out and handling resin and catalyst, and to observe the effects of different proportions of catalyst on gel time and cure time. This will enable you to better judge how much catalyst you need for a particular job.

### First trials

As stated in the previous chapter, the amount of catalyst that needs to be added to initiate the cure of polyester resin depends on the amount of resin, the ambient temperature, and the time required to get the job done before the resin gels. It's not an overly critical parameter, unless you add way too much catalyst and the resin batch gels before you've had time to apply all of it. The trick, therefore, is to calculate the size of the job and the ambient temperature, and add sufficient catalyst to the resin to give yourself enough time to complete the job without rushing. Ideally, in your temperature-controlled workshop you will not need to alter the percentage of catalyst you use too much. However, if, like me, you have a workshop which is significantly influenced by outside temperature, then in practice some adjustments to catalyst proportions will be necessary.

First, as a rough guide, Table 2–1 shows approximate pot life times for polyester resin with a medium reactivity catalyst. These figures are about right at 25°C.

### Table 2–1 Approximate pot life at different catalyst proportions

| % catalyst | pot life, minutes |
|---|---|
| 1/2 | 50 |
| 1 | 30 |
| 2 | 15 |
| 3 | 7 1/2 |

If the temperature drops by 10°C you can reckon on roughly doubling these pot life times. So in round terms, if you want to aim for a 15 minute pot life at 15°C, use 2 per cent catalyst. These figures are necessarily approximate because they will vary according to manufacturer and possibly even resin batch, as well as, quite probably, the age of the resin and catalyst if, for example, it has been in your workshop for a while; but they'll get you somewhere near to start with. However, there is no substitute for doing your own trials with the materials you have available, and that's what you're going to do next.

So as not to waste too much resin on these trials, only small quantities will be mixed. You will need four mixing cups, four mixing sticks, a large mixing stick to stir the resin prior to use, your weighing scales, and a workbench. You will also need a small offcut of plastic-faced chipboard (on which to dispense some of the catalysed resin mixes you're going to make), your thermometer, a watch to measure gel times and a notebook to record your experiments. Wear your gloves and overalls, and activate the workshop ventilation.

First, make a note of the workshop temperature. Stir the resin thoroughly in its storage container, then weigh out 25g of resin, as accurately as you can, into each of the four mixing cups. Next you need a method of measuring small quantities of catalyst. This is most easily done by dispensing it in drops. You may have been supplied with catalyst in a dispenser that enables drops to be counted out easily, but if not, a syringe can be used for the same purpose. A syringe is, in fact, a useful tool for calibrating the volume of the drops. For example, take up some catalyst in your syringe, then dispense 1ml of it back into the catalyst storage container, in drops, counting each drop. You will probably get about 40 drops per millilitre, and from that you can work out the following:

| 40 drops | = | 1ml | which is approx 1g |
|---|---|---|---|
| 20 drops | = | 0.5ml | ~ 0.5g |
| 10 drops | = | 0.25ml | ~ 0.25g |
| 5 drops | = | 0.125ml | ~ 0.125g |

If you get a different number of drops per millilitre from your dispenser, you'll need to adjust this table accordingly. For practical purposes, the volume is assumed to be equivalent to the weight of catalyst, and although this is not strictly true, it's a not unreasonable approximation.

Now, to the first pot of resin add five drops of catalyst (equivalent to 0.5 per cent weight for weight, or w/w). Stir gently but thoroughly, going round the sides and the bottom of the mixing cup with one of the mixing sticks, wait about half a minute, and then note the time. Leave the mixing stick in this pot so as not to contaminate any of the others. To the next pot of resin add ten drops of catalyst (1.0 per cent w/w), stir, stand and note the time. To the third add 20 drops catalyst (2.0 per cent w/w), stir, stand and note the time, and to the last add 40 drops (4.0 per cent w/w). Using each mixing stick, dispense a small pool of each of the catalysed resin mixes onto the plastic-faced wood offcut, then stand back and observe, occasionally prodding with the mixing stick in each pot and pool and noting what happens.

Possibly the first thing you'll notice is a gradual change in colour, possibly from a brown tint to a green tint (this obviously depends on the initial hue of your resin). Then, after some minutes, the resin with the most catalyst in it will start to get more viscous, until it rather rapidly ceases to be a runny liquid and becomes a lumpy gel. Note down the time at which this happens, because this is the gel time, and defines the useful pot life of the resin. It will be obvious that this substance can no longer be poured, brushed or otherwise dispensed. The polyester molecules have cross-linked, and the mix is going solid. You may also notice that the colour changes again at this point. In addition you will be able to detect significant heat being generated by the mix in

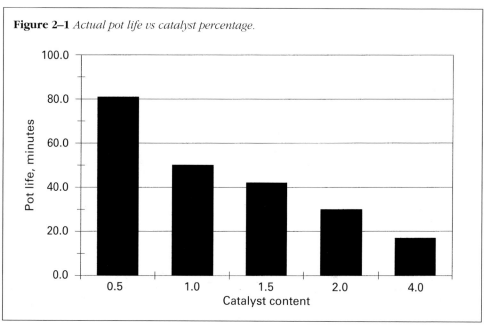

**Figure 2–1** *Actual pot life vs catalyst percentage.*

the pot – this is the exothermic heat of reaction. In fact the base of the pot will get almost too hot to touch after a while, before subsequently cooling again.

As each mix gels, note down the times, and if you're that way inclined plot these times on a graph against catalyst concentration, as shown in Figure 2–1. These particular results were derived from just such a trial that I carried out using a batch of resin and catalyst some months old, when my workshop was bathed in spring sunshine, and hence was a very workable 22 to 24°C. Notice that the gel times are rather longer than those in the table above. This is almost certainly because the chemicals were not fresh, but it shows that doing this exercise on at least one concentration of catalyst on a batch of chemicals of possibly unknown history can provide a useful yardstick to the reactivity of the resin/catalyst mix, and will also enable you to take the ambient temperature into account. Right, that's resin mixing. Now on with the first moulding.

As stated previously, to create a moulding you first need to have a mould, and for this exercise we're going to cheat

just a little by using what you might call a 'pre-fabricated' mould to make a test moulding. The reason for this is simple – moulds can often be made using similar techniques to those used to make mouldings, and it seemed more logical to describe the manufacture of a simple moulding as the first step along the learning curve. Hence we've jumped the mould making stage for now, but only so that we can develop the basic techniques that can be applied to making both moulds and mouldings. I hope that will make sense later, even if it doesn't right now.

**Mould preparation**

So, the material for our pre-fabricated mould is going to be another piece of plastic-faced chipboard (sometimes known by the trade-name Contiboard), which possesses all the essential qualities of a mould – it has a good surface finish (well, good enough for this exercise anyway), is strong and rigid, and is compatible with the chemicals and processes to which it is to be subjected. Always remember that preparation is everything, and whatever the standard of surface

*A basic prefabricated mould – plastic-faced chipboard.*

finish is on your mould, that is what you'll achieve on your moulding. And backtracking from that, the finish on the mould is entirely dependent on the finish on the master pattern. However, in this case we have short circuited the usual

*Apply several coats of silicone-free wax first. Allow to harden for about an hour between coats.*

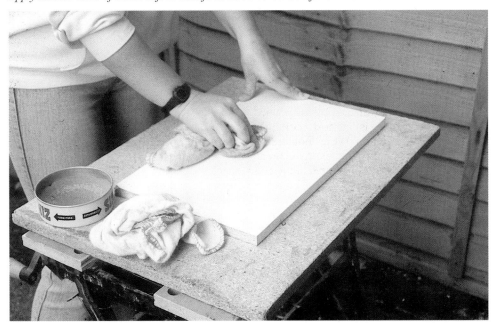

*For the 'belt and braces' approach, use PVA liquid release agent as well.*

process by using this pre-fabricated mould.

First of all, cut the panel of board to size (say 25 × 25cm, or 10 × 10in) and sand down the rough edges. Then the release agent must be applied. The first time a mould is used, it is wise to apply several coats of release wax, partly at least to minimise the risk of missing any areas; but thereafter a single coat of wax can be relied on. Between each coat buff the wax with a soft, dry cloth. Alternatively, if PVA release agent is used a coat of this should be wiped on with a clean cloth, and then allowed to fully dry. Other release agents which permit multiple releases from one application are also available, but are considerably more expensive in the first place, so are perhaps better suited to production runs.

## The gel coat

Once the wax has had a few hours to harden, or the PVA has completely dried, a gel coat can be applied. For this you will need a mixing cup, a mixing stick, the gel coat resin, catalyst, a syringe, pig-

ment if you intend to use it, a clean brush, and acetone solvent to clean the brush afterwards. Wear your gloves and overalls and get some ventilation going again (that's the last time I'll badger you on that topic – possibly).

How much gel coat do you need to use? The aim is to get an even coat about 0.4 to 0.6mm (0.016 to 0.024in) thick, and this can be achieved using between 450 and 600g/sq m, or 1.5 to 2oz/sq ft. (Note: It gets much easier if you stick to metric measurements from here on so that you don't have to work in impractical fractions of ounces and fluid ounces.) Too thin a gel coat may not fully cure, and the underlying reinforcing fabric may show through; and too thick a gel coat may crack and craze, and will be more prone to impact damage. So if your mould panel is 25 × 25cm, or 0.25 × 0.25m, its area is 0.0625sq m, so you will need between 28g and 38g. It is necessary to add an allowance to a small quantity like this to cater for some gel remaining in the brush, so add around 10–15g, which means you need to weigh out 50g in this instance. Put the top back on the gel coat container.

If you intend to add a pigment to your gel coat, now is the time to do it. You will need a pigment that is compatible with the gel you are using, and a whole range of colours is available from the manufacturers. Consult the instructions on the pigment container label to ascertain how much is needed (it is usually just a few per cent by weight, depending on the opacity of the pigment involved), then weigh out – or estimate, if you're feeling over-confident – the requisite amount and add it to the gel. Stir it in thoroughly but gently so as to minimise the introduction of air bubbles.

To this you typically need to add around 2 per cent catalyst, though as with resin this will depend primarily on the manufacturer's instructions and the ambient temperature. This is generally meant to be 2 per cent by volume, but once again it will be satisfactory to work this out on a volume to weight basis, that is 2cm$^3$ (the same as 2ml or 2cc, if you

prefer) of catalyst per 100g of gel coat. This amount is most easily measured out with a clear plastic syringe. Carefully draw up the catalyst in the syringe, put the top back on the catalyst bottle, and gently dispense the catalyst into the gel coat that you have weighed out. Stir the mixture thoroughly but gently, and then let it stand for maybe half a minute or so to allow the curing reaction to initiate. Then load up your brush and apply the catalysed gel coat to the mould surface in slow, even strokes. Gel coat is quite viscous, even when your workshop is nice and warm, and can only be properly applied with steady brush strokes if you're to achieve the consistent, even coating you are aiming for. If the gel coat is uneven, it will cure at different rates across the mould, which can create uneven stresses that lead to crazing and a patchy appearance.

Continue until you have used all the gel coat in your pot and are satisfied that you have an even coating, and then allow the gel to cure. Clean your brush

*Brush on the gel coat with slow, even strokes.*

*Aim for an even coat, not too thick, and not too thin.*

with acetone before the gel cures (it won't dissolve off the brush once it has cured). At this stage, beware of getting dirt, dust, assorted debris, and – in the case of an outside workshop – abseiling spiders or other suicidal bugs, onto the gel coat, because it will be difficult to remove such unwanted additions.

## Laminating

Once the gel coat has cured to a tacky but solid state (remember the fingerprint test from earlier), you can start to prepare for laminating the reinforcement fabric. For the purpose of this exercise, good old CSM will be used. The first thing you have to decide with any moulding job is how many layers of reinforcement fabric you are going to need. Once you've worked that out, you can then calculate pretty accurately how much resin you're going to need. So, for our simple, square, flat moulding, we will use two layers of 450gsm (1¹/₂oz) CSM, and for good measure we'll laminate a diagonal cross-shaped stiffening structure in place too. This will be dealt with later, however,

and for now we'll concentrate on just the first two layers.

Our square mould, you will recall, is 25 × 25cm, or 0.0625sq m in area. However, it is necessary to cut the CSM slightly oversize in order to leave a margin which, after curing, can be used to prise up and release the moulding from the mould. So allow, say, 2cm all round, which means we need to cut two CSM squares measuring 29 × 29cm, or 0.0841sq m. Referring back to Chapter 1, you'll recall the concept of the fibre volume fraction, which was actually expressed in terms of the percentage weight of the finished laminate that was reinforcement fabric, and examples of CSM fraction of 30 and 50 per cent fibre by weight were given. There is another way of looking at this fraction, and that is to regard it as a resin to fabric ratio, which at 30 per cent fibre weight fraction means that the resin to fabric ratio is 70:30, or 2.33:1. This means that the weight of resin in the final laminate is 2.33 times greater than the weight of fibre, and this is in the range of typical resin to fabric ratios achievable with CSM, which should ideally be between 2:1 and 2.5:1, though up to 3:1 is sometimes unavoidable.

You can now see how we calculate the resin requirement. We know that we are going to use two layers of CSM of 0.0841sq m, each weighing 450g per square metre. So the weight of CSM to be used is 2 × 0.0841 × 450g = 75.7g CSM. The amount of resin that will be needed will be between two and three times this, and will most likely be around 2.5 times this weight, which equates to between 151.4g and 227.1g, and ideally around 189.2g. So for convenience, weigh out 200g (if you are using kitchen scales, you will probably have 25g divisions on your 'readout', so you could guess where 189g is on the scales if you wish).

Get everything else you need ready, including catalyst, a clean 2in or 50mm brush, a paddle or washer roller, mixing stick, pigment if you're going to use it, and acetone for brush cleaning after you've finished. Mix the requisite amount of pigment in thoroughly at this point if you are going to pigment your moulding. Now work out how much catalyst to add, based on the earlier section or the manufacturer's instructions, or better still, on the results of your own trials. For the purpose of this paragraph, I'll assume you need 1 per cent catalyst, which will be 2g or 2ml for a 200g resin mix. Carefully add the catalyst to the resin, then mix it in thoroughly, let the resin stand for half a minute, then pick up your brush to apply the resin. Depending on workshop temperature you should have between 30 and 50 minutes pot life, which will be plenty for this job. If you want to give yourself more of a challenge or if it's cold, use a higher proportion of catalyst.

First, brush a generous, even coat of resin all over the surface of the gel coat. Then position the first layer of CSM fabric over the mould and lower it into place, leaving an even 2cm margin all the way around. Now take the brush and, using a stippling action rather than a brushing action, work all over the CSM to get the resin to soak up through and fully 'wet out', or impregnate, the fabric. As you

*Lay the CSM onto the resin-coated surface, and stipple with a brush to bring up the resin.*

work at this you will notice that the fabric becomes more conformable – this happens as the binder which holds the fibres together in the mat form actually dissolves in the resin, leaving nothing, for the time being anyway, to hold the mat fibres together. This not only makes the mat easier to work around any shape that the mould may include (not relevant in our simple trial here), but it also makes it more vulnerable to damage if you're not careful. That's why a stippling action is used in preference to a brushing action.

Add more resin with the brush if necessary to ensure full wetting out of this first layer of CSM, and wet out the overlap margins too. Your roller is actually a much better tool than the brush for impregnating the CSM with resin, and consolidating the laminate, and any trapped air bubbles are easier to dispel with the roller. It's very important that there are no trapped air bubbles next to the gel coat because these can blister and crack later, especially if the laminate is exposed to a source of heat, such as direct sunlight. But don't overuse the

roller – too much rolling can break the strands down into individual fibres, which can lower the mechanical properties of the laminate.

Once this first layer is fully consolidated, lay the second layer of fabric in place and press it down with the brush or the roller. Notice how this layer also wets from below as you work the brush or roller over its surface. Then add as much of the remainder of the resin as is needed with the brush (there's no point in using what is obviously an excess), ensuring an even distribution across the laminate, and stipple or roll to fully wet and consolidate the two layers of fabric together. Although not relevant to this trial, note that if you were making a thick laminate, you would need to pause every four layers or so in order to prevent a runaway generation of heat, known colloquially as an exotherm. By allowing four layers at a time to gel and cool, the chemically-generated heat from the curing reaction is allowed to dissipate for a while, and this potentially laminate-damaging or even dangerous situation can be avoided.

*A roller is a better tool for consolidating the laminate and removing trapped air bubbles.*

There is a point during the cure cycle when, for a limited period, the laminate is in a semi-hard state known as the 'green stage'. It is too soft to release from the mould in this condition, yet it can be cut without disrupting the laminate's integrity. This enables the overlapping edges of a moulding to be 'green trimmed' using a sharp bladed knife such as a Stanley knife, without creating the dust that accompanies this process later, and much more quickly than trimming the cured laminate. But don't forget to leave at least one overlapping edge so that you've got something to lever with when it comes to releasing the moulding from the mould.

### Reinforcing the moulding

Under normal circumstances the moulding could now be left to cure. The time this takes is, as we have seen, temperature dependent, and may occur within a normal working day. It is often convenient, though, to cure mouldings overnight, and providing a suitable tem-

perature is maintained that would usually prove to be no problem. However, as declared earlier, we are going to add a diagonal cross-shaped reinforcement structure to the back of our experimental moulding. This will require a suitable rib former that is compatible with the resin, and which provides a lightweight bridge over which more resin impregnated CSM can be applied. In this instance we will use corrugated cardboard, but you could use various other materials, including wood strips and those described in the section on cores in Chapter 1. These offer some stiffness of their own, but the majority of the stiffness increase will be obtained from the GFRP bridge that is going to be created over the top of these ribs. This type of stiffening bridge is obviously only suitable for flat sections of mouldings.

You could wait until the first layers of the laminate have fully cured before adding this reinforcing structure, but it's probably easier to do it after only partial cure has occurred, while there is still a

*Ribs over which stiffeners will be laminated. Wood or other core materials can, of course, be used.*

degree of softness in the first layers which allows the ribs to be set into the material. However, you should allow *some* hardening to take place, because if you don't there is the risk that the ribs could distort the laminate and leave a visible impression in the gel coat surface (though this is only likely to be noticeable with ribs applied to the back of thin laminates). There is a balance to be struck in the timing here, but it's only by attempting things like this in trials that you get a feel for what you can and cannot get away with.

First, then, you need to cut the reinforcement ribs to length and shape. One of them can be almost the full length of the diagonal of our square moulding, although it will not be extended right to the corners, while the other has to be in two pieces, shaped to fit against the longer section. If you're using wood, carefully sand down any rough edges, and taper off the bluff cut ends with your sanding block. Now prepare the extra CSM to cover the ribs. You will need two strips the length of the diagonals that cover the ribs and wide enough to provide about a 3cm overlap either side (say 10cm wide, then), tailored so that they do not protrude beyond the corners of the mould. To make a tidy job, you could then cover this with another full size square that goes out to the edges of the moulding with a very small overlap; or if you wanted to keep weight to a minimum, you could just cut another two further CSM strips, slightly narrower than the first two – say 6cm wide.

How much resin do you need to use this time? You can either work out the area of the CSM strips and calculate their weight, or just carefully fold them over (don't crease them) and put them on your weighing scales. Multiply their weight by the resin to fabric ratio – say 2.5:1 again – and add an allowance to cater for the coating of and absorption of resin by the ribs. The weight of CSM is about 50g, so we'll need about 125g of resin for that and, say, another 25g to cover the ribs, making 150g of resin. This job will be quite a short one, so a short pot life will be tolerable, and we'll use 2 per cent catalyst, or 3ml.

Weigh out the resin, add the pigment, stir, add the catalyst, stir, and let the mix stand for a short while. Then brush some resin onto the back of the moulding along the strips where the ribs will go, paint some resin onto the ribs, and then press them gently into place. Now you need to wet out the CSM strips, but this time you're going to 'pre-wet' them. Place the first wide strip of CSM on a piece of plastic-faced wood, old newspaper, or polythene sheet, and stipple on resin until the strip is wetted out. Make sure the top surface of the reinforcing ribs is also fully wetted with resin, and then, using the brush and a mixing stick, carefully lift up the wetted CSM strip and lower it into place on the back of one of the ribs, leaving it there for a few moments while you wet out the second wide CSM strip. Before you place the second strip onto the moulding, use your brush to stipple the first strip down onto the rib and moulding. You'll notice that by pre-wetting the strip and leaving it for a short time the binder has dissolved and the CSM has become highly conformable, which makes it easier to stipple down into place. However, if you leave a pre-wetted piece of CSM too long it will disintegrate when you try to lift it up. No, this isn't dropping you in at the deep end, it's just a case of increasing your experience as rapidly as possible…

Once the first strip is consolidated, lift up the second wide strip and place it on the opposite diagonal, then leave it whilst you pre-wet the first narrow strip, before going back and stippling the second wide strip into place. Repeat this process until all four strips are in place, and then work over them with the brush to make sure they are fully consolidated. You could use your roller for parts of the job, and if you've purchased a disc roller you can use that to work into the trickier corners.

Now you can leave the moulding to

*Stipple the covering layer of CSM down around the stiffening ribs.*

cure. Don't forget to clean all your brushes and rollers in acetone before any of the resin with which they've been in contact has the chance to gel, otherwise you won't get it off. It's a good idea to store the brushes and rollers you are going to be using in a pot, with the lid on and a small volume of acetone in the bottom. The lid prevents the volatile acetone from evaporating, and keeps the brushes pliable and the rollers rotating freely.

**Moulding release**

Once the moulding has cured it will be hard, and the overlap edges will have a stiff, brittle feel to them (and will quite likely have horrible, sharp, resin-impregnated fibres sticking out from the edges that will do their best to pierce you – wear thick gloves for handling cured GFRP mouldings). Don't attempt to release the moulding from the mould until this is the case. If the moulding still feels at all soft or sticky then it has not fully cured, even if, theoretically, it has had sufficient time to do so. A useful test

is the coin- or key-tapping test. Tap the moulding with the edge of a coin or key, and if there is a solid sounding noise then the moulding has probably cured, but if the sound is dead it certainly hasn't. Perhaps the temperature dropped too low for full cure in the time you envisaged. Or maybe (perish the thought) you miscalculated the catalyst amount. Then again, perhaps you even forgot to add any catalyst at all – you wouldn't be the first, and one even hears tales of professional laminators doing this from time to time. (If you do ever do this, all you can do is brush a coat of 'fast' resin – that is, resin with 4 or 5 per cent catalyst in it – onto the back of the moulding, let that cure, and hope it gives the whole sticky mess enough rigidity to be pulled out of the mould.)

But this will not have happened on your first carefully controlled trial! All will have gone smoothly, and you will now be able to release the moulding from the mould. Wearing the aforementioned sturdy gloves, prise the overlapping edge away from the mould with your fingers

*Wearing stout gloves, prise the edge of your moulding away from the mould.*

and pull the moulding away from the mould. Providing the release agent was correctly applied in the first place, there will be a satisfying cracking noise (as opposed to the sickening, dispiriting version in which it is the laminate itself that

*Hey presto! Your first successful moulding releases cleanly.*

cracks) as the moulding cleanly separates from the mould, and you get your first view of the surface of your maiden project. It has been said before that making composite mouldings is the only situation in which the material is made at the same time as the product, and this is why the release of a moulding is always a slightly nail-biting moment. In truth you really don't know how good the finished product is going to be until then. But, when everything has worked out well, it's also an immensely satisfying moment.

## Trimming and finishing

Having proudly surveyed your first moulding, you need to trim and finish it. Trimming can be done with a powered jigsaw, but, even though it's slower, I prefer to use a small handsaw such as that shown in the photograph, especially on thin laminates. Powered jigsaw blades can sometimes grab at the laminate, and the potential for causing irreparable damage just isn't worth the risk. On thick, flat laminates, however, jigsaws are fine.

On your test moulding, use the type of handsaw I've suggested so that you can develop a 'feel' for cutting a cured laminate. To mark the lines to be cut, apply masking tape to the gel coat side of the moulding along the proposed cut line, and use a pencil to mark the cut line on the tape. Then carefully cut down each line in turn to leave clean edges. It's better to cut from the gel coat side because it reduces the risk of chipping the gel finish.

You can now tidy up and round off the cut edges with a metal file or abrasive paper. It's also a good idea to run coarse abrasive paper on a sanding block over the back of the mould to remove any of the stray spiky fibres that have a habit of causing bodily damage to the unwary laminator.

If you want to drill holes in a laminate, again work from the gel coat side to avoid chipping the gel finish. Either use a piece of masking tape again on which to mark your intended target, or mark the gel with a sharp pointed tool or punch

*Trim the moulding with a handsaw like this, cutting from the gel coat side.*

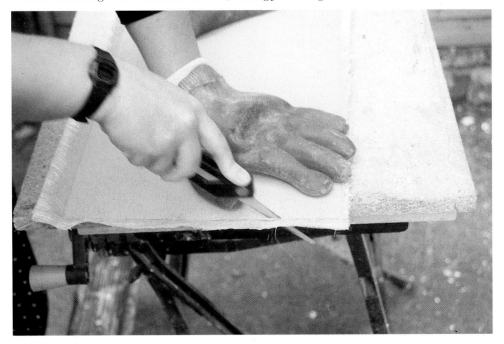

*The stunning finished article!*

(by hand, not with a hammer), then use light pressure on your powered (or hand) drill. Larger holes can be cut with a hole saw attachment on the drill, and non-circular holes will require a jigsaw (hand or powered) and filing as necessary. You can also employ powered disc cutters and sanders on laminates, but these should be used with care because they can remove a lot of material very rapidly. They also create vast clouds of potentially hazardous and irritating dust.

# Chapter 3

# Pattern making

AS PREVIOUSLY MENTIONED, the usual generalised process of creating a composite moulding is a three-step operation. The first step is to produce, or have readily available, a pattern, also variously referred to as a master, a buck, or a plug. This is either a full size, exact replica of what the end product will look like, or a component that you wish to copy (be aware of the possible existence of design copyright in such cases, otherwise you could end up with an irate designer's lawyer chasing you with legal documents). The second step is to make a mould on or in the pattern. And the third step is to make mouldings in or on the mould. There are instances where this can become a two-step process, where, for example, the end product required is so simple in form and shape that a mould can be made directly without first making a pattern, or perhaps where the end product is 'female' in form, and creating a 'male' mould from scratch is actually easier than making a female pattern. (In case there is any confusion about references to male and female parts, my Concise Oxford Dictionary states that a 'female' part is 'manufactured hollow to receive a corresponding male part', and a 'male' part is 'designed to fill a corresponding female part'.) The number of envisaged uses, amongst other factors, is also likely to influence the decision as to whether a mould should be made directly or from a pattern.

Patterns can be made from a fairly wide variety of materials provided they satisfy the requisite criteria. The most important point to remember, though, is that the time and effort spent achieving the best possible finish on a pattern will be reflected in the quality of finish of the mould, and hence, ultimately, the finish on the final moulding. You cannot make a decent mould from a poorly finished pattern, and you cannot make a good moulding from a poor mould. So make a substantial allowance for the time it takes to achieve a good pattern – it is a very time consuming process, especially if you have to create it with your own fair hands (as opposed to using a machine to make it). It is also important that the materials you select to manufacture your pattern are capable of yielding a good finish. Just what this means will be covered in detail as we go along. A pattern need not be made from just one material, though, and it is quite probable that you will use at least two or three materials in constructing it. The rest of this chapter will assume that you are going to make a pattern from scratch, rather than simply copying an existing component. If you do intend to do the latter, go directly to Chapter 4 to find out how to make moulds.

The general qualities you need from a pattern and its constituent materials are: the materials must be readily shapeable and capable of yielding a good finish without special tools being required; they must be resistant to the physical processes, materials and temperatures to be used in mould manufacture; the pattern construction should preferably be strong enough to withstand mould removal without disintegration or damage; it might also have to be durable enough to contend with more than one mould being made from it; and it should be possible to construct it from materials that are readily available and within your budget. Obviously, some of these criteria are dependent on the exact mould-making method you select, but for the time being we'll work on the assumption that moulds and mouldings will be made by wet lay-up contact moulding methods at ambient temperature, and leave examination of the different requirements of elevated temperature cure, vacuum consolidation, and pressure moulding to later chapters.

**Pattern materials**

The sorts of material that are most likely to be available for home workshop use include wood of various types, metal, plaster of Paris, builders' plaster, clay, plasticine, various plastics including GFRP, foams, wax sheet and fillet, and resin-based fillers such as car-body repair filler. As previously mentioned, you will probably combine a number of these materials in the construction of any one pattern. The surface finish may require further materials, such as cellulose or acrylic paint (applied with brush or spray), polyester or epoxy resin, or a specialist finishing resin formulated to produce a high gloss finish on a pattern. The latter type of product tends to be more expensive, but may save you time in achieving the shiny finish you'll usually be looking for. Other paint and resin finishes will almost always require rubbing down with progressively finer grades of abrasive paper and buffing with cutting compound to get the desired surface gleam. (Note: It is fair to say that it sometimes isn't vital to get a high gloss surface if the end product doesn't need such a finish, but mould release will almost

always be easier from a good surface finish.)

Depending on the size and shape of your pattern, wood can be a suitable material choice, especially if the pattern is to be small and solid. Expensive hardwoods such as mahogany are used by professionals with adequate budgets, these being stable, close-grained (guaranteeing a good finish), and relatively easy to work. The cost of mahogany probably isn't justifiable for most home projects, however. There are also other less expensive hardwoods, such as jelutong, which are similar to balsa in their properties and are easy to work. But providing very good long term dimensional stability is not necessarily a prerequisite, ordinary (and much cheaper) softwoods can be used for shaping solid patterns. Larger patterns tend to be hollow, and other forms of timber such as plywood, medium density fibre board (MDF), and plastic-covered chipboard (such as Contiboard) can all be useful in pattern construction, the last often providing an adequate surface finish to flat areas. MDF is advantageous because it can be fashioned into three-dimensional shapes relatively easily with conventional hand and power tools, though it seems you need to protect yourself from the dust it produces. The cheaper forms of plywood are useful for the bases and support frames of larger patterns in which other materials are supported by a wooden frame or box-work. However, *all* wood pattern materials, especially MDF, need protecting from humidity and dampness to prevent distortion and degradation.

Metals can certainly be used for pattern construction, either as a machined solid or in sheet form, though they are unlikely to be used as often as other materials because they are not as easy to shape and, in sheet form, are easily damaged and dented.

Plaster of Paris and builders' plaster make relatively cheap, easily worked filler materials that can be applied either onto a wooden box-work structure, or over expanded metal or wire mesh supported by dowels in a timber box-work. A disadvantage of plasters, however, is that they are water-based, and therefore take quite some time (weeks, even) to dry out, an essential requirement before resin-based materials can be applied over them. Furthermore, the drying process tends to cause shrinkage and cracking, necessitating repair and filling. Plasters can nevertheless be useful, especially on a large pattern where anything else might be very costly.

Clay and plasticine are handy materials, especially for small three-dimensional details where their ability to be shaped by hand can be exploited. Plasticine can also be used to form small fillets in otherwise sharp internal corners, which often facilitates a more efficient mould release. An even better material for this is wax fillet, tailor-made for the job, which comes in various sizes, and after being pressed into a corner is smoothed into a neat, radiused fillet with a ball-ended tool of appropriate size, warmed in hot water. Nor does the wax need to be treated with a release agent.

Plastics can also make useful pattern materials, particularly as some already have excellent surface finishes. Compatibility with the resin you intend to use for the mould must be checked if you have no data available, but, for example, one useful plastic that can be purchased from DIY stores in sheet form is Formica. This is well finished, compatible with polyester resin, and makes a good surfacing material on flat or gently curving areas. Using GFRP certainly shouldn't present any compatibility problems if the mould is to be made in the same material. It can be an effective reinforcement over other less durable 'bulk' materials, and can act as a substrate to finer finishing materials such as polyester resin-based body filler. CSM may produce too rough a surface, but woven cloth and glass tissue produce a much smoother surface that needs less filling to achieve a good finish.

*Larger hollow patterns can be constructed from MDF board.*

Certain foams make excellent pattern materials. For example, polyurethane foam is compatible with polyester resin, and is easily carved and sanded to shape. It is rigid enough to be virtually self-supporting, and readily available if not exactly cheap. It can be bought as a two-pack chemical kit that is mixed at the time of use, then poured into a retaining cavity wherein it expands to many times the liquid volume before it sets. Alternatively it can be bought in the form of pre-expanded blocks and sheets of various dimensions and thicknesses. It can be bonded easily to itself or to other materials, and it can be coated with GFRP to build a tough and durable surface which can then be finished appropriately. Polystyrene foam, as was stated in Chapter 1, is not compatible with polyester resin because it dissolves when in direct contact with it. But, providing it is sealed with something like PVA adhesive or epoxy resin before any polyester resin is brought anywhere near it, it can prove a useful, easily worked, readily available and cheaper alternative to polyurethane foam. It can be bought in pre-cut panels at various thicknesses from builders' merchants. You can bond sheet plastics such as Formica to flat or gently curving faces of polystyrene to create a sealed, smooth surface.

Resin-based fillers are essential for obtaining a suitable finish over areas of plaster or foam. Since they are usually based on polyester resin, you cannot apply them directly to un-sealed polystyrene foam because the foam will once again disintegrate when in contact with filler. General-purpose car body filler, obtainable from car accessory and DIY stores, is adequate for surfacing patterns, provided it is reasonably fresh and spreads easily, though you can also buy purpose-made pattern maker's filler, which claims to produce a smoother finish free of porosity. The choice is yours, and whether you will benefit from the purpose-made product depends on how many patterns you're likely to make and how big they are going to be.

Unless your pattern is made entirely of well-finished plastics, or is a pre-existing component that already possesses a good finish, you need to apply a suitable surface coating to it. The material you choose to provide this final finish needs to offer several characteristics. It must be capable of sealing any porous surface over which it is applied, be that wood, plaster or filler. It must again be compatible with the materials that have been used to make the pattern, and which are going to be used to make the mould. And most importantly perhaps, it must allow you to obtain the finish you want (or need).

Un-reinforced polyester resin is one suitable material, brushed (or sprayed, if you have the equipment) over the pattern surface, and allowed to cure before being sanded and polished. Epoxy resin could be used for the same purpose, but being more expensive is probably not the most sensible choice unless there is some reason why polyester cannot be used. You can purchase special finishing resins, formulated to create a high gloss surface, which will undoubtedly be the best materials for the job in a lot of cases, but which are also rather costly. Or, if the surface is already reasonably smooth and free from blemishes, you can use paint. Acrylic or cellulose paints can be either sprayed or brushed on, rubbed down between coats, and then polished with cutting compound to produce a high gloss surface at modest cost. Once the release agent is applied, the surface is ready to take a mould. PVA release agent on top of wax seals the paint surface thoroughly.

Although PVA acts as a very good seal on top of a paint finish, you would be well advised to check the compatibility of your paint with the underlying materials by making a small test sample and applying the paint you intend to use. And you also need to be certain that the painted surface is compatible with the mould making process, so a small test sample should be made, release agent applied, and your chosen resin brushed on and cured to check that all will be well. Incompatibility will show up either as a wrinkling of the paint, or an unwillingness on the part of the resin to cure properly adjacent to the painted surface. This would be *very* depressing if you only became aware of the problem when the mould failed to cure on your (previously) shiny pattern.

## Pattern design and manufacture

Probably the most important step in designing a pattern is drawing it. With very simple patterns this may not be necessary, but the process of actually drawing a design will help you to work out how it needs to be made, and how to avoid omitting minor but often important details. Drawings don't have to be accurate, or to scale – sketches on the proverbial paper napkin or cigarette packet are usually better than nothing. The drawing will end up showing not just the shape of the item to be created, but also some of the features that will aid the manufacture of the mould later on, like flanges (possibly removable) around the periphery, or a baseboard on which to mount the whole thing. A detail that you should also keep in mind at the design stage is the component's intended final thickness – this may affect the pattern in areas where this component sits very tightly over others, and you need to make allowance for the laminate thickness.

You will also be able to design in where mould 'split lines' will be needed. These cater for patterns that have an 'undercut' to them, which would prevent the mould being removed from the pattern unless it is made in two or more sections bolted or clamped together. (More on this in the next chapter.) Another related consideration is that even where there is no undercut, it can be difficult to remove a mould from a pattern with deep sides. The problem is eased somewhat if the pattern is designed with non-parallel sides which converge slightly in the direction in which the mould will be removed. This naturally creates a divergent shape to the mould. The angle of convergence need only be quite small, say a degree or so, and may therefore not even be noticeable in the end product, but it will save a lot of grief, not just when taking the mould off the pattern, but also when releasing mouldings from the mould later on.

## Two-dimensional patterns

A simple two-dimensional pattern should really be regarded as a mould, since this is one instance in which the 'tooling to production' sequence is just a two-step process. But let's consider it here, looking at how it can be made, and from what. To produce a flat composite sheet that has one 'good' surface, you only need to have a flat pattern or mould. The material you choose to make it from will quite probably be governed as much by what you can readily lay your hands on as anything else, because wet lay-up ambient temperature cure contact moulding doesn't really place many special criteria on pattern materials. However, the standard of finish you require may influence your choice.

If, for example, you want to cut out a two-dimensional shape to make a simple aerofoil end-plate in flat sheet, or a basic instrument panel, then you would perhaps select plastic-faced chipboard as a cheap, readily obtainable material which can be easily cut with hand or powered saws. You have the option of cutting the pattern to the exact dimensions of the required moulding, or leaving a margin around the outside. In the latter case you could carefully scribe a shallow 'trim line' in the surface of the plastic-faced chipboard, which would show as a thin, raised line on the moulding, and act as a guide to trim the moulding to. Once you have cut your pattern to shape and size, the only finishing required is to sand down any rough edges, and to apply the appropriate release agent. In this instance, four or five coats of good mould-release wax works well.

Other materials that can be used for simple 2D patterns include wood – once again an easily cut and shaped material, which then needs to be painted or resin coated. Either coating will need rubbing down with wet and dry abrasive paper, then buffing with cutting compound to as shiny a surface finish as you require prior to release agent application (several coats of wax again works well, as does PVA liquid release agent). Plate glass can also be used, needing only a few coats of mould release wax to produce a spectacular, shiny finish! Glass, though, is not

*A two-dimensional (well, almost) pattern made from plastic-faced chipboard, with a few add-on bits.*

easily cut to shape and size, but is ideal for making regular, flat panels that can be trimmed to the desired shape and size later. Sheet or plate metal can be used too, being relatively easy to cut to shape and needing only waxing or PVA coating to get a good release.

## Simple three-dimensional patterns

Making even the simplest three-dimensional shapes requires more thought and effort than 2D, but need not be difficult to create. For example, take a simple aerofoil or wing shape, which has a consistent cross-section across its width (or 'span', to use the correct aeronautical term). Such a shape is sometimes described as having 'single curvature', because the curvature is only in one direction. This feature enables simple tools and techniques to be employed in making a pattern. Let's assume that you want to create your own wing shape from scratch, and that you have no exist-

ing wing to mould from. You therefore need to decide what materials you are going to use to form the wing shape, and to obtain a high gloss finish on your pattern. You also have to choose whether to make the pattern in one or two pieces – it can be easier to make separate patterns for upper and lower halves, with each half fixed to a baseboard to provide stability whilst you work on it. An implicit assumption is that the pattern will be 'male' – that is, its curvature will be convex. This makes it very much easier to create by hand.

Selection of materials will once more be heavily influenced by what you have available, what is easily obtainable, what falls within your budget, and what you are used to working with. For all these reasons, wood usually plays at least some part in the process. But if you are limited to hand tools to carve out your wing shape, then making the pattern in solid wood would take a long time. It is generally easier to make wooden templates that are cut to the desired shape and fixed to a rigid baseboard at 'stations' along the span of the wing, and then to fill the spaces between the templates with a material that is easily carved, sanded or otherwise shaped and is capable of accepting the materials that will provide the outer 'shell' and requisite surface finish. Polyurethane foam comes straight to mind, and polystyrene foam also works well, with the usual proviso about sealing it if polyester resin is to be used. Don't forget to cut the profile templates slightly undersize to allow for the thickness of the outer shell finish, which should be the exact dimensions and shape of the final product.

Sheet metal also lends itself to being formed into single curvature components, and you may prefer to think about folding aluminium sheet into your wing profile, perhaps bonded and screwed to a wooden frame of ribs and spars (these could also be formed from aluminium sheet). At this point, you are almost bound to say to yourself: 'why bother to make a mould, because I've just made an aluminium wing?' Whilst this may be true, consider for a moment the disadvantages of using aluminium for items such as wings, or any other bodywork for that matter. Firstly, aluminium is easily dented, and dents not only look unsightly but also adversely affect the airflow around a wing, which is likely to make it a lot less efficient than you might have hoped. FRP moulded wings do not dent anywhere near as easily. Secondly, it is more difficult to exactly replicate a given shape each time when making it from scratch in folded metal, whereas moulded composite components come out identically each time you mould a new one. Thirdly, it is also difficult to put small radius curves and folds into metal sheet, which tends to compromise the shape of a wing's leading edge and limits one's ability to produce a decent aerodynamic profile.

This last point is a clincher when it comes to making a wing pattern, whereas the previous points relate to making the actual wings. So, if you want to create an efficient wing pattern, sheet aluminium, and sheet metal in general, is not your best option. Plenty of people will argue against this, and there are a lot of aluminium wings in use in motorsport. Aluminium does have its advantages, such as relatively low cost, the fairly short amount of time required to manufacture a product if you don't already have a mould, and (at least until you've read this book) probably a greater degree of familiarity in its handling and use. Where details in the shape and design of a component are less critical than in the case of aerofoils, aluminium can certainly be used successfully to make single curvature patterns.

Back to our wing pattern, though – and remember, the choice of a wing here is illustrative of techniques which you could apply to any single curvature pattern. First you need to define the shape of your wing (or whatever your simple 3D component is going to be). In this instance, you will probably have consulted aerodynamic reference books at the local library, or preferably bought a copy of my first book, *Competition Car Downforce* (published by G.T. Foulis), and you will now be in possession of the co-ordinates you need to draw out an accurate profile of an efficient wing shape. Having done that, you need to decide on the one- or two-piece pattern route. I think the two-piece route makes life simpler, so the descriptions and illustrations will cover this method. This means that you need to cut out two sets of templates, one to the shape of the upper wing surface, and one to the profile of the lower wing surface. Templates can be cut from plywood or MDF, but need to be thick enough to accept small screws driven up through the baseboard, so say around 9–10mm minimum (about 3/8in). Naturally, the templates not only need to match your drawn profile, they also need to be identical to one another too, so unless you are very good at cut-

*Cutting wooden templates for a simple three-dimensional pattern, in this case the lower half of an aerofoil.*

ting out shapes from wood, some time will need to be spent on finishing the templates so that they are identical.

The rectangular baseboard itself must be rigid and stable so as not to distort or move around during any of the processes

*Templates cut to shape.*

*Finishing a template.*

that follow. Sturdy plywood or chipboard just about suffices, but can be made much more rigid by screwing sections of finished 50 by 25mm (2in by 1in) timber 'end on' to the underside at the front and back edges.

Next, you need to position and fasten your templates carefully onto the base-

*The templates positioned at their stations on the baseboard.*

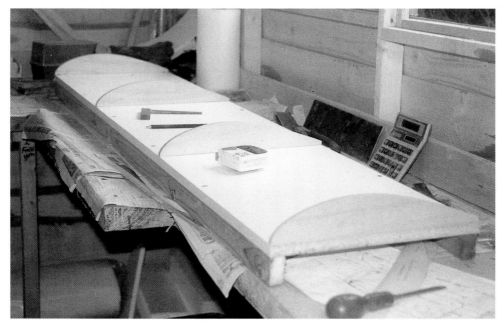

board. The number of templates you need will be governed by the maximum width (or span) of the pattern, but as a rough guide fix one template at regular intervals of about 300mm (approximately 12in). The leading edge of the templates should be aligned along one long edge of the baseboard, and at right angles to it. For convenience, in this instance the baseboard should be no bigger, front to back, than the wing profile – I find it's easier to finish a wing mould right at the trailing edge, and put a flange standing upright (approximately) at right angles to the surface at the trailing edge. But more of that in the next chapter as well, because this will not always be the case.

Once the templates are securely fastened to the baseboard, the shapeable material can be positioned between them. Whatever material you use, it must start out protruding above the templates at all points and be shaped down to the required profile by one or other of the methods described here. The illustrations show polystyrene foam blocks, cut to fit between the templates, but polyurethane

foam block is probably a better choice, if more costly. You could also use two-pack expanding foam to fill the gaps (do one gap at a time to keep everything under control...), maybe using sheet plastic held down over the gaps between templates to force the foam to preform roughly to the profile of the templates. By the way, before attempting to use two-pack expanding foam carry out some trials using small quantities, to see just how much it does expand. Then you could get technical and try to calculate how much you'd need to mix to fill the volumes between templates.

In the case of polystyrene foam you can, if you have a mind to, go to the modest expense and less modest trouble of making a 'hot-wire bow' to cut it to shape. This is a handy tool to have if you are likely to want to cut more shapes out of polystyrene foam block, but probably not worth the effort for a one-off job. It does, however, create a lot less mess than sawing and sanding polystyrene. It can be used to cut polyurethane foam as well, but the fumes generated are evil-

*Preparing polystyrene foam block between templates prior to cutting.*

smelling and toxic, so this, most assuredly, is *not* recommended. The fumes evolved during hot-wire cutting of polystyrene are acrid enough, and good ventilation is essential.

To make a hot-wire bow you need a length of electrical resistance wire – such as that from a defunct electric fire, suitably straightened out – to form the 'hot-wire bowstring' that heats up and cuts the foam; a wooden frame that has a means of adjusting the 'bowstring' tension to keep the hot-wire straight; and a 12-volt battery, plus some cable to make connections to the bow. Some form of variable resistance that can adjust the current in the hot-wire, and hence the heat generated, is useful – I raided a scrap toaster for this purpose and removed the small element that heats up the bi-metallic strip; I adjust the current, very crudely, by altering the position of a crocodile clip connector on the coil. In fact the whole thing is very crude, but it is functional, and cuts polystyrene blocks like a hot knife cutting butter. Notice that you need the wire to pro-

trude slightly beyond the bow frame so that the frame does not get in the way when cutting blocks that are wider than the bow. The bow can then be used to shape polystyrene to template profiles very easily, by connecting it up to its battery, letting it get hot, and then simply dragging it over each block in turn, using the templates as the guides.

To shape polyurethane foam, the safest way is to sand it to profile using a purpose-made sanding block that is at least as wide as the pattern. Use a section of smooth 'finished' 50 by 25mm (2in by 1in) wood, with coarse abrasive paper stuck to one surface by means of double-sided adhesive tape, and gradually sand down through the foam block until you get to the templates. But take care not to sand down your accurately-shaped templates!

Now you are almost ready to apply the outer shell to the pattern. But given that this shell will have a thickness of its own, you need to sand down the foam block, whatever type it is, between the templates to allow for building up the surface

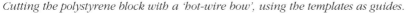

*Cutting the polystyrene block with a 'hot-wire bow', using the templates as guides.*

to come level with the profile of the templates. So you have to decide what the outer shell materials are going to be, and roughly how thick the shell will be. The shell will usually consist of a reinforcing fabric in resin, followed by some form of filler, and finally a few coats of paint, so allow about 3mm (about 1/8in), and sand down the foam about this distance below the templates.

To give the pattern some toughness and durability, a good choice to cover the foam would be a layer of GFRP. One or two layers of CSM in polyester resin will do the job, and this can be applied directly onto polyurethane foam once all the loose dust from the sanding operation has been cleaned off. If you've used polystyrene, you can either try sealing it with a few coats of PVA adhesive (wood glue) – which you must let dry completely before applying CSM and polyester resin – or apply a coat of epoxy resin, which will make an effective seal and also put some strength into the surface. You could lay down some glass fibre fabric at the same time, but make

sure that the fabric is compatible with epoxy resin – CSM, for example, often isn't. Don't cover the wood formers with fabric and resin by the way, unless you cleverly made an allowance for the thickness that this would add when you first cut them out.

When the resin supporting the glass fabric has cured, you can start to apply filler. This is a fairly laborious process, but having chosen this route to making a pattern there's no escaping it now. And in order to avoid it you would have had to use a medium such as wood in the first place, itself far more laborious to carve and sand to shape. The filler is best applied in plenty of thin coats that build up to just above the required thickness, and then sanded back to the profile of the templates. The process tends to be an iterative one of filling and sanding, followed by more filling and sanding, until you produce a satisfactory, defect-free surface finish to which you can apply the final coat. The sanding will be with progressively finer grades of abrasive paper too, ending up with something like a 240

*Covering the polystyrene with woven glass cloth and epoxy resin.*

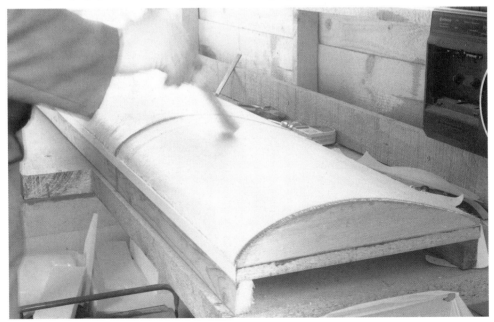

*Applying body filler to the pattern surface.*

grit dry abrasive, before switching to 400 grade wet and dry if you intend to apply paint as the outer layer.

If you choose a thin coat of resin as the outer layer, you will be looking to obtain your high gloss by means of this

*Using a wide sanding block (a piece of straight timber with abrasive paper held on by double-sided tape) to sand down the pattern surface.*

coating. As mentioned previously, you can purchase special finishing resins designed for this job, or you can use cheaper polyester resin and obtain a similar result. It's a case of horses for courses, and the 'correct' choice is budget-dependent as much as anything. Generally, however, you get what you pay for. The rubbing down process is the same as described below.

If paint is to form your outer coat, then typically you can use automotive spray paints as sold in aerosol cans at motorists' spares stores, but as mentioned earlier, you should carry out some trials to make sure the paint doesn't react on the surface to which you apply it, or under the resin and CSM that will be applied on top of it later to form the mould. I have used these paints, and others like filler/primer spray paint, to successfully coat patterns, but there is no substitute for making your own test samples – if things go wrong, don't say I didn't tell you to experiment first! Assuming your test samples look good and reveal no problems, then basically you need to spray several even coats of paint over the filler surface, and then rub it down with finer and finer grades of wet and dry paper, starting with 400 grade, then 600 grade, before finally working through to 1200 grade. After that you switch to cutting compound, and buff away until you get a gloss finish. It's very good for the arms.

If, during these final stages, you spot defects such as slight indentations or high points, you will regret it if you don't deal with them there and then, because they will be *at least* as visible in the finished product. To remove them add some more filler, and do some more sanding and some more painting, all the while telling yourself how obvious the defects would have been if you'd ignored them. There is no *easy* way to make a good pattern.

Once you've achieved the best surface finish you can, you are ready to apply the appropriate release agent, as described in Chapter 2.

## More complex three-dimensional patterns

Shapes that comprise more complicated geometry, or complex ('double') curvature, are obviously not so simple to create. On the assumption that you, like me, do not have the luxury of a multi-axis machining centre residing in the shed at the bottom of the garden, these more complex shapes are, once more, going to have to be tackled the old-fashioned way – by hand. But creating a satisfactory complex pattern is not necessarily that difficult; it just takes care and time. Those most skilful of craftsmen and women, the pattern makers, have a blend of knowledge, experience and intuitive ability that probably make our best efforts appear slow and even amateurish by comparison, but then that's why they get paid for it while we're doing it in our spare time in the shed. The fact that these wonderfully accomplished folk exist should not deter the rest of us from having a go.

The technique involved in creating a three-dimensional pattern is, in principle at least, not very different to that described in the previous section. Depending on the size of the project, you have the choice of carving a shape out of a solid material such as wood or metal, or for larger projects you can assemble materials together to make a hollow pattern. For example, you could screw together carefully cut pieces of MDF to form a hollow box structure if your component shape is comprised of flat panels. But for larger shapes it's back to the template and foam method, except that this time you will have to apply a bit more thought and effort to the templates and the supporting structure.

As an example of a more complex three-dimensional shape for which to make a pattern, think of a single-seater racecar nosecone. Parts of a nosecone, such as some of the sides and perhaps the underside, may be flat, so flat panels of MDF could be used as the pattern surface for these (with an appropriate surface finish applied, of course). Other parts will be curved, and almost certainly the curvature will be complex. For these areas you need to use a material that you can carefully carve and sand to shape, and, as already stated, the rigid foams are eminently suitable for this purpose. You could therefore simply build up these areas in solid foam, and then sand away until you have the required shape ready for surfacing. This would be fine if the actual shape and dimensions were not critical, and if you have a good eye that needs no guidance to maintain symmetry and form. You're probably already a sculptor if that's the case. But in most cases you will be better off working from drawings, because you can than make your templates from these drawings, and build a structure that will provide the guidance that you'll probably need (unless you're a sculptor) to get the desired finished shape.

Back to the nosecone pattern. The shape is three-dimensional, so draw it out in plan view as well as side and front elevations. Then mark transverse cross-sections on the drawings, spaced at 'stations' of around 250 to 300mm (10 to 12in), or perhaps considerably less where your shape curves rapidly. These cross-sections are going to be used to make transverse templates (from ply or MDF) that

you will screw to a baseboard at the requisite spacings (assuming the underside of the nosecone is flat for the purposes of this exercise). If there is longitudinal curvature too, then you will also need to draw longitudinal cross-sections at intervals, perhaps one at the centre line and maybe one or two more either side of the centre line, depending on the size and curvature of the nosecone. These are again used to make the longitudinal templates you will need.

Number each template from a datum such as the rearmost or foremost transverse template, and maybe from the left and right of the centre longitudinal one, then mark them out in turn to the shape and dimensions defined in your drawing, and cut them out. Also cut out your baseboard to the plan shape, plus a generous extra border of 50 to 75mm (2 to 3in). Now you have to assemble your templates onto the baseboard in the designated order. Here you need to use one of two methods to join the longitudinal and transverse templates together. You can either fix the centre longitudinal to the rear (largest) transverse template, then cut all the other transverse templates in half (removing half the thickness of the centre template from each) and join them to the centre one. Or you can do the job properly, cutting half-height slots the

**Figure 3–1** *Schematic of a simple nosecone pattern, showing templates at stations.*

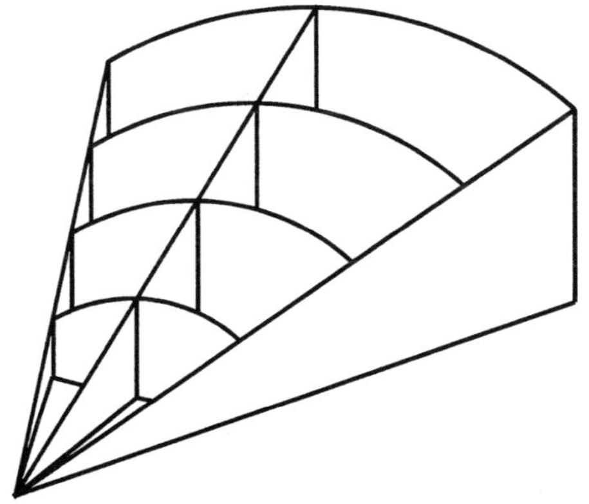

thickness of the template material into the longitudinal centre template, and reversed half-height slots in the transverse ones so that the templates slide together and interlock in a lap joint. The templates are then screwed to the baseboard, and the remaining longitudinal templates are then fitted in position between the transverse templates.

You now have a box structure that forms the skeleton of the hollow pattern, and which defines the approximate shape. Now you have to fill the spaces between the templates with the material that you will carve to the final shape and to which you will apply the durable surface, just as with the simpler patterns discussed in the previous section. Obviously, you don't need to fill the whole structure with rigid foam, but you do need to fix the foam blocks (if that's what you are using) in such a way that they are rigidly and immovably attached to the box structure, and protruding above all the templates slightly. Depending once again on the size and shape of your pattern, you might find that the best way to do this is to attach further horizontal (and possibly vertical) pieces of board to the templates, set below the 'surface', onto which the foam blocks can be firmly glued. This will provide the necessary support to the foam to

allow you to work on shaping it.

And shaping the foam is the next step. Clearly, sanding between the templates is going to generate a slightly angular surface at this stage, especially in areas of pronounced double curvature, but since you'll be sanding the foam down to just below the 'surface' defined by the templates, this is not yet critical. To sand to the level of the templates, make up a sanding tool from a piece of 50 by 25mm (2in by 1in) timber with coarse abrasive paper stuck to it again, this time making the tool slightly longer than the gaps between templates, and be careful not to sand down the templates themselves. Then use a smaller sanding block to rub down the foam to just below the templates.

Now, as with the simple 3D pattern described previously, a layer or two of CSM or woven glass cloth in polyester resin can be applied to give the pattern surface strength and durability. Once this has cured, the process of applying filler can be started. Sanding the filler is going to be the hardest part of this job, not because of the physical effort, but because you will have to start using those sculptor's attributes of a good eye and a confident hand to get the desired surface curvature. Clearly the filler needs to be built up between templates to allow the

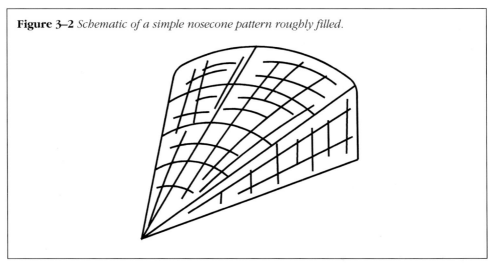

**Figure 3–2** *Schematic of a simple nosecone pattern roughly filled.*

requisite curvature to be accommodated, and then careful sanding can commence. You can see now why areas of rapid curvature change require closer template spacing, and why areas of double curvature demand more time at this stage. But, to reiterate, time is probably the most valuable component of a pattern, so don't skimp on it. The chances are you will need to exercise a high degree of patience in order to do a good job.

Once the filler surface has been rubbed down to a medium grit abrasive paper finish, you can apply whatever material you have chosen for the surface finish, and finally flat it down and buff it up until you get the gloss that you want to see in the end product. This process is the same as described in the previous section.

The observant reader will have noticed that the pattern thus created will, ultimately, enable the manufacture of a bottomless nosecone. To make a pattern for the underside is simple, especially if it is to be entirely flat, because you can use the 'direct to mould' approach described earlier in this chapter to make a mould for the underside from plastic-covered chipboard. The surface finish won't be as good as your masterpiece for the upper section, but being practical, how often is the underside of your nosecone going to be visible? Not too often, I hope. So just mark around the baseboard of the upper pattern directly onto the shiny surface of a piece of plastic-covered chipboard, and cut to shape. And that's it – one mould for the underside. This will be bolted to the flange of the upper mould once that has been made so that a complete nosecone can be laminated, and unbolted again to aid release of the finished component; but more of this later.

## The professionals

Now may not be the time to say this, as the blood, sweat and tears slowly dry on the surface of your handiwork, but once you've made a pattern using what we might call 'traditional methods', as described above, you begin to realise the

*Epoxy block being prepared for machining into a chassis pattern at Benetton Formula.*

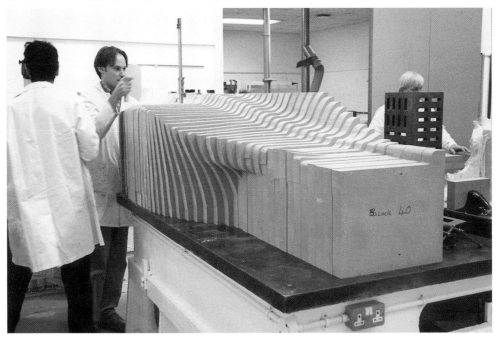

advantages that fully tooled-up professional pattern makers are able to enjoy these days employing computer-aided techniques. By transferring drawings electronically from computer aided draughting (CAD) packages directly to computer-controlled multi-axis machining centres, the top Formula 1 teams are able to carve out pattern shapes large and small from special epoxy block, thereby eliminating many labour-intensive hours of work, and guaranteeing dimensions and symmetry that exactly match the drawings. We'll take a closer look at this fascinating technology in Chapter 9, just for interest's sake, but if you want to equip your own shed similarly, first buy a bigger shed, and second, keep buying those lottery tickets.

# Chapter 4

# Making moulds

IN THIS CHAPTER we'll look at how you perform the second phase of the basic three-step composite component production sequence – making moulds. For the time being the methods and materials that we'll go into will pertain solely to the wet lay-up, ambient temperature cure, contact moulding process, concentrating primarily but not exclusively on moulds made in GFRP. Consequently the practical techniques mastered in Chapter 2 will get you through this chapter, and enable you to make moulds that will permit moulded composite components to be made from a wide range of materials. Mould construction is a lot less time consuming than pattern making, but, like all the processes described in this book, requires no less attention to detail.

**Mould requirements**
The design of a mould must obviously reflect its intended use with regard to the size, shape and particular characteristics of the component to be made from it, and the intended number of uses to which you envisage subjecting it. In all likelihood your mould will be female in shape (though that does depend on which surface of the finished product is to have a smooth finish), and it will be laminated over a pattern such as described in the previous chapter. The surface of the mould has to be smooth, to facilitate component release and to minimise the amount of work needed to achieve an appropriate surface finish on

the end product. The mould must physically allow the lamination, release and removal of the component following cure, and this may demand that it is made in more than one piece. It generally needs to be stronger and stiffer than the component which is to be laminated in it will be when cured. And, if it is reasonably large, it will probably need reinforcing with an external structure bonded to the outside, which will usefully double up as a stand on which the mould can be placed whilst you work on it.

Let's take a look at facilitating component lamination and release. We have already alluded to this point in the previous chapter, in a brief discussion of moulds that need to be made in more than one piece, with external flanges set along 'split lines' at which the pieces of the mould are bolted or clamped together. We'll consider the detailed construction of these flanges in the next section, but their positioning is something that has to be considered at this early mould design stage, if not during the making of patterns. The need for split lines and flanges in a mould is to enable the production of a moulding that could not otherwise be manufactured or released from a single-piece mould because of difficult access, undercut, or 'internal' features such as return flanges, or just a deep 'draw' which would make release extremely difficult. As a large-scale (in motorsport terms) example, consider making a mould for a single-seater monocoque chassis – you can visualise straight away that the mould would need to be in at least two parts, maybe upper and lower, with a flange at a split line about half-way up the sides, or where there was a suitable change of angle or curvature of the sides that dictated very obviously where the split line should go in order to avoid undercut in one or other half. Similarly, as mentioned earlier, aerofoils are conveniently made in upper and lower half-moulds which are clamped together in order that the two halves of the component may be joined.

Notice that the component may or may not be made in one shot. In the examples quoted above, the chassis and the aerofoil would probably be made in two separate pieces which are subsequently bonded together, whereas in the case, say, of a racecar nosecone, the base and any return flanges along the back face that butt up to the chassis or the cockpit cover would be laminated along with the other surfaces of the component in a one-shot process. The former examples are where laminating the product in one piece would be impossible because of access, whereas the latter is where release of the component would be impossible without unbolting the mould sections.

The desired location of split lines is often fairly obvious. In the case of the nosecone example again, if the shape is fairly simple, with a basic triangular appearance when viewed from above and from the side, then split lines would most conveniently be at the baseboard and along the back edge. A mould flange would be laminated onto the baseboard around the bottom edge of the pattern, and a further flange with a bolted mating return flange would need to be added to the back edge (more on the details of this a bit later). Then the underside mould can be bolted to the lower edge flange to enable the underside to be laminated in the same process as the rest of the nose, and in the case of the back edge the

*Our simple pattern, with split-line flange on the top (back) edge.*

internal return is laminated against the bolted mould return flange. Thus the nosecone mould becomes a three-piece mould – the main section with flanges around the base and rear edge, plus the underside mould and the back edge internal return flange mould. All three pieces are bolted together at the flanges to facilitate one shot lamination, and following component cure the pieces are unbolted to allow the release of the finished, single-piece component. Notice, too, that the flanges around the lower and rear edges help to make the main mould much stiffer and stronger than if it had no flanges.

As stated in the previous chapter, in the case of an aerofoil the mould would most probably have a flange at a split line along the leading (front) edge, and possibly a further flange along the trailing (back) edge. Each half would then be laminated separately, and ultimately the upper and lower halves would be joined in the mould halves, which would then be bolted together while the adhesive cured.

The materials to use in making a mould by wet lay-up will depend once again on the envisaged use of the mould, but will most probably be glass fibre chopped strand mat (CSM) in a polyester resin matrix, possibly with one of the less expensive core materials to help stiffen and strengthen larger unsupported areas. These are the cheapest materials, and are certainly quite capable of being laminated up into a tough, stiff and strong mould able to endure many repeated uses. You can make a lighter, stronger mould with woven glass fibre cloth, or even carbon fibre fabric, and also by using epoxy resin instead of polyester. But for ambient temperature cure contact moulding, there aren't really any good reasons why the extra cost of these materials should be borne. Only once you start contemplating higher temperature curing and vacuum consolidation do you need to think about more sophisticated mould materials, and we'll go into that in later chapters.

## Pattern preparation

Whatever you are going to take a mould from, be it an item you are replicating or a pattern you have made from scratch, usually the first job that needs doing is to apply the mould release agent (though see the next section on split lines). As discussed in Chapter 2, the most common types of release agent for this kind of moulding work are either a proprietary mould release wax, an automotive wax if you can be certain it is not silicone based (and such traditional silicone-free waxes are harder to find nowadays), or a polyvinyl alcohol (PVA) dispersion. My personal preference, especially where a high gloss finish is desired, is a mould release wax, but I also use PVA, usually on simple components and internal sub-assemblies. But it's up to you which you use. PVA has the advantage that it is water soluble, and is easily washed off a cured moulding, necessitating minimal preparation before painting. Wax residue, on the other hand, must be removed with a suitable solvent, rubbing compound, or fine abrasive before paint will adhere. So there are pros and cons to each type of release agent.

If you are using mould release wax, and the pattern on which you are going to make your mould is new, then you need to apply several coats. This not only helps to ensure complete coverage of the pattern, it also helps to do a thorough job of sealing the surface should there be any remaining porosity. The manufacturer's instructions should be followed with regard to the specific method of application for any given product, but in general waxing involves plenty of soft, clean cloths, and copious quantities of elbow grease. It is imperative that you avoid using cloths which have been used for any other purpose, especially ones that have been used to apply and buff fine abrasive rubbing compounds. Wax is usually applied to relatively small areas at a time, then buffed until a hard shiny coat is achieved. The whole process should be repeated several times, perhaps applying

*Several coats of mould release wax should be applied.*

five or six coats. It is then best to leave the wax to harden for at least a couple of hours, and preferably overnight, before any resins are applied.

If you are using PVA release agent, it can be applied by brush, soft, clean cloth or sponge (it can be sprayed too, but unless you are geared up to do this it probably isn't the most convenient application method). A thin smear of PVA is applied over the entire surface of the pattern, and is then allowed to fully dry. Be especially careful to make sure that the PVA dries completely in corners, where surface tension tends to pull it into liquid fillets which take longer to dry than the thin surface smear. Warm moving air accelerates the drying process, so a fan heater can be used to speed things up if you're pressed for time – but beware of blowing dust and debris onto the pattern surface.

### Split lines

Depending on which release agent type you use, split lines will either be attached before PVA application, or after waxing. Split lines are added to the pattern as temporarily adjoined flanges, and as such they will impede thorough waxing if they are attached first, but do not normally interfere with PVA application. There are numerous ways you can apply split line flanges, and the choice of material will depend on the complexity of their shape. Whatever material you use, though, it must be resistant to the chemicals that are going to be applied to it (release agent, gel coat, and resin), and it must be possible to attach it temporarily to the pattern surface in such a way that it forms a sturdy enough backing for a fibre-reinforced flange to be laminated onto it without sagging or falling off during the process. It must also be possible to remove the temporary flange without damaging the permanent laminated flange once the first part of the mould has cured, because the adjacent part of the mould is then laminated up to the first flange to complete the assembly. Clearly the second part of the pattern and the exposed area of new flange must have release agent applied before this second phase of mould lamination, otherwise the two mould parts will not be separable.

Metal or plastic angle strip can be a useful split line flange material, which can be stuck to the pattern with double-sided adhesive tape along reasonably flat sections. But you can use strips of plywood, Formica, or even stiff cardboard. Porous materials like wood and card can be sealed with clear adhesive tape, which is usually resistant to release agents and resins (do a test sample first to be certain). You may need to make a flange out of several pieces of wood, card or whatever, but they can be joined with suitable tape to form a continuous surface. If a flange requires curvature, then strips of sheet aluminium can be a good choice, and would, for example, be ideal for making the external flange around a

wheel arch on a saloon, sports or sports racing car body pattern. Clearly the wheel arch pattern would need a suitable internal return to which to stick a protruding external flange. Aluminium need only be wiped over with PVA to get a good mould release.

The width of the flanges needs to be a minimum of about an inch (25mm), and can usefully be 2 to 3in (50 to 75mm), depending on the overall size of the mould. The minimum width should allow for whatever size of bolts you intend to use to hold the mould parts together during lamination, plus an extra allowance to provide adequate strength around the drilled bolt holes. Metal washers or plates can be used to reinforce the areas where these bolt holes are to be drilled, and can be laminated into place during the lay-up of the flanges.

**Gelling the mould**

The release agent has been applied, the split line flanges are in place for the first

*Gel coat applied to the pattern.*

part of the mould, and the flanges have also had release agent applied. The next job is to apply the gel coat. The gel coat for a mould is usually a bit thicker than on a moulding, to allow for any repairs or rubbing down that might be needed during the mould's working life, and you should calculate the quantity of gel coat required on the basis of the upper end of the range quoted in Chapter 2 – that is, around 600g/sq m, or 2oz/sq ft. This will create a gel coat thickness of around 0.5 to 0.6mm (around 0.02in or so). It sometimes isn't easy to obtain as even a gel coat as you would like, especially if the ambient temperature is a bit low, in which case it might be better to apply a double gel coat at a slightly lower surface coverage rate. This helps to ensure a reasonably thick, continuous gel coat over the whole surface.

Remember to only weigh out as much gel at a time as you can reasonably apply within the expected pot life, which you will, of course, have determined with a small trial before you started to apply gel to the pattern. And make up each mix in a new pot, otherwise you'll end up with lumps of partially cured gel from the previous mix contaminating the fresh mix. By the same token, wash your application brush in acetone between mixes or the same contamination problem will result, and you'll produce a horrible, lumpy finish. If you are going to add pigment to the gel coat – and it's a good idea to use a pigment colour that will contrast with the colours you expect to use in the mouldings, and also with the pattern colour – then add it to the gel in the manufacturer's recommended proportions, and stir it in thoroughly before adding the catalyst.

Next, add catalyst at the requisite rate (usually 2 per cent by volume with gel, but manufacturers' recommendations or variations in temperature may require modification to this value), and stir it in slowly but very thoroughly, ensuring that you mix down the sides and around the bottom of the mixing cup to distribute the catalyst thoroughly. Then brush the gel onto the pattern in slow, steady strokes so that it forms as even and continuous a coat as possible over the whole surface, including the flanges. The gel is then left to reach a tacky cure (remember the test – if your finger tip leaves its imprint but no gel is left on your finger, you can proceed to the next stage). If you can see the pattern surface through the gel coat (this is why using contrasting colours helps) then the gel is not thick enough, and a second coat is needed. It should be applied once the first coat has reached the tacky cure state as described above. The second coat, if needed, is then left to cure.

## Defining the mould lay-up

Now you are nearly ready to apply the fibre reinforcement. But first you have to work out what materials you are going to use, and how many layers will be needed – these are interdependent to some extent. The thickness of the mould determines, in part, how stiff and strong it is going to be, and also how heavy and how costly, and these are factors you will have to weigh up, if you'll pardon the pun, in relation to the envisaged use of the mould. Clearly a bigger mould will need to be thicker than a small one in order to achieve adequate rigidity, although a mould of complex shape will gain some of its rigidity *from* its shape. As a rough guide, one source suggested making the mould approximately twice as thick as the intended thickness of the components to be made in it, but this advice is only useful if you already know how thick your components need to be, and it is limited to non-sandwich components.

The truth is that there really is no substitute for a bit of experience here, even if it is somebody else's and comes to you by way of advice. Alternatively, examine or estimate (using your fingers and thumb as a gauge if nothing else is available) the thicknesses of some GFRP composite components on competition cars in the paddocks at events, and you will begin to get an idea of the thicknesses that other manufacturers have used in some products. You might be lucky enough to speak to people who have made their own components and who actually know how many layers of whatever type of fabric they used. Any information like this will help guide you towards making your own choices. And if all else fails, the following very approximate guidelines might help to get you started: work on the principle that small moulds designed for the production of thin, lightweight components will probably need to be in the range of 3 to 4mm thick (around 1/8in), while larger moulds will probably fall in the range 5 to 8mm (say 3/16 to 5/16in), or maybe even thicker in the case of full-size body moulds for enclosed wheel racecars. If in doubt, err on the side of thickness when laying up a mould.

As has already been stated, the decision as to which reinforcing materials to use is usually strongly influenced by the desire to minimise cost, so the bulk of

the mould will probably be glass fibre CSM in polyester resin. But there are practical reasons why other materials need to be employed adjacent to the gel coat. The first material to laminate over the gel coat should be a glass fibre tissue. This is a lightweight non-woven material comprised of fine glass fibres with a mass per unit area of around 30gsm (approximately 1oz/sq yd). Placed on the back of the gel coat, glass tissue prevents coarse, stiff fibres of CSM penetrating through to the surface.

It is important that you do all you can to avoid entrapped air in the ensuing laminate, particularly in the layer immediately adjacent to the gel coat. Why? Because air bubbles which get trapped in the cured resin act as weak spots, and perhaps more importantly can expand and cause cracks if the mould gets hot, as in strong sunlight, or if elevated temperature post-curing is planned. I have one mould which seemed fine for a while when it was made in the winter, but which developed a few blisters beneath parts of the gel coat during the following

*Roughly cutting CSM plies for the pattern.*

*Trimming the CSM to shape on the pattern.*

summer, simply due to the temperature inside my workshop getting high enough to expand some of the bubbles that negligent technique had left behind. For this reason it is definitely worth putting down a layer of CSM next, whatever material you plan for the rest of the mould, because it is easier to get a continuous all-over bond to the gel and tissue than with woven cloth, and this can help to avoid the problem of entrapped air adjacent to the gel coat.

Next you must work out what you need for the bulk of the reinforcing material, which, as we have already said, will probably be CSM. As another rough guide to how many layers will be necessary, one layer of 450gsm (1¹/₂oz) CSM will end up at approximately 1mm thickness when contact moulded by wet layup, so small moulds will require three to five layers, bigger moulds will need more. If you now work out the approximate surface area of the pattern to be covered, you will be able to calculate how much CSM is going to be needed,

and from that, how much resin will be required to fully wet out that amount of glass mat (using the guidelines given in the laminating section of Chapter 2). It can be a help at this stage to make templates out of brown wrapping paper or newspaper, cut and possibly stuck together with adhesive tape to the size and shape of each piece of CSM that will be needed for each layer. This will assist with cutting out the requisite pieces of CSM in the most economical way. Allow for about a 25mm (1in) overlap between adjacent pieces of CSM rather than butt jointing them, and also allow for about the same amount of overhang beyond the pattern edges, to guarantee that the mould is at full thickness right to its extremities when it is eventually trimmed. For the flanges, cut enough strips of manageable length to about 2cm (³/₄in) more than the flange width, to lay up the flanges to at least the same number of layers as the main mould. Some people reckon on making the flanges thicker than the main mould in order to make

*In this case Coremat is being used for the bulk of the mould laminate.*

sure that they are really stiff when you bolt the mould parts together later, and there would certainly be no harm in following this approach.

## Laminating the mould

Finally, on to the practical part of the lamination. The general techniques will be just as described in the practical exercise given in Chapter 2. You will, by now, be surrounded by the fabrics cut to size and shape, resin and catalyst, cleaning solvent, mixing pots, brushes and other tools that you need, and in front of you is the gel-coated pattern. Remember to only mix as much catalysed resin at any one time as you can conveniently use within the pot life of the mix. If the ambient temperature is markedly different to when you last made a test batch, or you are going to use a new batch of resin and/or catalyst, then make a new test batch and check its pot life before starting the main job. You will be glad you did so later, especially if the pot life is shorter now than it was last time. There is

nothing as irritatingly wasteful as throwing away half a mix of resin simply because it gelled faster than expected – except, perhaps, overestimating how much resin you needed for the job in the first place.

As suggested above, the first layer to be laminated onto the pattern will be a layer of glass tissue. At about 30gsm the resin consumption of this lightweight material is not very high, so your first resin batch will be small. Allow for about a 3:1 resin to tissue weight ratio – this is more than you will need just to impregnate the tissue, but allows you to cover the pattern with a liberal coat of resin first. Brush resin all over the pattern (or, if it is a large multi-piece pattern, over the area you are going to laminate in this session), and then lay the tissue carefully in place, taking care not to crease or damage it. Overlap any joins by about 25mm (1in). Carefully press the tissue into the resin with a clean, soft laminating brush, and gently stipple it down so as to completely saturate it with resin, and so that it fully bonds to the gel coat beneath. Cover the whole area in this way, including the flanges.

Next, apply the first layer of CSM strips to the flanges. The reason for doing this now is so that you can butt the strips of CSM into the tight corners between the flanges and the main surfaces, thus ensuring that you have fibre reinforcement right into those corners. You may first need to carefully brush on extra resin to ensure that the surfaces of the flanges are thoroughly 'wet'. When laid down on the wetted surface, the CSM strips will soak up the resin from below, a process that you encourage by stippling with your brush. Only when you have brought up as much resin as possible from below do you add any extra resin on top. This reduces the chance of trapping air bubbles.

Now you can apply the layers of CSM to the mould surfaces, overlapping the flanges. Put one layer down at a time, lightly pressing it into place on the pre-wetted surface beneath and then stippling with your brush to bring resin up from

below before adding more resin to completely wet out the newly applied layer. Make up extra batches of catalysed resin as you need them, working on the basis of around a 2:1 to 2.5:1 resin to fabric weight ratio with CSM. Alternatively you can estimate the resin requirement by assessing the thickness of the number of layers you are going to put down, and assume that the resin quantity needed will amount to the same thickness. Multiply this by the surface area, and that will give you a volume of resin required. For example, if you are going to use four layers of 450gsm CSM, that will be about 4mm, or 0.4cm, thick. Over one square metre, that corresponds to 100cm × 100cm × 0.4cm, or 4,000cm³, which approximates to roughly 4,000g, or 4kg. By comparison, four layers of 450gsm CSM at one square metre weighs 1,800g, and at 2:1 to 2.5:1 resin to fabric weight ratio this would imply that 3,600 to 4,500g, or 3.6 to 4.5kg of resin would be needed, which nicely brackets the 4kg worked out using the first method. Both methods only provide approximate fig-

*Laminating the first layer of CSM.*

*Laminating the Coremat layer.*

ures, so be prepared to make up extra small batches if you're the parsimonious type, or waste small amounts if you're an extravagant sort. Again, you are not so concerned with the optimum strength to weight characteristics with a mould – if

*Laminating the top layer of CSM.*

it's a bit heavier than it needs to be, it still isn't going to slow your car down because it won't be fixed to it!

If you are going to apply layers of woven glass cloth, these are best alternated with layers of CSM to ensure that good inter-laminar bond strength develops (the CSM fills the holes in the woven cloth), and should be applied over all the main surfaces of the pattern. The resin consumption of woven glass cloth is lower than that of CSM, and can be generally calculated on the basis of between a 1:1 and 1.5:1 ratio, or anywhere from the same weight to 50 per cent more resin than glass cloth. In this situation, work on the high side of the ratio range, because the main aim here is not so much to achieve optimum strength as to avoid getting any air bubbles or voids. And the subsequent layer of CSM will soak up any surplus.

Again, first make sure that the surface is thoroughly coated with resin, and then lay the cloth in place, ensuring that it too butts right up to the flanges and doesn't 'bridge' the corners anywhere. A bridge such as this leaves a bubble of trapped air underneath, which means the mould is not properly reinforced at that point. Overlaps between adjacent pieces of cloth should again be about 25mm (1in). Woven glass wets very easily with resin, so all you need to do with your brush is make sure that the cloth is pressed firmly onto the CSM layer, and that there are no bubbles, creases or bridges anywhere. With care, you can actually use brush strokes on woven fabrics, but do not use so much pressure that you distort and damage the weave, because that could leave an unsupported void. Don't be tempted to use a roller on cloth, because once again you are more liable to cause damage to the weave and rucks in the fabric. Some people use squeegees on woven cloth to spread the resin and saturate the cloth fully – personally I've never got on very well with these, and prefer brushes, but by all means try them out. Cover the

whole surface of the pattern or section of pattern you are working on with woven glass cloth, and brush it out so that it is fully impregnated with resin and completely bonded to the CSM layer beneath.

You can beneficially use a roller to help wet out and consolidate the CSM layers, and more easily dislodge any trapped air bubbles, though entrapped air in subsequent layers of fabric poses less risk to the mould quality than air trapped near the gel coat. Overlap joints can be thinned to near the same thickness as the rest of the surface by working on them with your brush or roller once the mat binder has fully dissolved. By stippling or rolling across the join, the overlap can be spread out and thinned. To obtain good flange strength it is necessary to overlap some layers onto the flange, rather than butting all layers up to them. This can be achieved by laminating some of the strips of CSM you cut for the flanges so that they do bridge the corners.

With small to medium-size moulds, or mould sections of low to medium thickness, it should be possible to laminate the whole job in one session without undue difficulty. With bigger and thicker moulds it may be necessary to laminate up to about 5mm (0.2in) thickness and then allow at least partial cure to occur so that the heat of curing doesn't build up too much. As stated previously, this situation, known as an exotherm, can damage moulds and mouldings, and is consequently to be avoided. Once the whole mould or mould section has been laminated up, you need to leave it to cure. If you wish, you may be able to 'green trim' at least some of the rough overhangs prior to full cure, as described in Chapter 2, and this will save a little time when you come to apply the finishing touches later on. Otherwise, the first part of your mould needs to be left at least overnight and possibly a full 24 hours, or even longer – depending on your workshop temperature – before you can do anything else to it.

## Constructing subsequent mould sections

Once the first part of your mould has cured to a satisfactory degree (hard, rigid, not even slightly soft or sticky), you can move on to the next phase. First, remove the temporary barriers which you stuck to the pattern, onto or up to which you laminated the mould flanges. They should release easily enough from the moulded flange if gently prised with gloved hands, using a wooden stirring stick to initially lift the edges if necessary (*don't* be tempted to use sharp metal tools to lever any part of a mould or moulding, because you are likely to damage the surface). Then treat the new mould flanges and any untreated sections of the pattern with release agent, in the same way as described in the earlier section on pattern preparation. Flanges can be treated with wax or PVA, whichever is going to be quicker for you. If you originally waxed the whole pattern, re-wax wherever you stuck the temporary barriers in case the adhesive strip or tape that you used has lifted any wax away. Then repeat the

whole gelling and lamination exercise on the next section of the mould.

If you are just laying up the second part of a flange to make an internal return on a moulding, you also need to prepare the surface of the pattern onto which that will be made. For example, with our hypothetical nosecone, you would mark up on the back of the rear-most station of the pattern the shape and depth of the return below the main mould surface, and prepare the pattern surface to a little beyond this line, as well as the upstanding mould flange made in 'step one' above, with release agent. Then you would gel over the upstanding mould flange and where the internal flange mould is to be laminated, and finally laminate strips of CSM over that whole area, with a suitable overlap. When this has cured, it will be possible to remove it and trim it to the required size and shape.

When all the remaining sections of your mould have been laminated up and cured, the next job is to drill through the flanges where they are to be bolted together for

*The flange at the top has now been laminated.*

subsequent moulding manufacture. This job is best done now for the simple reason that all the mould sections are, by virtue of being stuck reasonably firmly to the pattern, held in exactly the right positions relative to one another. You could release each section in turn and then place them back on the pattern for drilling, but why not use the fact that they are held firmly in place at this stage to make this job easier? The size of holes you drill will obviously depend on the size of bolts you plan to use, but will probably be around 6mm ($1/4$in). Use high speed steel drill bits, and start with a small bit, such as 3mm ($1/8$in). Use light pressure and a high cutting speed if you have a choice, and hold a piece of wood against the flange to back up where you are drilling. Then switch the drill bit for one the next size up, and repeat the process until the holes are the size you want.

## Mould release

To commence the release of the mould from the pattern, first prise the overlapping edges of the mould away from the edges of the pattern, using gloved fingers only. Then, usually, a direct pull away from the pattern will release the rest of the mould. Sometimes moulds prove a bit more reluctant than this, and you need to work your way around the edges, prising a little more firmly as you go until the whole mould comes away from the pattern. What seems like adhesion of the mould to the pattern is just the result of slight shrinkage during curing, and is generally easily overcome by determined tugging. Again, do not be tempted to use any sharp tools to lever the mould off, even at the flanges, because it's all too easy to damage the mould surface if the tool slips under the flange. If some form of tool really is necessary, use flat wooden mixing sticks and tap them in at the flanges, where they act as wedges. But again, be very careful if you do this, because the resin and gel coat are still likely to be relatively soft so

*The main mould section has been released and trimmed.*

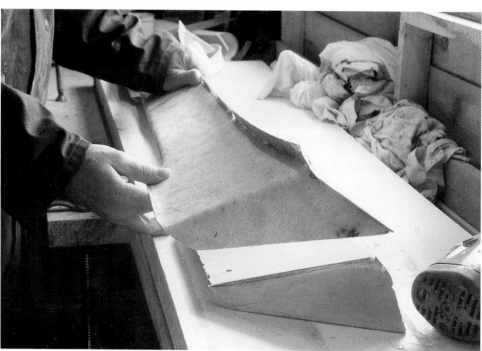

*The mould surface is as good as the pattern's.*

soon after initial hardening. Larger moulds may need a little more persuasion to release, and sometimes a few judicious but not over zealous blows with a soft headed mallet can assist by jarring the mould loose. If you have an air compressor, prising up an edge and blowing compressed air between the mould and pattern will often pop the mould off very easily. (Note: If, on a big mould, there are areas that will subsequently be cut out of the component, it is possible to drill 'blow holes' in the mould – covered with clear adhesive tape prior to moulding – through which compressed air may be blown to facilitate release.)

With split moulds, you first have to prize the mould sections apart at the flange joints, again possibly tapping in some wooden mixing sticks as thin wedges before working round each section of the mould in turn as described above. Once the first section has been removed, the rest follow more easily.

## Mould reinforcement

Nearly all moulds require some form of reinforcement to be attached to them, even if only to provide a stable base on which to stand them once the moulds have been upturned to be worked on. But a suitable structure attached to the back of a mould also greatly enhances its stability, strength and rigidity. Some people make and attach their reinforcing structures to moulds before releasing them from patterns. However, there are two reasons against doing this: firstly – and perish this thought – it is always possible that a mould may prove to be unusable because of major defects or some other quality problem, in which case there is no point in going to the lengths and expense of attaching a reinforcing structure; and secondly, the mould becomes rather more unwieldy once the structure is attached to it, which may impede the release operation. Conversely, prior to release the mould is firmly attached to the pattern, which can facilitate the reinforcement operation. In your early laminating days it might be better if you release and inspect the mould first before placing it back on the pattern just as soon as you have inspected it (so it cannot distort whilst it is still not fully cured) and then reinforcing it. Once you are more experienced and have a relatively defect-free record, you will feel more confident about bonding on the reinforcing structure before mould release, in those instances where this is more convenient. If the mould is dimensionally critical, *always* reinforce it before releasing it from the pattern.

You can make a suitable reinforcing structure out of some form of wooden board, like exterior or shuttering grade plywood, MDF, or even chipboard. You need to cut out pieces of board to the transverse profile (or profiles) of the back of the mould (the number of sections you need will depend on the size of the mould), and also cut two longitudinal pieces that you can attach with nails or screws to the ends of the transverse sec-

tions to make a hollow box structure. Depending on the size of the mould, you may also need intermediate longitudinal sections, which you can lap joint to the transverse sections. Assemble the reinforcing structure, and once you are happy that it fits onto the back of the mould, lay it in place ready for bonding to the mould. Bonding can be done with one or two layers of CSM and catalysed resin laminated to form a right-angled fillet between the box section sides and the back of the mould.

So as not to cause any possible distortion of large, unsupported areas of the mould, some people prefer to attach the reinforcement structure only at the mould flanges, where the mould is at its most rigid. This approach would actually alleviate the need for any intermediate transverse reinforcement sections at all. However, other people favour bonding all the sections into place along their full length, including the transverse ones. Clearly the most appropriate method will depend on how thick, and thus how

*This Penske Indycar chassis mould shows how stiffeners should be designed if they are needed.*

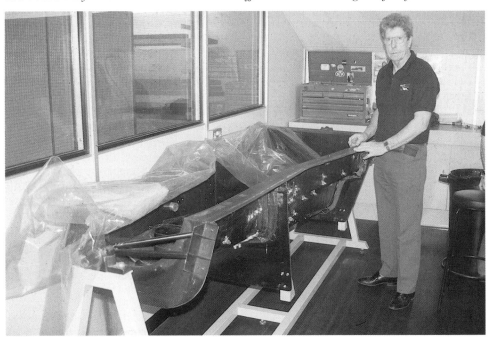

inherently rigid, your mould is. A compromise might be to bond the transverse sections at intervals with short strips of CSM, to minimise the risk of distortion showing through onto the mould surface, and to bond the outer pieces to the flanges – which are already strong and stiff – along their whole length. Once the reinforcement structure has been bonded in place, it is left to cure. You can then upturn it, and trim, sand or plane the box structure as necessary so that it rests flat and stable on the floor or workbench.

## Trimming and finishing

The mould, or mould sections, can now be trimmed and finished. The first job is to remove those unpleasant spiky edge overlaps that will already have done their best to impale you. Wear thick gloves for this. The overlaps can be removed by hand with a hacksaw or a padsaw with a fine toothed blade, or using powered tools such as a jigsaw or an abrasive disc cutter so long as great care is exercised. However, powered tools remove material very rapidly, and can also 'grab' a GFRP product whilst it is being cut and, if you are unlucky, can crack or even break it. Although most of my projects are relatively small, I prefer to invest more time and use hand tools. If this seems impractical for bigger projects, just think how much more time it will take to make a new mould. To get a better feel for cutting GFRP, try the various cutting tools at your disposal on the trial project piece you made back in Chapter 2. To cut to a line, stick a strip of masking tape along the approximate line of the cut on the gel coat side of the mould. Mark the cut line on the tape (it's easier than trying to mark on the gel coat itself), and then make the cut from the gel coat side (this helps to minimise the risk of chipping the gel). For cuts to critical dimensions, cut not quite to the line, and then file or sand precisely to the line afterwards. Trim up all the mould sections and flanges in this way, and dispose of the trimmings in line with local rubbish disposal regulations.

It is quite likely that the backs of your

*Our spoiler mould components, finished and trimmed.*

moulds or mould sections will also be afflicted with at least occasional sharp resin-impregnated fibres, and these can be removed with dry, coarse grit aluminium oxide abrasive paper, held on a sanding block and run over the surface. The trimmed edges can also be sanded with dry, coarse or medium grit abrasive paper to remove any sharp corners, and even to round off edges where this doesn't alter the fit or important dimensions of any components. Standard metal files can also be used for this job, though make sure that you either file from the gel coat side and only use pressure on the forward stroke, or file carefully along the edges to avoid chipping the gel. Together with the edge trimming mentioned above, these operations make moulds much safer and more comfortable to handle.

It is possible that you may need to make some small repairs to your mould before it can be used. For instance, there may be small areas that, in spite of all reasonable care being taken, adhere to the pattern and cause some localised damage to the gel coat of the mould. Or

if the gel was a bit thin in places it may not have cured properly, and there may be some localised surface wrinkling. Sometimes, too, the gel coat may not bond very well to the laminate, perhaps because of a lack of consolidation or inadequate 'wetting' of the laminate, and the unsupported gel coat may fracture and flake off in places. Hopefully, if these problems do occur they will be very localised, and repair is a viable recovery option. If the faults are more widespread, then it will probably be better to start again. But, this won't happen because of the care you're taking!

Small faults can be repaired with care. Depending on the exact nature of the fault, it needs to be scratched out with a penknife or similar tool, and any loose or unsupported areas of gel coat, resin or fibre reinforcement should be removed. Then prepare the underlying surface with abrasive paper, clean it with acetone and let it dry, prior to filling the defect with polyester-based body filler. The filled area is then very carefully sanded back and blended in with the mould surface, then polished up with progressively finer

*Flange detail on the top, back edge of a nosecone mould.*

*Base flange and split line on a nosecone mould. Polyurethane stiffeners are also visible.*

grades of wet and dry abrasive paper, and finally buffed to a shine with rubbing compound. The repaired surface will have a slightly different texture to the bulk of the mould surface, but this hopefully will not show in the finished product. Alternatively, minor faults can be repaired with a small quantity of catalysed resin applied just to the prepared area, and held in place with a patch of cellophane or clear adhesive tape. Once the resin has cured this patch can be peeled off, leaving a smooth resin patch that will need relatively minimal finishing. The type of defect, and its location on either a flat or curved part of the mould, will determine which repair method to use.

## Alternative mould-making techniques

Despite what has been written in the previous two chapters, there are some occasions where it is worthwhile making three-dimensional moulds directly, rather than going through the pattern-to-mould sequence. One such situation is where the component is essentially a female shape, such as a 'NACA duct', when it is simpler to make a male mould directly,

and take the female component off that. Cheap, easy to obtain DIY materials can be used to make a mould like this, and get a good result. One such mould is illustrated here. Other, more complex three-dimensional male moulds can be made using the same materials and methods as described in the preceding pattern-making chapter, with the proviso that you need to make the mould durable enough to withstand the envisaged number of uses.

Another example is where you possess, or more likely have access to, the capability to machine a female mould from a suitable solid material, such as aluminium. The aerofoil moulds shown here were machined out of two very expensive solid aluminium blocks, using a large computer-controlled three axis mill, which had been programmed via a CAD drawing of the aerofoil profile extruded electronically into a three-dimensional shape. Then a 'tool path' programme was fed into the machine's controller, and the shape was slowly cut out of the metal block, without any direct human intervention. After a final polish the moulds were ready for use.

*A NACA duct mould. This is a male mould, made straight from Formica over chipboard templates and polyurethane foam block, with the edges finished using body filler.*

*A pair of aluminium moulds CNC-machined from solid, then hand polished. A high level of precision is possible using this method, and with much effort a mirror finish can be achieved.*

However, the former example would probably have more relevance to most DIY moulders, and could usefully be borne in mind for shapes that lend themselves to a simplified production sequence. The latter example, whilst interesting, is a technique that is unlikely to be available to many of us!

# Chapter 5

# Component manufacture

**Aspects of product design**

For the time being, we'll carry on with the assumption that you are using CSM reinforced polyester resin, but later in this chapter we'll look at how you might modify things with woven glass fabrics, and in the next chapter we'll consider the use of more advanced fibres, fabrics and resins in greater detail.

The design of a product, that is to say the choice of laminate lay-up and reinforcement materials and methods, obviously depends largely on the product's intended use. You need to decide how strong and stiff it has to be, how it is to be fixed to the car, how long you intend it should be capable of lasting (one event, a whole season, or several seasons), whether low weight is a primary criterion, what type and standard of finish is required, and how much you can budget for it. Collectively, these criteria will determine how you make your component.

Let's again take an example of a typical competition car component: a single-seater-style, non-structural nosecone (that is, one that doesn't carry aerofoils, or fulfil the role of a frontal impact structure). Such a component needs to be as lightweight as possible, but robust enough to take minor knocks without disintegrating, and stiff enough to maintain its shape under aerodynamic loads at speed. It will require fixings to hold it directly to the car and/or to an adjacent body section. It will also need flanges, maybe with dowels or pegs, or possibly a joggle, to butt or overlap with the adjacent panels, and it may need to partly support front aerofoil mountings. And given that it is a particularly vulnerable component, it would be better if it was inexpensive, because you will almost certainly come to regard a nosecone as a consumable item!

The shape of a nosecone, with a front end that is usually tapered in side view and often in plan view as well, possesses considerable integral rigidity by virtue of that shape, rather like the ends of an egg. The shell of an egg is very thin, but it derives immense strength from the curvature around the tapered ends. However, a nosecone, like an egg, is much weaker in areas of less curvature, and may well need supplementary stiffening in these regions. Right-angled flange returns around the edges at the rear can also add considerable rigidity to the 'open' end of the nosecone. These flanges may have dowels or recesses moulded into them which, by slotting into recesses or onto dowels similarly moulded on the adjacent panels, serve to accurately locate the components. Whether this is the case or not, the flanges need to be pretty robust, if only to withstand the nosecone being picked up and carried, and therefore these areas need reinforcing too. If the joints with adjacent panels are via joggles, additional stiffening may be needed close to these areas.

From all of these parameters, and from

the samples you made earlier, you can now begin to develop an idea of how many layers of CSM will be required to construct a suitable nosecone. If this is the first such component you have decided to make, your best guess on lay-up will be just that. But that doesn't necessarily matter, because if you err on the lightweight side, and upon release from its mould the nosecone seems to be too flimsy, you can always put it back in and add some additional reinforcement by way of extra layers, or stiffening ribs. If you err on the side of excess, however, you'll be stuck with a heavy component. To avoid this, you need to bear in mind that the whole idea of making competition car components is to keep them as light as possible for the job they have to do, and for the life expectancy you impose on them. That is, after all, one of the reasons why composites – and especially advanced composites – have found such wide acceptance in motorsport. Remember Colin Chapman's doctrine: if it lasts more than a race, it's too heavy! Then apply a bit of real world common sense, and come up with the best performance/cost compromise you can.

Let's get down to practical guidelines. If you are using typical 450gsm CSM, your common-or-garden general purpose weight of glass matt, let's say you use two plies over the whole area of the nosecone to start with. The tapering front section will probably be strong enough at that, but flatter areas may need additional material. Perhaps the most efficient way to strengthen and stiffen these regions is to use something like Coremat, which is a versatile, easy-to-use core material which works well with polyester resin. You can obviously choose from any of the core materials that are compatible with the materials and resin you are using, and which can accommodate the shape and curvature of your nosecone. But strips of Coremat – cut to a width of perhaps 1 to 2in (25 to 50mm), laid-up onto the back of the two-layer laminate along the directions where extra robustness is required,

and then covered over with an overlapping strip of CSM – take up curvature very easily and form good stiffeners.

The flanges and edges usually need to be quite a bit thicker than the main areas, and you can stiffen them up by using, say, another two or three layers of CSM, cut into strips wide enough to cover the flange width, or around an inch wide (25mm) for un-flanged edges. This will give a total thickness of four or five layers around the flange margins, which, as you'll recall, will correspond to a thickness of about 4 to 5mm (0.16 to 0.20in). You may also want to add an allowance for extra strips of CSM about 50mm (2in) wide, to overlap along internal corners, such as at the side/base joints, where the main plies are butted. This will ensure the sides and the base are well bonded together.

Then you'll need to reinforce areas such as aerofoil attachment points. Sometimes aerofoils can be carried in metal tubes which are mounted in moulded bosses in the sides of nosecones. These bosses need to be reasonably thick too, not less than three or four layers in total. If wings or flaps bolt through the sides of a nosecone, then local reinforcement in the form of thin (say 3mm) plywood can be employed, bonded to the inside of the two main plies with the resin being used, then laminated over with another layer (or two) of CSM. Obviously, if the sides are curved plywood will not be useable, in which case you might consider thin sheet steel, pre-curved to shape, or, as a lighter alternative, sheet aluminium, though the latter will not bond as well in a polyester resin matrix.

We are now in a position to estimate materials quantities. For the sake of the calculations here, a very simple nosecone shape will be used, as shown in Figure 5–1. You can substitute the dimensions of your own project and make the same calculations, and keep in mind that this does not have to be super-accurate. Our hypothetical nosecone here is 0.6m wide at the back, 0.4m high, and the sides are 0.8m long. Using the 'sum of squares' rule, this means that the nosecone is 0.74m from front to back along the underside, and 0.84m from front to back along the upper surface. By calculating the area of the four triangles involved, we can work out the entire surface area of the nosecone. The area of a triangle is half the base times the height, so the area of the nosecone underside is $1/2 \times 0.6 \times 0.74$sq m, or 0.22sq m. The top surface is $1/2 \times 0.6 \times 0.84$sq m, or 0.252sq m, and the area of the sides is $(2 \times 1/2) \times 0.4 \times 0.8$sq m, or 0.32sq m, making the overall surface area 0.792sq m. Assuming it runs around the whole periphery, the flange around the rear of the nosecone is $(2 \times 0.6) + (2 \times 0.4)$, or 2m long, by 0.025m (25mm) wide, which makes 0.05sq m. Thus the total surface area of the whole nosecone is 0.842sq m.

There are, however, two different things to be worked out. On a theoretical basis, you can now calculate the weight of gel coat, CSM and resin that will finish up in the complete, trimmed nosecone on the basis of weight per unit area per layer of gel and CSM, and an assumed resin uptake value for the CSM. This will give you a reasonable estimate of the likely weight of the cured product. But on a more practical level, you can also work out how much CSM you will need to cut from your roll, which will not be the same as the surface area of the nosecone multiplied by the number of layers, because you need to allow for a trimming margin. You also need to work out how to cut out the necessary pieces from the roll in the most efficient, least wasteful way.

Let's make the weight estimate first. There are three main components that will go to make the nosecone: gel coat, CSM, and resin. For this sort of rough estimate you can ignore pigment and catalyst. The quantity of gel coat can be estimated on the basis of a coverage rate of around 500gsm. Thus, 500gsm $\times$ 0.842sq m = 421g, or 0.42kg of gel. (We'll convert to pounds at the end of the calculation so as to avoid 'rounding' errors.)

The weight of CSM will be the weight of the two main plies plus the extra strips at the flanges, corners and stiffeners. At 450gsm the two main plies of 0.842sq m weigh 450 $\times$ 0.842 $\times$ 2 = 758g, or 0.758kg. The extra weight of the flanges will be 0.05sq m $\times$ 2 plies (say) $\times$ 450gsm = 45g, or 0.045kg. The weight of the corner overlaps and stiffeners will be around 2.34 $\times$ 0.05m = 0.12sq m $\times$ 450gsm $\times$ 2 plies = 105g or 0.105kg. This makes

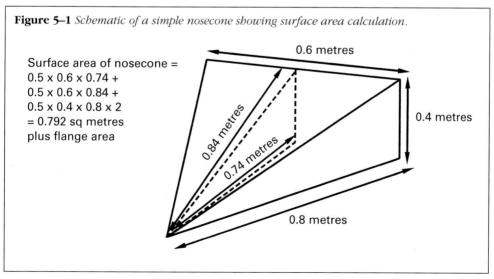

**Figure 5–1** *Schematic of a simple nosecone showing surface area calculation.*

Surface area of nosecone =
0.5 x 0.6 x 0.74 +
0.5 x 0.6 x 0.84 +
0.5 x 0.4 x 0.8 x 2
= 0.792 sq metres
plus flange area

0.6 metres

0.84 metres

0.74 metres

0.4 metres

0.8 metres

0.908kg of CSM to add to the gel weight.

The weight of resin can be calculated on an average uptake ratio of around 2.25:1 resin to fabric weight, so the weight of resin needed will be 2.25 × 0.908kg = 2.04kg.

Finally, an allowance for the stiffeners should be added. Say 3mm Coremat is used, which itself weighs next to nothing, but which takes up 1.8kg of resin per square metre. If we use one central strip running along the top surface of dimension 0.74m × 25mm, or 0.0185sq m, it will soak up 0.0185 × 1.8 = 0.033kg of resin.

The cumulative total of these various weights is therefore 3.4kg, or 7$^{1}$/2lb. You are now in a position to judge whether this seems heavy or light, and to make adjustments to the lay-up if you deem it necessary. For example, you could replace one of the main plies of 450gsm mat with a 225gsm layer, and save about 0.7kg, or 1$^{1}$/2lb, overall. But at least using this principle you can put some real numbers into the design process, which will enable you to increase your 'feel' for what you think is about right. You can also identify the major contributors to the weight of the finished product – clearly the resin is the biggest of these, and whilst the resin to fabric ratio can be improved from 2.25:1, don't bank on big savings here. The real weight savings, as we shall see later, come from using fabrics that consume significantly less resin while at the same time providing better physical properties.

You can also work out what amount of CSM you will actually need to perform the lay-up you devise. This is most easily done by drawing out the shapes and dimensions of the pieces you need on a representation of the fabric you are using as if it was rolled out on a cutting table, as in Figure 5–2, and adding about 20mm overlap to each piece to ensure full coverage of the mould (you can always trim to size prior to lamination if you need to butt pieces together). This is where any tailoring skills you possess will come to the fore. As you can see in the drawing, laying out the pieces in this way allows you to fit them together efficiently, wasting as little as possible. In this case, and indeed in most cases, what looks like waste will be cut into the strips you need for the flanges, corners and stiffener overlaps, so there will be very little real wastage. You can see that about 2.5 linear metres of CSM will be needed from a roll which may be about 0.92m wide, making the actual area used about 2.3sq m. As was stated earlier, this is a lot more than the surface area of the mould multiplied by the number of plies used, so it pays to do a rough tailoring pattern.

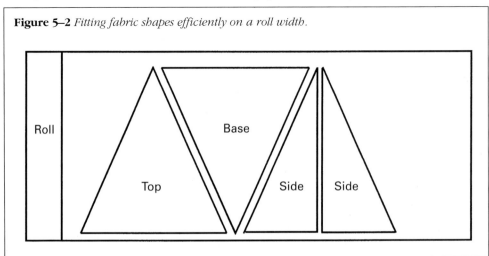

**Figure 5–2** *Fitting fabric shapes efficiently on a roll width.*

**Table 5–1 Cost estimate for a hypothetical nosecone in GFRP**

| Component | Quantity | Unit cost | Cost |
|---|---|---|---|
| Gel | 0.42kg | £5/kg | £2.10 |
| CSM | 2.3sq m | £1.50/sq m | £3.45 |
| Resin, polyester | 2.04kg | £3/kg | £6.12 |
| Catalyst | 0.03kg | £6/kg | £0.18 |
| Coremat | 0.0185sq m | £3/sq m | £0.06 |
| Pigment | 0.02kg | £20/kg | £0.40 |
| Sundries | eg brush, acetone, wax etc | Estimate | £2.00 |
| | | **Total cost of materials** | **£14.31** |

You can now work out the component costing if you so wish. All you need to do is list the quantities of each component that goes into the recipe, multiply them by their unit costs, then add them all up to get a total, as shown for this example above.

The unit costs are for illustration purposes only, but they represent the approximate prices I was paying for these materials in 1998/9. The catalyst quantity is based on 1 per cent in resin and 2 per cent in gel coat, and the pigment quantity is based on 5 per cent in the gel coat only. Keep this table in mind, because we'll be doing cost comparisons using more advanced materials later on.

**Preparing for work**

If the component you are going to make is anything other than a very simple shape, it helps if you take the time to make some cutting templates. Using newspaper or brown wrapping paper, for example, cut out reasonably accurate templates of the pieces of fabric you will need to achieve full coverage of your mould, allowing perhaps 20mm (3/4in) overlaps between adjacent pieces. For the hypothetical nosecone discussed in the previous section, you would probably cut a template for the top, one for the base, and one for the sides. Doing this not only makes cutting the reinforcing fabric to the right size and shape easier and less wasteful, but it makes it faster, and you can store the templates away to use on the next component you make from the same mould.

Preparing the mould starts with making sure that the surface is clean and free from any damage or residue from a previous job. Your chosen release agent is then applied to all surfaces. It pays to be very methodical here, and whichever type of release agent you use, make sure that every bit of every surface is adequately coated. With wax coating, applying more than one coat (which you'll be doing anyway if this is the mould's first use) helps to ensure total coverage. If you're using a liquid release agent such as PVA, then going over the surfaces twice or more before the PVA dries also helps to ensure complete coverage. If your mould is in more than one part, apply release agent to the parts – including any flanges – while they are separate. That way, if gel or resin seeps between the mould sections it will release easily from the mould joint faces. Alternatively, if you do not wish any gel or resin to get into the joints at all, you can run a small fillet of plasticine along the joint lines prior to applying the release agent. This can help to achieve neat, void free, small radius rounded external corners in some cases (see Figure 5–3). As stated previously, you then need to leave the release agent to harden or dry. Wax is beneficially left for at least a couple of hours, and preferably overnight, whilst the liquid release agents must physically dry. Allow extra time for the release agent which has seeped into mould joints to dry, because if you don't, it will seep back out into the gel when you apply that, and will ruin the component in those areas.

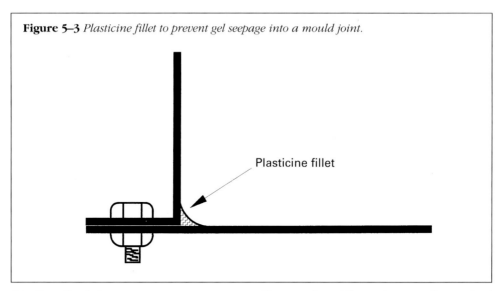

**Figure 5–3** *Plasticine fillet to prevent gel seepage into a mould joint.*

Plasticine fillet

## Starting the job

You are now ready to apply the gel coat. The calculations on material requirements you did earlier will have given you a figure for the approximate total amount of gel coat you will need. Add perhaps 5–10 per cent to this amount to allow for some wastage, and this will be nearer to the amount you actually need. Don't forget, though, that you should only mix the amount that you can apply within the relevant pot life time. So, to be thorough, make a small test mix of gel with the requisite amount of catalyst (2 per cent normally, or 2ml per 100g of gel for convenience) and record how long it takes to cure to a lumpy consistency. Now you know the approximate pot life in the prevailing ambient temperature, and you can adjust your mix sizes accordingly. On smaller, more intricate jobs I tend to use 250ml paper drinking cups as mixing pots, and this is a convenient quantity to make and apply at 2 per cent catalyst addition rate and at 20 to 25°C. Larger, simpler components with bigger areas to cover enable bigger mixes to be made and used before they start to go off, although the prevailing conditions may require adjustments to catalyst proportions and mix sizes.

You mix your gel coat as described in Chapter 2, adding pigment if required before adding the catalyst, and then apply it to the mould in steady brush strokes, aiming to get as even and smooth a coat as possible. The warmer it is, the easier this will be to achieve, because the viscosity of the gel coat drops as the temperature goes up. The shed in winter is consequently a difficult working environment, and it is essential to rig up a supplementary heat source to achieve as equable a temperature as possible. If it's uncomfortably cold, it's not much good for moulding work. However, if your gel coat is rather viscous, and not too amenable to being brushed out into a nice even coating, you can thin it down with a proportion of ordinary laminating resin. Never add too much – no more than 25 per cent resin at most – and mix it carefully into the gel you have dispensed for the job. This gives you a slightly less viscous gel to deal with, which from here on you treat as if it was normal gel – you use the same pigment and catalyst proportions, for example.

The gel coat must then be left to cure, which will take a few hours depending on workshop temperature. The usual 'fingerprint test' tells you whether or not the gel coat has cured sufficiently (your finger leaves a print, but no gel sticks to your finger). Before going any further, inspect the gel coat over the whole mould surface. If there are any obviously thin areas (if you pigmented your mould surface a different colour to the intended component pigment, as suggested in the previous chapter, this will be easy to spot), it will be necessary to go over them again with another small batch of gel. The reason for this, as was stated earlier, is that thinner areas of gel take longer to cure, and can cause wrinkles to appear on the surface of the finished component, or, worse still, patches that have not cured at all when you release the component from the mould. This is not easy to rectify, so it is far better to prevent it from occurring at all. If needs be, therefore, go over the entire mould with another thin coat of gel – you may add a few tens of grams weight, or maybe a few hundred grams on a bigger item, but better that than end up with a defective component.

## Laminating the component

The general laminating procedure follows the guidelines set out in the exercise in Chapter 2 and enlarged upon in Chapter 4, but we'll go through some of the details again here to deal with the specifics of making a particular item. Once more, let's consider the hypothetical nosecone. You will have cut the requisite fabrics already, as described above, and calculated the likely quantity of laminating resin you are going to need. A test mix will determine the pot life you're going to have to contend with at the appropriate catalyst addition rate (probably 1 per cent, or rather 1ml per 100g of resin) in the prevailing temperature, and you will now be able to figure out how many mixes of what size will be needed.

With a component like a nosecone – which in our hypothetical example has a separate bolt-on mould section for the base, as well as bolt-on flange moulds around the back face – you have the choice of whether to bolt all the sections together and mould the entire component

in one session, or whether to laminate the component in stages. The former isn't always easy, because it is sometimes difficult to physically reach inside the assembled mould to laminate the front portion properly. You can also end up with your arm, shoulders and, worst of all, your head inside the mould for some time whilst you are laminating it, which is not only uncomfortable, but also means you get to inhale fairly concentrated styrene vapour – definitely *not* recommended.

So, why not take advantage of the mould being in separate parts, and mould the main areas separately? You then, of course, have to join them, which again means reaching inside the mould, but for less time than if you were laminating the whole thing in one piece. If you elect to follow the latter route, then the idea is to leave a margin around the edge of the fabric and resin, let them cure, join the mould sections together, then gel over the joint, let that gel cure, and finally laminate strips of fabric and resin over the joints to the same lay-up of plies as the main areas. The final strength of a component made this way will not be quite as good, but in most non-critical components the difference will be insignificant.

The general laminating process follows the earlier guidelines. First of all you brush a generous coat of resin over the area you are going to laminate, then you carefully position the first section of CSM, and if necessary, using gloved hands, slide it into the exact position in which you want it. Make sure you butt the CSM right into the corners where there are flanges, and avoid bending any CSM over these tight corners where it might form a 'bridge' which has a void beneath it (see Figure 5–4). You will be overlaying strips to bridge the corners and create full strength in these areas later on. Then, using a laminating brush or a roller, start to consolidate the layer of CSM until you have soaked up the resin, and add more resin with your brush, stippling and rolling to fully wet out the CSM. Then move onto the adjacent section, brushing on a coat of resin, then once more carefully sliding the CSM into position, overlapping the previous section by about 20mm. Stipple and roll, add more resin, and stipple and roll again until this section is consolidated. The overlap joins can be worked on with brush and/or roller until they are scarcely any thicker than the overall lay-up.

Treat the flanges in exactly the same way as the main areas, laminating strips of CSM into place, and butt them tightly into the corners. Once again, you will be overlapping slightly wider strips of CSM onto the flanges so that these bond to the main areas and build up full strength.

Once the first layer has been laminated, don't wait for it to cure, but commence with the second layer immediately (or go to the section below on 'stiffeners and sandwich panels' if such a construction is to be used). This time you don't brush on any more resin, because you already have a 'wet' surface on which to apply the next layer of CSM. Carefully, without disrupting any of the material you have already laminated, position the first section of CSM over its predecessor. Using a brush, stipple it onto the first layer so that you bring resin up, then, once no more resin soaks through, add some more with your brush and continue to stipple and roll until this layer is fully wetted and consolidated. Move onto the adjacent sections as before until all the main areas and flanges have been laminated.

Next you need to reinforce the flanges with further strips of CSM. These will need to be a little wider than the strips butted into the corners to allow for some overlap – make them at least 20mm wider. It's sometimes easier to pre-wet these strips with resin on a suitable piece of board before picking them up with your brush and a spare mixing stick and positioning them over the relevant flanges. Once they are in place, stipple them down with the brush, and press them into the corners so that they bond to the layers already in place. You will notice that the inherent stiffness in the fibres tends to fight against being pushed into tight corners, but you just have to persevere and keep pushing them into place if they spring out and form little bridges and voids.

If you elected to make your component in sections, then you will join the sections with strips of resin-impregnated CSM that extend at least 20mm and probably nearer 40mm onto each part of the component. In this event, you will be overlaying these strips onto a cured surface, so you will need to pre-wet the joint areas with resin before applying the CSM strips.

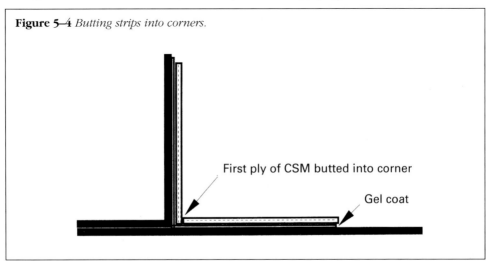

**Figure 5–4** *Butting strips into corners.*

First ply of CSM butted into corner

Gel coat

## Stiffeners and sandwich panels

Depending on what material you have chosen for your stiffeners, you may now have to let the component cure, or at least, part-cure; but if you use a material such as Coremat, which soaks up resin and therefore shrinks at much the same rate as the rest of the laminate, you can get on with this part straight away. You will need to cut strips or pieces of your chosen core material to whatever width and length you decide is necessary, then pre-coat them with catalysed resin and position them onto the back of the CSM laminate in the required position. If the core material is resin-absorbent, like Coremat, you then brush on resin and stipple until the stiffener is saturated. Next you overlay further strips of resin-impregnated CSM that overlap the stiffeners by a sufficient margin to bond them fully to the main surfaces.

If you are making a much larger component which does not possess much integral rigidity by virtue of its shape, you may need to make the large – and especially flat – areas by means of sandwich construction. As discussed in earlier chapters, there is a wide range of materials to choose from for the core of the sandwich, but perhaps the more commonly used are some of the rigid and flexible foams. If our hypothetical nosecone was

deemed to require sandwich construction over larger, flat areas, one of the best core materials from the strength to weight point of view would be polyurethane foam. This can be supplied in various thicknesses down to $1/2$in (12.5mm), and is relatively light, is compatible with CSM and polyester resin, and, since it does not absorb resin, remains fairly light even after lamination.

In order to get the stiffest and lightest construction possible, the foam panels would be cut to shape for the areas that need extra stiffness, bevelled with a sanding block so that overlaying CSM does not have to cope with sharp radii, cleaned of dust, and placed on the back of the first layer of laminated CSM once partial cure had occurred. Putting the panels in place prior to partial cure risks damaging that first layer of reinforcing fabric. The second layer of CSM would then be laminated over the back of the PU foam panels in just the same way as the rest of the component's non-sandwich parts.

If curved areas require sandwich construction, then one of the flexible foams like PVC foam, or even Coremat, might be used. The latter does not yield the lightest laminates because of its resin absorbency, but it does enable a lighter, stiffer laminate to be manufactured than the equivalent thickness of CSM.

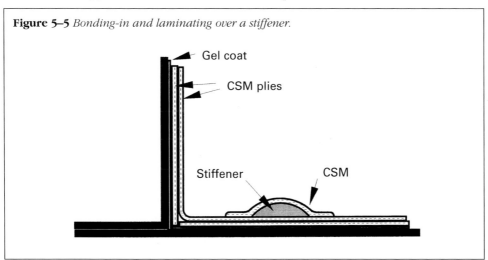

**Figure 5–5** *Bonding-in and laminating over a stiffener.*

Gel coat

CSM plies

Stiffener

CSM

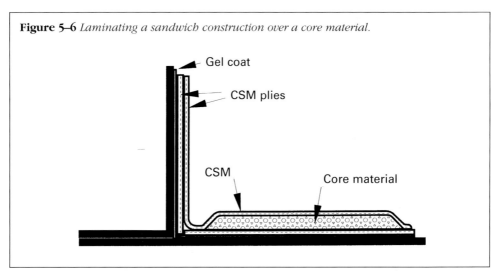

**Figure 5–6** *Laminating a sandwich construction over a core material.*

Gel coat

CSM plies

CSM                                    Core material

## Improved glass fabrics

In Chapter 1 we saw that woven glass fabrics produce higher performance laminates for two reasons. Firstly, the fabrics themselves are inherently stiffer, at least in the direction of the fibres. And secondly, their resin uptake is significantly less, leading to a stiffer and stronger laminate per unit weight. So what could we expect from our hypothetical nosecone if woven glass was adopted instead of CSM? What weight fabric would we need to use, and how many layers would be needed?

Table 1–7 in Chapter 1 gives us some pointers, although we must be careful in drawing conclusions from the resin to fabric ratios stated therein. The key figures for our purposes are that a laminate made from woven E-glass at a glass content of 70 per cent by weight (equivalent to a resin to fabric ratio of 0.43:1) was 2.8 times stronger and twice as stiff as a laminate made from CSM at a glass content of 30 per cent (a resin to fabric ratio of 2.33:1).

Now, working by hand it would be pretty well impossible to get a resin to fabric ratio as low as 0.4:1, even with woven glass. More likely a ratio of about 1:1 or 1.5:1 would be achieved, or say around 1.25:1 as a practically achievable average. This corresponds to a glass con-

tent of 45 per cent by weight. So how can we work out what strength values a woven glass laminate with this resin to fabric ratio would have? Fortunately there is a relatively simple formula that can be applied here, called the 'Rule of Mixtures'. In essence this states that the tensile strength of a laminate is the sum of the value of the tensile strength of the resin matrix multiplied by the matrix fraction (by weight), plus the value of the tensile strength of the fibre multiplied by the fibre fraction (by weight). In other words, the relative proportions of the matrix and the fibre, and their respective tensile strengths, determine the tensile strength of the laminate. Forgive the mathematical representation below, but it does help in calculating theoretical strengths of various fibre fractions if it is stated as a formula. We'll use the specific tensile strength – that is, the tensile strength divided by the density – of the materials involved, so that we have a direct comparison of similar weights of the materials we're interested in; abbreviating specific tensile strength to STS, and using the subscripts $_L$ to represent 'laminate', $_F$ to represent 'fibre' and $_M$ to represent 'matrix', the Rule of Mixtures becomes:

$$STS_L = (STS_F \times W_F) + (STS_M \times W_M)$$

Thus, providing we know the properties of the resin and the laminate at a given fibre fraction ($W_F$), it becomes possible to calculate what the properties of the laminate at other fibre fractions would be, and to save time the specific tensile strengths of various glass fibre/polyester resin composites are given in the table below. The first three values are extracted from Table 1–7, and converted to specific values by dividing by the materials' densities, whilst the last column is calculated from the woven at 70 per cent fibre fraction value and the non-reinforced polyester resin value using the Rule of Mixtures.

### Table 5–2 Estimated comparative specific tensile strengths of some GFRP laminates

|                        | PE resin | CSM | Woven | Woven |
|------------------------|----------|-----|-------|-------|
| Fibre fraction         | 0        | 30% | 70%   | 45%   |
| Specific tensile strength, MPa | 48 | 78 | 176 | 130 |

Right, enough of the maths for now, and on with the material comparisons. The values we are really interested in are the specific tensile strengths of a CSM laminate and a woven laminate at practically achievable fibre fractions. Thus, the figures for CSM at 78MPa and woven (45 per cent) at 130MPa tell us that the same weight woven laminate is 66 per cent stronger than the CSM laminate, or conversely that the woven laminate, when made to the same strength, is 40 per cent lighter. These are the sorts of numbers that we should be interested in for our competition cars! Essentially, if we make all the body panels using woven glass instead of CSM, we could save up to 40 per cent of their weight. But what are the disadvantages of doing this? Well, woven glass fabrics are more expensive than CSM, and a bit more fiddly to cut and handle. They do wet-out with resin quite easily once they are in position, but more care must be exercised when applying resin, so as not to disrupt the weave pattern and leave weaknesses. We'll go into this in more detail shortly. Another advantage of woven fabric is that because its resin uptake is lower than CSM, the resin cost element is reduced.

The table below is the same as Table 5–1, but this time using woven fabric for the construction of the hypothetical nosecone. The weight of woven glass fabric chosen is 390gsm, which at 45 per cent fibre fraction will produce a laminate roughly 40 per cent lighter than 450gsm CSM at 30 per cent fibre fraction, but which according to our sums will be of a similar strength. The flanges and stiffeners still utilise CSM because of the ease of handling this material in strip form, and to give the flanges some bulk. The end product is only slightly more expensive in materials, but will weigh 40 per cent less over the main areas, saving about 1kg (over 2lb) overall.

### Laminating with woven glass fabrics

As was hinted in the previous section, in some respects woven glass fabrics are not as easy to work with as CSM. Because

### Table 5–3 Cost estimate for a hypothetical nosecone in woven GFRP

| Component | Quantity | Unit cost | Cost |
|-----------|----------|-----------|------|
| Gel | 0.42kg | £5/kg | £2.10 |
| Woven glass, 390gsm | 2.3sq m | £3.50/sq m | £8.10 |
| Resin, polyester | 1.2kg | £3/kg | £3.60 |
| Catalyst | 0.02kg | £6/kg | £0.12 |
| Coremat | 0.0185sq m | £3/sq m | £0.06 |
| Pigment | 0.02kg | £20/kg | £0.40 |
| Sundries | eg brush, acetone, wax etc | estimate | £2.00 |
|  |  | **Total cost of materials** | **£16.33** |

CSM is held together with a binder, it possesses some inherent stiffness that actually makes it quite a stable, not too-drapeable material to cut, handle, and position in a mould. Woven glass, on the other hand, is more drapeable, has a tendency to fray along cut-lines, and can be rather awkward to position in a mould. The drapeability of woven glass can also be an advantage if a mould has a degree of complex curvature, and different weave patterns can be exploited to this end, as described in Chapter 1.

So, care needs to be taken when cutting woven fabrics, to ensure that the fabric does not distort as you cut pieces from it, which can lead to these being misshapen and irregular. Some laminators find it easier to cut woven fabric if it has been pre-wetted on a sheet of material first, and cut it when wet. Then, when you come to laminate it into the mould, you need to take great care that it makes contact only where you want it to. If a draping corner happens to come into contact with a resin-coated surface somewhere other than where you intended, it will not only adhere to it but will distort out of shape as it is removed, however careful you are. In no time at all you will find yourself becoming intimately acquainted with a sticky tangle of fibrous threads, and it will become obvious that the only course of action is to start again.

Once you have your piece of woven glass in place in the mould you will find that it wets very easily, using careful brush strokes to apply the resin. Don't be tempted to use rollers or squeegees, because these can snag, distort and disrupt the weave pattern, creating weaknesses. In more complex concave moulds it is possible for creases to develop if the weave pattern cannot accommodate the curvature. The best way to handle these is to cut through them and overlap the 'spare' bits rather than trying to take up the creases as tucks. The propensity of edges to fray is best dealt with by laminating with woven material nearly to the edges of your mould, and to overlap the edges with narrow strips of resin-impregnated CSM. This ensures complete reinforcement coverage right to the component edges.

When the cured moulding is observed in oblique lighting, or at an oblique angle, the weave pattern of the fabric can often be seen in the gel coat as a series of minor ridges and depressions. This may not concern you, but if it does, one way of avoiding it is to use CSM on the back of the gel coat, and laminate woven glass onto the back of the CSM. This will obviously halve the possible weight saving (unless you use a lighter weight CSM plus one ply of light woven fabric and one of heavier woven fabric), but you will usually obtain a better surface finish. Another method of reducing this weave effect is to put down a ply of glass tissue on the back of the gel coat before laminating the woven glass layers.

The nature of woven cloth means that the plies only make occasional contact with each other where the threads coincide, and with polyester resin this means that the inter-laminar bond strength is not particularly high. As was mentioned during the discussion on mould making, it is better to alternate CSM and woven glass so that the CSM fills the gaps in the weave pattern, and provides a better inter-laminar bond.

## Curing, releasing, trimming and finishing

Once your component has been fully laminated, it should be left to cure at least overnight, preferably for 24 hours and possibly longer if ambient temperatures are on the low side of the ideal working range. You will be able to feel if the laminate is still at all soft, and if it is, allow more cure time, or try to raise the workshop temperature. Don't be tempted to take the thing inside your home, though, because the resin smell will linger and you will not be allowed in again (or, if you live alone, you won't *want* to go in again).

As mentioned in Chapter 2, 'green

trimming' is possible if you catch the right moment of partial cure, but, whilst this can save a little time at the final trimming stage, I prefer to leave the overlaps that protrude beyond the mould, because once they have cured they provide a surface against which you can lever when removing the component from the mould. And component release is the next job. Once the component has fully cured, more or less the same process as that described in the previous chapter (for releasing moulds from patterns) is used to release it from the mould. First you need to undo and remove the nuts and bolts holding the mould flanges and the main mould sections together. Then you prise the component away from the edges of the mould, using the overlaps if applicable (beware of spiky fibres!). Hopefully it will separate from the mould very easily with a direct pull at the edges, although more determined tugging is often required. If it does not release easily, try tapping gently over the surface of the mould with a soft-headed mallet – this sometimes jars a tight component loose. Failing that, you could try using flat wooden mixing sticks and maybe strips of hardboard as wedges, and tap them in gently between mould and component, though great care is needed when doing this, because at this stage the component will not yet have fully hardened. Alternatively, if compressed air is available try squirting a jet between the mould and the component, or through 'blow holes' in the mould (if you pre-

pared any). But if all your preparations were thoroughly carried out prior to gelling and laminating, the component will come out of the mould relatively easily.

Now you can get busy with your hacksaw, or padsaw, or – if you are brave – your jigsaw or angle grinder with cutting disc fitted, and trim off the spiky overlaps. Remember to cut from the gel side so as not to crack or flake the gel coat. Then clean up and smooth off the cut edges with a file or medium to coarse grit abrasive paper on a sanding block, and dispose of the trimmings in accordance with local rubbish disposal regulations.

If you haven't already done so, thoroughly inspect the component to see that it is defect free (hopefully), or to spot any minor defects which might require repair. As with the mould, small defects can be repaired by removing any loose gel or fibres with a knife or file and filling the defect with everyday automotive body filler, before sanding and buffing back to a suitable finish. The final task is to prepare the surface of the component, which may just mean washing and polishing if a coloured gel coat is to constitute its outer finish, or washing and finely abrading if it is to be painted.

We have seen in this chapter how woven glass fabric could enable improved components to be made. In the next chapter we will investigate the benefits of aramid and carbon fibres, as well as more sophisticated resins and core materials.

# Chapter 6

# Material upgrades

IN THIS CHAPTER we'll look at the materials that can be combined with the same wet lay-up contact moulding techniques we've been using, to gain further advantages of weight savings, mechanical property improvements, or both. We will concentrate on those materials that are readily available from commercial suppliers, namely aramid and carbon fabrics to replace CSM glass and woven glass; epoxy resin to replace polyester resin; and more sophisticated cores such as honeycombs.

**Fabric upgrades**
It is pretty clear from the calculations done using the 'Rule of Mixtures' that it is the reinforcing fabric which provides the majority of both the strength and the stiffness of a composite laminate material. This is as you would expect. So, in order to make rough comparisons of these relative mechanical properties we need to compare the respective fibre types in which we are interested. Table 1–3 shows values of the specific tensile strength and modulus (stiffness) values – where 'specific' means that the values appertain to equal weights of each material, taking into account their densities – for E-glass, high strength carbon and aramid fibres, and from this we can construct another set of values, shown in Table 6–1, of these figures relative to E-glass.

We could therefore use these figures to make reasonable assumptions about some of the properties of laminates made from fabrics comprising these fibres, if we assume that the weave types and fibre fractions are the same in each case, and that the resin bonds equally well to all the fibre types (it doesn't, but let's assume parity for now). In other words, let's suppose that the E-glass figures relate to a plain woven fabric at 45 per cent fibre fraction in a polyester matrix laminate, as discussed at the end of the previous chapter, and that the HS carbon and aramid values in Table 6–1 are for similar weave fabrics also at 45 per cent fibre fraction in a polyester matrix. Now we can estimate the laminate weight needed to achieve a similar strength nosecone to that hypothetically made from woven glass fabric in the previous chapter. Let's kick off by discussing carbon fibre fabric, and also look in more detail at the practicalities of laminating components with this material as a reinforcement in polyester resin.

**Table 6–1 Relative mechanical properties of reinforcing fibres**

| | Specific tensile strength | Specific tensile modulus |
|---|---|---|
| E-glass | 1 | 1 |
| HS carbon | 1.41 | 5.09 |
| Aramid | 1.52 | 3.13 |

**Carbon fibre reinforced polyester components**
Using the assumptions stated above, the figures in Table 6–1 indicate that a carbon

fibre laminate would be 1.41 times stronger, and about five times stiffer, than the equivalent weight woven glass reinforced laminate. But turning this around, we can work out that a laminate of equivalent strength would be approximately 30 per cent lighter when made from carbon fibre rather than woven glass, and it would still be more than three-and-a-half times stiffer. These once again sound like worthwhile gains for competition car components if weight-saving is what matters on your car – and when doesn't it matter?

What carbon laminate weight is needed, then, and what carbon fabric weight does this correspond to? In the last chapter, the woven glass fabric cited for use in our nosecone project was 390gsm. At 45 per cent fibre weight fraction, equivalent to a resin to fabric ratio of around 1.25:1, this would create a laminate weight of 390 + (390 × 1.25) = 877.5gsm per ply. If we can get similar strength from a carbon reinforced laminate that is 30 per cent lighter, this implies that our carbon laminate will weigh 614.25gsm, and if the fibre content of that is 45 per cent, then this corresponds to a carbon fabric weight of 276gsm. Carbon fabrics are commercially available at 280gsm, which is close enough for our purposes.

So, on this basis we expect that two plies of 280gsm carbon will enable us to make our nosecone as strong as if we used two plies of 390gsm woven glass; that it will be approximately three-and-a-half times stiffer; and that we should save some weight as well. As with the woven glass exercise, we'll assume that the flanges, corners and edges of our nosecone will be made in CSM, and that the same stiffener is used (it probably won't be needed, but it adds very little extra weight). We can thus calculate what the theoretical weight of the nosecone will be. The gel coat and resin-impregnated CSM strips will weigh the same; only the two main plies and their resin impregnation will be different. In fact, it is helpful to tabulate the comparative figures for the weights of the main plies and the resin needed to impregnate them so that we can see where the weight savings come from – see Table 6–2. In each case, remember, there is 0.842sq m, multiplied by two plies of fabric.

We know by calculation that the original all-CSM nosecone weighed 3.4kg (7½lb), so from Table 6–2 we can see that using woven glass saves about 1kg, and the switch to carbon fibre saves just over 0.4kg more, or almost another pound. The total saving achieved by switching to carbon is therefore 1.4kg, or just over 3lb, representing a weight saving of more than 40 per cent.

But we'd better examine the costs involved in using this more sophisticated material, and once more we can compile a table showing the various cost elements. As with the changes in weight, it is really only the changes to the fabric, and the resultant change to the resin consumption, that have an effect on the total cost, as shown in Table 6–3.

There are a couple of ways of looking at this final cost figure. You can either say, 'Hey, it only costs another £55 to make a carbon nosecone instead of a chopped strand mat one', or you could view it rather differently, and say, 'Clearly there is a substantial premium to pay for using carbon fibre fabric in this instance, and the extra 0.4kg of weight-saving costs a lot more than the first 1kg saved by switching from CSM to woven glass

## Table 6–2 Weights of main plies in hypothetical nosecone

|  | Fabric weight | Resin weight | Weight of laminate |
|---|---|---|---|
| 450gsm CSM | 0.758kg | 1.706kg | 2.464kg |
| 390gsm woven glass | 0.657kg | 0.821kg | 1.478kg |
| 280gsm carbon | 0.472kg | 0.589kg | 1.061kg |

**Table 6–3 Cost estimates for a hypothetical nosecone in carbon fibre reinforced polyester**

| Component | Quantity | Unit cost | Cost |
|---|---|---|---|
| Gel | 0.42kg | £5/kg | £2.10 |
| Carbon fabric, 280gsm | 2.3sq m | £27/sq m | £62.10 |
| Resin, polyester | 0.93kg | £3/kg | £2.80 |
| Catalyst | 0.02kg | £6/kg | £0.12 |
| Coremat | 0.0185sq m | £3/sq m | £0.06 |
| Pigment | 0.02kg | £20/kg | £0.40 |
| Sundries | eg brush, acetone, wax etc | estimate | £2.00 |
| | | **Total cost of materials** | **£69.58** |

fabric'. Which material you choose to use, therefore, will depend on whether you go for the best cost-performance compromise, in which case woven glass wins easily, offering as it does an almost 30 per cent weight saving for virtually no cost penalty; or whether you are on a no-compromise weight saving programme, and the extra cost is not a problem. If you consider all the body panels you could save weight on over the whole car,

and the actual cost of using carbon fibre, you might have to spend maybe £300 or so on carbon fabric to make all the bodywork of, say, a single-seater (rather more if you have a sports racer, or if you are making a saloon or sports car body). But then again, the weight saving for the whole body kit will be fairly substantial, and going the extra mile by using carbon could maybe save you an extra 2–3kg. At least by working through exercises like

*One of the author's early efforts – a carbon fibre aerofoil. The sandwich-construction skins were laminated with polyester resin, though the sub-structure and mounting plates were bonded in place with structural epoxy adhesive.*

this one you will be able to assess the benefits and costs and come to an informed decision as to the best route for you.

## The practicalities of using carbon fibre fabrics

Using carbon fibre fabrics with polyester resin is no more difficult, and in some respects is actually easier, than using glass fabric to make composite components. If we restrict ourselves in this discussion to the use of conventional woven fabrics, then, as outlined in some detail in Chapter 1, there is a choice of weave pattern as well as fabric weight and fibre type, although you will almost certainly be using the high-strength form of carbon fibre rather than the more specialised high modulus variety. An important point to mention now is that when you are purchasing your carbon fibre fabric, you should tell the supplier that you intend to use it with polyester resin, so that he doesn't supply you with a fabric that has

an incompatible finish applied to it.

The various weave patterns boil down to three basic types: plain, twill, and satin weave. Plain weave carbon fabrics are fairly stiff and relatively stable, which makes them quite easy to cut and handle. All carbon fabrics cut easily with scissors, or a sharp knife on a suitable baseboard that won't damage the fabric (vinyl floor covering offcuts are quite good as a cutting substrate). Plain weaves are the least drapeable of the weave types, which makes them less suitable for components with deep or complex curvature, but well-suited to larger, flat or simple curvature panels.

Satin weaves are the most drapeable of the weave types, but this also makes the fabrics very unstable to handle, and particularly prone to fraying. They are therefore the best type for complex or deep curvature components, but are awkward to use.

Twill weaves are a good compromise between the stability of a plain weave

*Preparations are just the same – a new mould needs several coats of mould release wax before you put resin anywhere near it.*

and the drapeability of a satin weave. Their characteristic diagonal herringbone pattern also looks good on a component that is made with a clear gel and clear resin to reveal the carbon fabric, though plain weaves are also aesthetically pleasing.

As with woven glass fabric, appropriate care must be exercised when cutting out the pieces of carbon fibre you need, and special care is required when handling the cut pieces in order to minimise fraying. Some laminators place a strip of masking tape along the line they wish to cut to, then cut along the tape, which prevents the edges from fraying. Such taped edges will either overlap the edges of the mould, or be removed once the carbon is fully wetted out with resin, at which point the tape adhesive usually gives up and you can peel it off fairly easily. It will, nevertheless, be impossible to avoid fraying altogether. Similarly, placing the pieces of fabric onto your resin-coated mould requires equal care, but in the case of carbon fabric the inher-

ent stiffness of the fibres helps a little, by reducing the propensity of unsupported corners to droop onto the mould before you intended contact to be made. This makes placing carbon pieces onto the mould somewhat easier than with glass.

The basic lamination process is very similar to that used with woven glass, commencing with brushing a generous coat of catalysed resin onto the already gel-coated mould, positioning the fabric as described above, and then gently pressing the fabric into place on the mould with your brush while at the same time avoiding distortion of the fabric weave. In this respect carbon handles slightly differently from glass by virtue of its inherently greater stiffness, because the fibre bundles that constitute the threads in the weave are more reluctant to adopt curvature. Thus, if you have any tight radius curves it can require careful but firm persuasion to ensure that the fabric is in contact with the mould in these areas, and has not 'bridged' them, leaving a void between the gel and the

*Rough tailoring the carbon fabric to the mould shape – see how easily dry carbon fabric frays.*

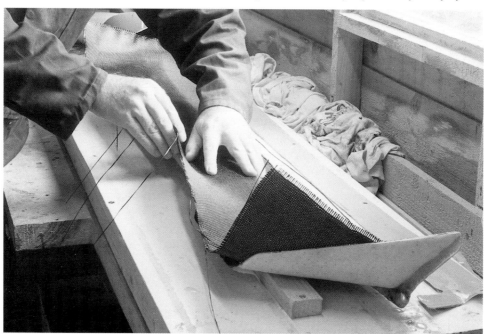

*Trimming to shape.*

fabric. This problem can occur even in areas of fairly gentle contour change, and requires diligent but careful application of the brush over the whole surface being laminated, to ensure intimate contact between carbon and gel. Sometimes it will be useful to apply the carbon fabric rotated at 45°, so that the stiff fibres are not trying to bend into tight curves.

As you brush the carbon onto the resin-coated gel, you will notice how the surface appearance of the fabric changes as the fibres wet out with resin, taking on a different type of shine to that of the dry fabric. Again, as with woven glass, don't be tempted to pick up a laminating roller or squeegee to use on woven carbon – your brush is all you need. Once you have been over the whole surface of the piece being laminated, and made sure it is in full contact over its entire area, you can then brush on more resin as needed. Use light brush strokes to apply the resin, then when you've applied as much as is required (you will, of course, have worked this out beforehand), use slow,

firm strokes over the carbon to gently force the resin into the fabric and simultaneously squeeze out any trapped air bubbles. Once again, this process requires some diligence but is well worth the effort, especially if you are using clear gel and clear resin. It is possible to force out the vast majority of air bubbles in this way. If any air is left behind, not only is it very visible and unattractive, but it also leaves the gel unsupported, and in time it will probably crack off over the bubbles. In a sense such bubbles are worse if you are using an opaque gel or resin because they are not visible until they crack or burst, and if this happens during painting, for example, when a two-pack epoxy paint finish is being heated to cure and dry it, it can lead to a lot of extra work at that stage.

Earlier it was stated that carbon is reluctant to adopt tight curvature radii, and this is generally true when using contact moulding techniques. It also applies to tight internal corners. Some variations in technique are therefore needed in

*Start laminating with light brush strokes, then use slow, firmer strokes to expel air bubbles. Do not stipple.*

order to ensure fibre reinforcement of such areas. Perhaps the easiest thing to do is to cut the carbon pieces slightly smaller than necessary along the edges that are to go into radii or corners, and overlap them onto strips of resin-impregnated CSM that you previously butted into these corners. You would then overlap a further ply of CSM around the corner, over the carbon, to provide full strength.

If you are using clear gel and resin so that you can see the carbon fabric, this treatment of corners would obviously show through, and look very odd. A simple trick to get around this is to apply a thin strip (10 to 15mm, or roughly ½in, wide) of black-pigmented gel onto the mould before the main, clear gel coat is applied, using masking tape to define a neat, straight edge to the black strip. Peel away the tape as soon as the black gel has been applied, and then let that cure before brushing on the main gel coat. This then gives a neat, black and totally

opaque border behind which you can hide the edge of your carbon pieces and lay up your CSM strips.

Another means of reinforcing corners is to remove some individual threads of carbon from offcuts, and apply them to tight corners in the mould once you have brushed on the first coat of resin. Then use your brush and a little resin to impregnate these fibre bundles and gently press them into the corners, prior to placing the main pieces of fabric onto the mould. However, this method obviously requires greater accuracy in the cutting and placement of the main fabric pieces, which is not something that is easy to achieve with dry carbon fibre. A compromise between these two methods might be to buy some woven or unidirectional carbon tape, and apply it to the corners as with the CSM strips. The route you choose will depend on your application and personal preferences.

The second ply of carbon can be positioned and gently pressed into place on

*Black gel coat margins can make a neater-looking job easier to achieve.*

the back of the first, and, as with glass, gentle pressure with your brush will start to bring up a little resin from the first ply.

Once more, make sure that there is intimate contact over the whole area between the plies, then brush on the

*This aerofoil has a black gel coat leading edge.*

remainder of the (carefully calculated quantity of) resin, using the brush to persuade it into the fibre bundles and force out the air as before, and also to ensure a good bond develops between the two plies. With care it is possible to use a laminating roller at this stage, and this allows you to be more certain that you have consolidated every square inch of the moulding. Components with complex curvature, of course, may not lend themselves to being rolled in this way.

We have assumed in earlier calculations that corners and flanges are still being laminated with strips of CSM. To obtain a neat looking finished moulding (when viewed from the inside or back), it is a good idea to lay down the first one or two flange plies before the carbon plies, and then finish off by laminating strips of CSM over the edges of the carbon pieces to hide any frayed edges. Similarly, you will have laminated tight internal corners with CSM strips prior to putting down the carbon plies. But to add a neat finish, lay strips of CSM into the corner over the butted carbon pieces, to cover over any frayed joints and to build up a strong corner joint.

Your carbon-reinforced polyester matrix moulding should now be left to cure in exactly the same way as any other polyester matrix moulding, and, once cured, needs to be removed from the mould, inspected, trimmed and finished. The only practical point worthy of mention here is that carbon seems to blunt hacksaw blades and the like much more rapidly than glass, so be prepared to change blades more frequently if you laid carbon fabric right up to the component edges. Otherwise the finishing process is the same as with any of the previous materials discussed.

You will be pleasantly surprised and impressed with the lightness and stiffness of your carbon fibre reinforced components, and hopefully you will also be pleased with the visual appearance if you elected to use clear gel and resin. But don't be too surprised or downhearted if your first attempt with a clear finish isn't

*The carbon fibre product, released from its mould and awaiting trimming and finishing.*

perfect – I know my first efforts were annoyingly bubble-ridden, and it took me a while to develop my application of the techniques described. Even now, releasing a component from the mould is slightly nerve-wracking (most honest laminators will tell you the same).

## Aramid fibre reinforced polyester components

We can apply the same principles as described in the foregoing sections to show how to work out the respective properties and costs of using aramid fibres in a composite component, again using our hypothetical nosecone as an example. Table 6–1 shows us that aramid fibres are 1.52 times stronger than woven glass, and 3.13 times stiffer, and as with carbon we can make the assumption that a laminate utilising these fibres will possess similar relative properties, and then do some calculations to work out what weight of aramid laminate is needed for our particular component.

If an aramid laminate is 1.52 times stronger than a woven glass reinforced one of the same weight, then an aramid laminate of the same strength as the glass one could be 1/1.52, or 0.658, times the weight, representing a 34 per cent weight saving where aramid replaces woven glass. Such a laminate would, theoretically, be approximately 3.13/1.52, or 2.06, times as stiff as the woven glass laminate. However, as we saw in Chapter 1, the inter-laminar strength of aramid reinforced laminates tends to be a weak point, so these values may not quite be achieved, particularly when the laminate is subject to appreciable bending loads. Nonetheless, the comparison we want to make here is probably valid for unstressed components like bodywork panels.

So, our aramid laminate can be 1/1.52 the weight of the woven glass laminate, which corresponds to 877.5/1.52 or 577.3gsm per ply. If this is again assumed to be at 45 per cent fibre weight fraction, then a 260gsm aramid fabric would fit the bill. However, as an example of how reality doesn't always match ideals, the nearest aramid fabric weight in the catalogues in my possession is 320gsm. For the sake of the calculations here, I'm going to be lazy and assume that this is as close as we can get, just to see what influence this has on our component's properties. It may well be that a 260gsm fabric is obtainable, but since it won't always be possible to match requirements exactly, it's useful to see how the 'next best available' might affect things.

We can now calculate what the weight of the main areas of our component would be using 320gsm aramid fabric, and add the values to those in Table 6–2.

We can now see that an aramid reinforced composite nosecone using 320gsm fabric would be just a little heavier than a carbon one, but would possess much improved impact resistance and greater toughness. But what would the cost of the whole component be? Again, we can put together a costing table similar to Table 6–3, but with the prices for aramid substituted.

It is now possible to compare the properties of all three composite laminate types discussed herein, and make judgements on their suitability according to the performance of the end product, and their respective costs. Only you can decide on the relative merits of each, and how they measure up to the require-

## Table 6–4 Weights of main plies in hypothetical nosecone

|  | Fabric weight | Resin weight | Weight of laminate |
|---|---|---|---|
| 450gsm CSM | 0.758kg | 1.706kg | 2.464kg |
| 390gsm woven glass | 0.657kg | 0.821kg | 1.478kg |
| 280gsm carbon | 0.472kg | 0.589kg | 1.061kg |
| 320gsm aramid | 0.539kg | 0.659kg | 1.198kg |

**Table 6–5 Cost estimates for a hypothetical nosecone in aramid fibre reinforced polyester**

|  | Quantity | Unit cost | Cost |
|---|---|---|---|
| Gel | 0.42kg | £5/kg | £2.10 |
| Aramid fabric, 320gsm | 2.3sq m | £17/sq m | £34.00 |
| Resin, polyester | 0.89kg | £3/kg | £2.67 |
| Catalyst | 0.02kg | £6/kg | £0.12 |
| Coremat | 0.0185sq m | £3/sq m | £0.06 |
| Pigment | 0.02kg | £20/kg | £0.40 |
| Sundries | eg brush, acetone, wax etc | Estimate | £2.00 |
|  |  | **Total cost of materials** | **£41.35** |

ments of your projects, but at least the method used here enables such comparisons to be made.

### The practicalities of using aramid fibre fabrics

The general procedures to follow when laminating with aramid fabrics are pretty much the same as those for carbon fibre fabrics, but there are some important differences to be highlighted along the way. The weave options with aramid fabrics usually tend to be twill and satin weaves, though plain weave options are available, and the fabrics are much more drapeable than carbon. But the biggest difference between aramid and all other fabrics is its reluctance to be cut, a quality that goes hand in hand with its amazing impact resistance. Conventional scissors just do not want to know about cutting aramids, but a fresh scalpel blade used on a resilient backing such as an offcut of vinyl floor covering can be made to do the job (*but take great care when doing this*). So too can certain short-bladed snips, such as those illustrated. If you intend doing much work with aramids,

*Short-bladed snips like these can be used to cut aramid fabric.*

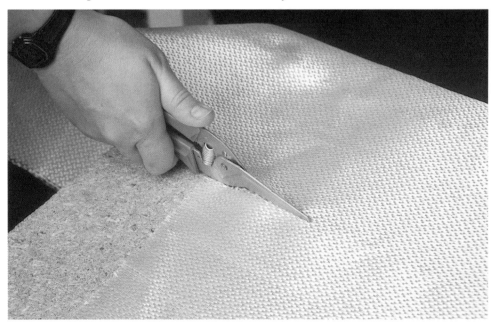

specialised shears can be purchased which, though expensive, will save a lot of time and cursing. This reluctance to be cut is not lessened after impregnation with resin, cured or not, and this is one reason why, ideally, aramids should not be taken right to the edge of components. Aramid fabrics also fray very easily, an attribute that is exacerbated by the use of all non-dedicated cutting implements.

Because of aramid's propensity to fray and resistance to cutting, it is always better to cut the main plies undersize and laminate to the margins with strips of CSM. If you do laminate aramid fabrics right to an edge that has to be trimmed, not only will it be difficult to trim, but you will also end up with a 'fluffy' edge, about which you can do nothing.

The actual lamination process will start off with laying down strips of CSM into corners, up to edges and over flanges, and will be followed by the first ply of aramid, cut to overlap onto, but not beyond, the edge strips. Brush a coat of resin over the main surfaces in just the same way as with woven glass and carbon, and lay on each piece of aramid fabric. Incidentally, you probably won't want to use clear gel in front of aramid because of its horrible yellow colour, but there is, in principle, nothing to stop you from doing so. Laying the aramid pieces into place requires plenty of care again because of the drapeable nature of the fabric. But once in position, this drapeability does allow aramids to conform to fairly complex curvature and quite tight radii.

Aramid fabrics are somewhat less willing to wet out with resin than glass or carbon, and careless brushing can actually lift the fabric off the back of the resin-coated gel. So a careful, methodical approach is needed when brushing resin onto aramids, to ensure that the whole area is wetted without disrupting or lifting the fabric. Once the first ply is on, the second is positioned and the brush is used over the whole area to press it down onto the first. The remainder of the resin is brushed on, and slow, careful but firm brush strokes are used to consolidate the plies together and force out any trapped air bubbles. Careful rolling can be done to ensure all areas are consolidated. Finally the edges, corners and flanges are finished off with resin-impregnated CSM strips, as described previously. Curing happens exactly as it does with glass or carbon fabrics.

Once cured, the component is released and inspected. Trimming should be easy if you laminated CSM right to the component edges, but if aramid fibres have reached the edges anywhere, these areas will be more difficult but by no means impossible to trim, and will end up looking fluffy – there is no other word for it.

## Hybrid fabrics

The hybrid fabrics you are most likely to come across are those comprising a mixture of carbon and aramid threads, which are available in a variety of proportions of the two fibre types. It will come as no surprise to know that the handling and lamination of these materials requires a combination of the above mentioned techniques for each fabric type.

## Real laminate properties

To illustrate the relative properties of some wet lay-up polyester matrix composite materials, some samples were made and subjected to some rather crude, but nevertheless interesting tests in my workshop (OK, shed). It can often be more helpful, I think, to see relative strengths and stiffnesses than to quote values of megapascals and gigapascals, and the accompanying photographs and graphs are reproduced to that end. The samples were two plies of CSM, aramid and carbon fabrics in polyester resin, hand-laminated on a flat piece of Contiboard, with no gel coat.

50mm wide strips were cut from each after curing, and 100mm lengths were overhung from the edge of the workbench and clamped in place. In the first test, equal weight objects were suspended from the ends of the test strips so that bending deflections could be measured as an indicator of stiffness. These figures were then adjusted to normalise them for equal laminate weight in order to give a relative specific stiffness indicator, and the results relative to CSM were as follows, and as shown in Figure 6–1:

*Crude but instructive tests of relative stiffness on two-ply laminates of CSM, aramid, and two samples of carbon.*

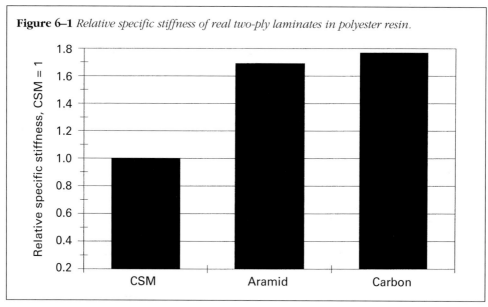

**Figure 6–1** *Relative specific stiffness of real two-ply laminates in polyester resin.*

CSM      1.00
Aramid   1.69
Carbon   1.77

Clearly both the aramid and carbon samples were significantly stiffer than the
CSM, as might be expected. These figures
could actually be inverted, so to speak, to
give relative weights for equivalent stiffness, and the values would then be:

CSM      1.00
Aramid   0.59 (41 per cent lighter than CSM)
Carbon   0.56 (44 per cent lighter than CSM)

The relative strengths of the laminate
samples were then measured by hanging
increasingly heavy weights from each
sample in turn until breakage or permanent deformation occurred. The results
were again normalised to equate to equal
weight laminates, and expressed relative
to CSM to give a specific indicator of
bending strength (see also Figure 6–2):

CSM      1.00
Aramid   3.41
Carbon   1.04

The aramid sample was significantly

*The aramid-reinforced sample was tough to break!*

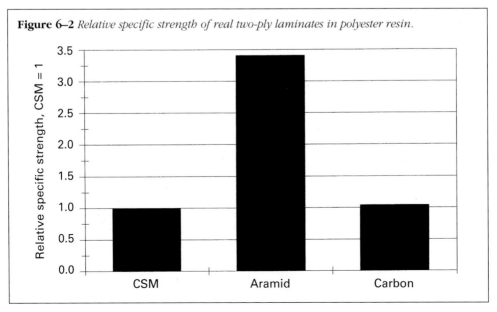

**Figure 6–2** *Relative specific strength of real two-ply laminates in polyester resin.*

stronger than the CSM, as we would expect, but interestingly the carbon sample was only slightly stronger than CSM, and exhibited a brittle fracture. This may have been a result of the quality of the sample lamination, or a less than ideal resin to fibre ratio, but whatever the reason, it suggests that practical tests are even more valuable than theoretical assessments of material properties.

However, the general conclusion from tests like this is that laminates of these more advanced fibres provide enhanced properties and potential weight savings compared to chopped strand mat glass fibre, and are therefore definitely worthy of consideration when making moulded components for competition cars, even when you intend to use the cheapest resin system available.

## Resin upgrades

Still greater improvements in laminate properties may be obtained by using more sophisticated resins. For our purposes here, the only resins we will discuss will be the widely available hand lay-up epoxy resins. These are available from a number of manufacturers (see appendix), and offer some significant performance improvements for your composite components.

As we saw in Chapter 1, epoxy resins provide strong adhesion between reinforcing fibres and between plies of fabric, which is what lends laminates their improved structural properties. The resins themselves are also much tougher, although, as we have seen, a laminate's properties depend largely on the properties of the fibre. In addition epoxies shrink less during curing than polyesters, which can be important if the dimensions of the finished component are especially critical. Epoxies are also more expensive than polyesters, far more critical on mixing proportions, generally cure more slowly, and involve increased health hazards by virtue of the chemicals involved. Nevertheless, the benefits often outweigh the disadvantages in more demanding

applications, and wet lay-up epoxies are so good that top race teams – in Indycar and Formula 1, for example – often do running repairs with them at race meetings when they don't have access to the 'pre-preg' facilities back at their factories.

Using epoxy resin in wet lay-up lamination is not really a great deal different to using polyester resin. Some people will tell you that it is pointless using epoxy resin unless you are going to use vacuum consolidation as well (covered in the next chapter), but you can obtain enhanced properties using contact moulding techniques with epoxies. Talk to the suppliers about your application and intended use, and they will be happy to advise on a suitable resin system, the best rate of hardener to use for the size of job and ambient conditions you are operating in, and so forth.

Amongst the practical advantages of epoxy resins is that you can use them in moulds made from polyester resin and use the same types of release agents, though specialist release agents are also available. This is another case where small-scale trials would be wise before committing a coat of epoxy resin to your mould.

Epoxy gel coats are available, but nobody seems to produce a clear epoxy gel. However, if you wish to make a clear matrix component there are a number of options open to you. If the component is flat, or nearly so, you could brush on a thin, even coat of epoxy resin first, and let it cure before proceeding to the lamination phase. (This technique will not work on a curved mould because the resin will run off high points and pool in low areas.) You will also need to prepare the surface of the cured resin layer as described in the supplier's instructions, to ensure that subsequent layers bond fully to this unreinforced layer. Alternatively you can laminate a slightly resin-rich first layer of fabric into your mould, and work the resin into the fabric with extra care so as to remove air bubbles. This can often produce a very good, void-free clear surface layer. Or you could use a polyester gel coat. Again, most people will tell you that this doesn't work, but providing you allow the polyester gel to cure well past the 'still tacky' stage, epoxy resin will then adhere to it (extremely well) and cure properly. If you are not concerned with having a clear matrix, opaque epoxy gel coats that take a painted finish are available, and can be treated in virtually the same way as a polyester gel, being brushed on and left to cure to a tacky state before continuing with the lamination of reinforcing fabric.

Epoxy resins would not normally be used with anything other than woven fabrics. Chopped strand mat, as we have seen, is held together with a binder that is soluble in styrene, the solvent that makes up a large proportion of polyester resin, and so is unsuitable for use with epoxy resins. In any case, it is highly improbable that you would want to use an expensive epoxy resin with CSM, which just doesn't have the mechanical properties to justify the use of a costly matrix. But if your choice of reinforcing fabric is woven glass, aramid, or carbon, then epoxy resin can certainly be used.

The practical techniques really differ only in the weighing out and mixing of the two resin components, often referred to as resin and hardener. The required proportions may be expressed in terms of weight or volume, and you need to equip yourself to follow the suppliers guidelines exactly. So if you need to mix two parts of resin to one part of hardener by weight, make sure you have a set of laboratory, kitchen or postal-type scales that allow you to weigh it as accurately as possible. On the other hand, if the relative proportions are by volume, then obtain (or make) some suitable graduated pots, beakers or measuring cylinders. The two components must be mixed just as thoroughly as with polyester resin and catalyst, which means stirring around the sides and base of your mixing pot with whatever mixing stick you might be using. Again, try not to

incorporate too many air bubbles. Remember, epoxy resin is a thermo-setting resin just as polyester is, which means heat is generated during the curing reaction. This means that it is also possible to create exotherms with epoxy, and the resultant fumes and smoke are rather unpleasant, as I can attest from personal experience!

Applying resin to the mould, and then to the fabric, is pretty much the same with epoxy as with polyester. Resin viscosities may differ slightly, and with one or two of the epoxies I've tried the viscosity gradually increases during the pot life, which can make it a little harder to spread evenly, but does give you an indication of how much pot life is left. Resin can be applied to the mould, the fabric then being laid on the 'wet' mould and more resin brushed on; or sections of fabric can be pre-wetted with resin by laying them on a sheet of Contiboard or polythene, and then brushing resin on. By carefully using a squeegee of some sort, excess resin can be wiped to the edges of the board or sheet so that you get as close as possible to the optimum resin to fabric ratio. The fabric then has to be carefully lifted off the sheet and positioned in the mould, which can be messy and difficult. With larger pieces of fabric it is easier to use polythene sheet for this purpose, then lift the wetted fabric and polythene sheet up together, press the whole thing against the mould, and then remove the polythene sheet as if it was a release paper on the back of a self-adhesive label. This facilitates fairly accurate positioning of the fabric pieces (but consumes polythene sheet).

Resin uptake can be assumed to be the same as with polyester, which is to say that fibre fractions will be calculated in the same way, so that laminate weights and costings can be calculated in just as with polyester. With this thought in mind, we could produce another costings chart incorporating epoxy resin into the construction of our hypothetical nosecone. But if we assume that the only thing that changes is the resin price, we can tabulate the costs more simply, thus:

## Table 6–6 Cost estimates of hypothetical nosecone with different resin types

| Fibre reinforcement | With polyester | With epoxy |
|---|---|---|
| Woven glass | £16.33 | £30.73 |
| Carbon | £69.58 | £80.74 |
| Aramid | £41.35 | £52.03 |

These figures are based on the earlier costings using polyester resin, and a cost of £15 per kg for epoxy resin, a typical 1998/9 price for a reasonable small job quantity of around 10 to 15kg. Smaller quantities of around 5kg would probably cost nearer £20 per kg.

Clearly the cost is considerably greater with a resin that costs about five times more, but the relative increase depends on the initial cost, and in that respect the percentage increase is obviously greatest with the woven glass reinforced component, and least with carbon fibre. This type of information again allows a better informed judgement to be made regarding the desirability of the respective mater-

ials you are thinking of using. You could look at Table 6–6 and say that epoxy resin nearly doubles the cost of a woven glass reinforced component, or you could equally well say that with carbon or aramid fabrics it only adds £10–£11 to the cost.

In the previous section the mechanical properties of some wet lay-up samples were given, as determined by very simple testing. By way of comparison, a sample of carbon fabric in epoxy resin was also tested, and its relative specific stiffness and strength values make interesting reading, certainly when compared to carbon in polyester. The stiffness values found were:

| | |
|---|---|
| CSM | 1.00 |
| Carbon/PE | 1.77 |
| Carbon/Ep | 1.98 |

And the strength values were:

| | |
|---|---|
| CSM | 1.00 |
| Carbon/PE | 1.04 |
| Carbon/Ep | 2.12 (see also Figures 6–3 and 6–4) |

It is evident that epoxy resin made a significant improvement to the stiffness of

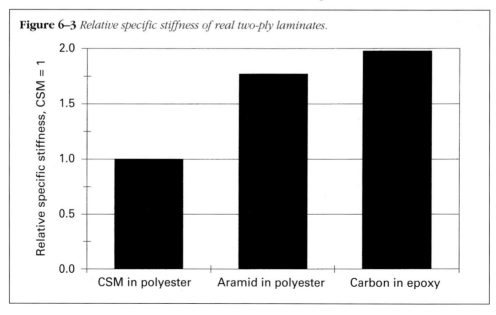

**Figure 6–3** *Relative specific stiffness of real two-ply laminates.*

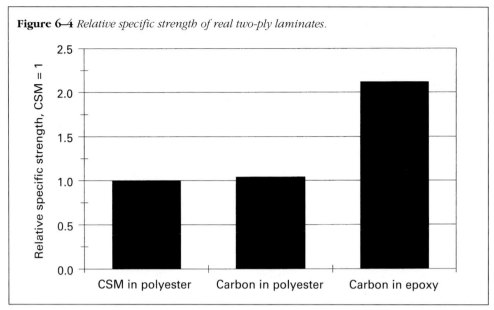

**Figure 6–4** *Relative specific strength of real two-ply laminates.*

the two-ply carbon laminate, but doubled the ultimate bending strength. Such test figures could be used, as previous relative values of strength have been, to re-engineer the lay-up of our nosecone, perhaps by reducing the required fabric weight, which would in turn reduce the resin consumption weight, to the benefit of reduced component weight and slightly reduced cost. Or they could be used to the betterment of strength and stiffness for a given weight of component.

### Trimming and finishing

There are no particular differences in the trimming and finishing of epoxy resin laminates. The resin is tougher, which helps to produce neater trimmed edges with less chance of chipping occurring as you trim. The finished surfaces take paint very easily, and by virtue of better chemical stability, epoxy resin-based components are more durable and less prone to distortion over time than their polyester-based counterparts.

### More core materials

The use of epoxy resin facilitates the use of a couple more core materials that, for

different reasons, do not work with polyester resin, namely expanded polystyrene foam and honeycomb materials.

Polystyrene foam cannot be used with polyester resin because the styrene in the resin dissolves away the foam – it literally disappears before your eyes. However, it is compatible with epoxy resin. It weighs next to nothing, it doesn't absorb any resin, and it can be cut, sanded and otherwise shaped into all kinds of formers for stiffening structures. It doesn't itself have significant structural properties, but it can be used to create structural improvements. For example, square-section strips, with the corners suitably rounded off, can be shaped and bonded onto the back of laminates, either during or after initial cure, and then additional strips of resin-impregnated fabric can be laminated over them, overlapping onto the main laminate to form top hat-section stiffeners. The additional strength and stiffness comes entirely from the shape of the top hat section itself.

Honeycombs are one of the most widely used core materials in the world of professionally manufactured composite components. Usually made from either aluminium foil or Nomex paper, these

## Table 6–7 Relative stiffness and strength of honeycomb sandwich panels

Source: *Honeycomb Sandwich Design Technology*, Hexel Composites

| Ply thickness = t | 2 ply laminate thickness = 2t | Core thickness = 2t + 1 ply skins = 2t Total thickness = 4t | Core thickness = 6t + 1 ply skins = 2t Total thickness = 8t |
|---|---|---|---|
| Stiffness | 1.0 | 7.0 | 37.0 |
| Flexural strength | 1.0 | 3.5 | 9.2 |
| Weight | 1.0 | 1.03 | 1.06 |

materials also weigh virtually nothing, yet by effectively increasing the thickness of a laminate without adding anything to the weight they increase stiffness enormously, whilst adding significant flexural strength. The table above illustrates the gains that can be achieved.

These figures relate to a two-ply generic laminate compared to sandwich panels faced with one-ply skins either side of two different thicknesses of honeycomb core. The thinner core, of equivalent thickness to the combined skin thickness, offers substantial increases in stiffness and strength, whilst the thicker core, which is three times the combined skin thickness, offers an outstanding increase in stiffness in particular for only a 6 per cent increase in panel weight. Such benefits have to be taken seriously in the context of their potential use on competition cars. As we shall see in Chapter 9, it is no wonder that these materials find extensive use in the construction of the world's leading racecars.

The performance of honeycomb cored sandwich panels depends on the bond between the thin honeycomb material and the outer skins of a laminate over the very small contact area. For this reason their application in wet lay-up systems is limited, because full contact between the respective materials is difficult to achieve, let alone guarantee, particularly where there is any degree of curvature – the honeycombs have an inherent stiffness of their own prior to encapsulation in a sandwich construction, which tends to fight against efforts to persuade them to lay on curved moulds. However, in the case of very simple components, such as flat sheets, or perhaps components with a large radius single curvature, there are ways in which honeycombs can be exploited. But it is only the bond strength that can be achieved with epoxy resins that enables honeycombs to be exploited properly, the bond achievable with polyester resin not being really sufficiently strong to construct reliable sandwich panels.

In the case of flat components, it is possible to lay up resin-impregnated plies on either face of a section of honeycomb sheet, and then press the laminate mechanically with a board weighted or clamped in place to ensure that there is sufficient pressure to provide full contact between the laminate layers and the mould. Strictly speaking, this is a form of pressure moulding rather than contact moulding, but as it involves little in the way of specialised equipment, it can be regarded as a legitimate DIY technique. Polythene sheet can be used as a 'release film' to prevent the weighted or clamped board from bonding to the back of the laminate. With simple curved mouldings, it is possible to use something like a sandbag to provide a conformable weight to press on a honeycomb sandwich laminate and ensure full contact is maintained over the whole laminate area during curing. Whilst neither of these methods should be used for critical structural components, there is nothing to stop their successful use in non-critical items to facilitate the exploitation of honeycomb materials in wet lay-up composite mouldings.

Honeycombs are not cheap materials, although compared to the price of aramid and carbon fabrics on a square metre basis they are not dissimilar. Typical prices for 3mm thick Nomex or aluminium honeycombs in 1999 were around £45 for an 8ft by 4ft (2.4m × 1.2m) sheet, representing about £15 per square metre. So if we were able to add a layer of honeycomb to our hypothetical nosecone project between the main plies, the additional cost would be about £12.63. But the tests I did on sample strips illustrate how components can be improved, even using low contact pressure with weighted boards. A sample strip of carbon-skinned 3mm Nomex honeycomb was laminated up using

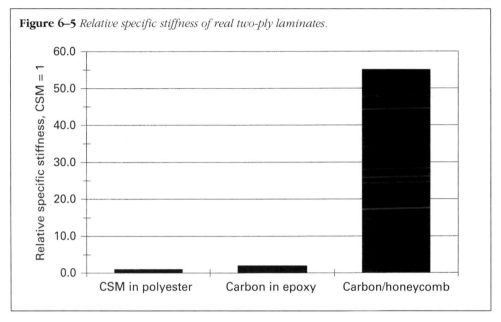

**Figure 6–5** *Relative specific stiffness of real two-ply laminates.*

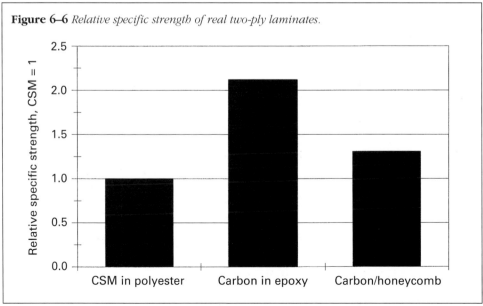

**Figure 6–6** *Relative specific strength of real two-ply laminates.*

epoxy resin. When cured it was tested in the same way as the previous laminates, and produced a specific relative stiffness some 55 times greater than CSM in polyester, and nearly 30 times stiffer than two plies of carbon in epoxy with no core material, as shown in Figure 6–5. As if to illustrate my earlier point about the difficulty of getting full strength using contact moulding methods, the specific relative bending strength was 1.31 times better than CSM in polyester, but less than the two plies of carbon in epoxy which was 2.12 times stronger than CSM in polyester (see Figure 6–6). The Nomex seemed to collapse over the bench edge in this test. Nevertheless, it is evident that very stiff laminates can be made using this method, and careful application may provide you with very positive benefits.

# Chapter 7

# Technology upgrades

WITH SOME MODEST investment in time or equipment, or both, it is possible to achieve upgrades in technology which can be combined with basic wet lay-up lamination to obtain improvements to composite components. These upgrades include positive pressure moulding (hinted at during the previous chapter), elevated temperature cure, and vacuum consolidation. We'll take a look at each of these methods in turn and see how and when they can be applied, with the usual emphasis on home workshop facilities.

## Pressure moulding

The phrase 'pressure moulding' perhaps brings to mind substantial machine presses, with expensive precision-made matched female and male tools which may either be cold, exerting just pressure, or heated to effect a more rapid cure of a moulded component. This technology is indeed used in industry for the bulk production of accurate moulded components that have carefully controlled thickness and good finishes inside and out. But a version of pressure moulding applicable to the home workshop, which involves nothing more grandiose than some more time at the mould-making stage and relatively minor additional expense, is also a practical possibility.

Very basic pressure moulding methods were discussed at the end of the previous chapter, in which flat components were pressed between pieces of board, and simple curved components could be pressed against a mould with something like a sandbag. The former method for making flat components is, in effect, a form of 'matched mould' pressure moulding. But to perform matched mould techniques with curved components requires that a male mould is constructed which allows a component to be laminated in the original female mould, and then be pressed against it with a male mould, weighted or clamped to achieve even pressure. (As in a modern household, male and female mould roles could be swapped here, if appropriate.)

The advantages of this technique are that a consistent laminate thickness can be achieved with a well consolidated laminate, and a good finish may be obtained on both faces of the laminate if required. The disadvantage is obviously that more time and materials are needed to produce the male mould as well as the female, and as such the method is only really applicable to components that require this level of thickness control, consolidation, and/or finish, and where sufficient numbers of components are going to be produced to warrant the extra time and expense at the tooling stage.

This technique can be used with polyester resin or epoxy resin, but its applicability should be limited to components with a simple, not too deep shape from which the mould halves can be easily separated. Components like aerofoil top and bottom halves, cycle-type mudguards, dash panels and such like would lend themselves to this process, if, as was stated above, it is going to be worth the extra effort in the long run. However, matched moulds *can* be worthwhile for one reason alone, and that is when working with carbon fibre fabric, which, as we have seen, is stiffer than other fabric types. Applying pressure by means of a male mould on the back of a laminate can make sure that the stiff fibres are fully pressed into areas of tighter curvature that they might otherwise be reluctant to conform to. This helps greatly in avoiding unsightly or structurally deficient air bubble voids between the first fabric layer and the outer surface, or within the laminate.

To make a matched male mould, you first need to have a female mould. It is then necessary to have a good idea of the laminate thickness you will end up with. This may require making a test component, or at least a sample laminate to the same lay-up. The reason that you need to know the laminate thickness is that, in order to exert even pressure over the whole surface when it is lowered onto the back of the laminate, the shape and size of the male mould has to allow for the component thickness. Perhaps one of the easiest ways of achieving a correctly-sized male mould is to actually lay it up on the back of a laminate already made in the female mould. This obviously requires an appropriate release layer on

the back of the laminate, which could be a generous coat of PVA, or perhaps a sheet of polythene, or you could use specialist release film, which we shall go into in more detail later. With this method, the finish of your male mould will be the same as the back of your laminate, or the sheet of polythene or whatever, which will probably not be particularly smooth, unless you finished off the laminate with a layer of glass tissue. Even so, the surface may not be all that good, and this may not matter. But if you want to achieve a good finish, there are other methods.

One such method is to screed the back of the laminate with filler and sand it back, and if necessary buff it until it is as smooth as you require. This is time consuming, but requires no special materials. Another method is to use sheet wax as a dummy laminate. Sheet wax, already alluded to in Chapter 3 as a pattern-making material, can be purchased in a range of thicknesses, from about 0.8mm (0.03in) up to about 6mm (1/4in), so obtaining a near-equivalent to your expected laminate thickness should not be difficult. This material can be made to conform to curved shapes with gentle warming, and being wax it requires no further release treatment. So, with wax sheets of an appropriate thickness (slightly thinner than the likely component laminate, to ensure the actual laminate is slightly compressed over its whole

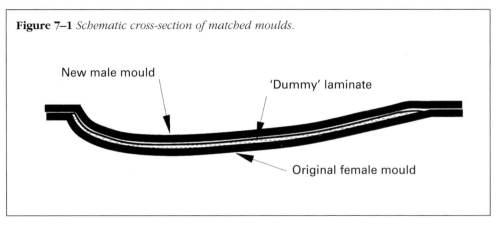

**Figure 7–1** *Schematic cross-section of matched moulds.*

New male mould

'Dummy' laminate

Original female mould

area when the male mould is applied), a dummy laminate can be laid in place on the female mould, yielding a smooth surface. A male mould can then be taken directly from this. Alternatively, male moulds can be cast in the female mould, on the back of a laminate or wax dummy laminate of appropriate thickness, using casting resin or rubber moulding compound. Where flanges exist on the female mould the matched male mould should also have such flanges, laminated in as part of its structure. These allow it to be clamped or bolted to the female mould.

Once the two matched moulds are made and prepared for use, component manufacture proceeds as described in preceding chapters, until it is fully laminated. At this point the male mould is carefully placed on the back of the laminate, and if equipped with flanges with bolt holes (useful for ensuring good alignment), the bolts are installed and the nuts are gradually tightened to bring the two matched moulds into pressure contact, gently squeezing the laminate between them. If the moulds are not equipped with bolt clamping, they must be carefully aligned, then squeezed with clamps or pressed together with suitable weights such as house bricks, or whatever is to hand and appropriate to the size of the component.

It is not necessary, nor is it a good idea, to try to exert massive pressure – the thickness of the component laminate in relation to the slightly lesser thickness of the dummy laminate used to make the male mould will effectively determine the appropriate amount of pressure, and any excess is just likely to distort the moulds and create too thin a laminate. The aim is to exert *some* pressure over the whole of the back of the component, thus ensuring full contact between reinforcing fabric and component outer surface, and obtaining even laminate consolidation.

Mould release, trimming and finishing are done in just the same way as with ordinary contact moulding, with the obvious difference that the male mould must first be released from the back of the laminate.

## Elevated temperature cure

The extent to which ambient temperature wet lay-up resin systems can be assisted by elevated temperatures is, if you will pardon the pun, a matter of degree. Both polyester and epoxy resins can be made to cure significantly faster with the application of modestly raised temperatures around 30°C, and the mechanical properties of mouldings made from both resin types can be greatly enhanced by a medium temperature post-cure that might fall somewhere in the range 50° to 80°C, depending on the resin and the manufacturer's recommendations. Tables 7–1 and 7–2 below illustrate both points for one epoxy resin, and we have already seen in Chapter 1 how polyester resin curing can be accelerated with similar temperature increases, and also how post-curing at temperatures up to 80°C can fully 'mature' a polyester-based moulding in as little as three hours. There is also the benefit that a consistent cure temperature will provide both a consistent cure time and consistent mechanical properties in your components.

## Table 7–1 Demould times for an epoxy resin with standard rate hardener

| Temperature | Demould time |
| --- | --- |
| 15°C | 16.8 hours |
| 20°C | 9.3 hours |
| 25°C | 5.0 hours |
| 30°C | 2.8 hours |

## Table 7–2 Effect of post-curing an epoxy matrix laminate

| Laminate treatment | Inter laminar shear strength |
| --- | --- |
| 28 days at 21°C | 54.4MPa |
| 24 hours at 21°C + 16 hours at 50°C | 66.2MPa |

The information in Table 7–2 is interesting when compared to a point made in Chapter 1, which was that a polyester resin-based moulding can be made to reach full hardness, or 'maturity', with a post-cure of 15 hours at 50°C. Thus, the ability to post-cure at 50°C can be seen to be particularly beneficial, whichever resin system you are using.

The main advantage of a shortened cure time is obvious – the component can be released from the mould sooner, permitting quicker finishing and the rapid re-use of the mould for the next component, if that is important. The improved mechanical properties that can be derived from a post-cure may or may not be necessary, but given that, in the example in Table 7–2 and the comparable effect on polyester resin-based laminates, a modest temperature post-cure performed overnight can yield significant improvements in laminate properties, then if you are suitably equipped it would be a shame not to take advantage of these benefits.

Already, then, we have two different temperature requirements that bring their own advantages, and which can be achieved by different means. Let's start off by looking at how to achieve temperatures of around 30°C, which will enable more rapid cure times to be realised. In order to be reasonably energy efficient, it makes sense to only heat as big a space as is necessary to accommodate the moulding in its mould, and which offers sufficient room to load and unload your components. For this reason, I would suggest building some form of 'warm box', electrically heated and thermostatically controlled. The alternative is to section off part of your workshop with plastic sheeting and heat that area with a fan heater or oil-filled electrical convector heaters, but this is bound to use more energy, and therefore cost more, especially as you really must make provision for good ventilation as well. You would probably also find that 30°C is an uncomfortably warm temperature to work in when wearing overalls and gloves (if you

work in the UK, where 30°C is a summer rarity; if you live somewhere warmer you may not need supplementary heating to achieve this temperature).

I once built a very basic 'warm box' from a pair of old wooden packing cases nailed together, with slatted shelves (facilitating air circulation by convection) on which to place components. It was heated with four 60 watt light bulbs and controlled with the kind of room thermostat used for central heating systems. I bought all the components at the local DIY centre, and despite being a hopeless electrician managed to make it all function safely. I always kept a wary eye on it when in use, but in all probability it generated insufficient heat to cause a serious fire hazard. Crude though this first effort was, it enabled a consistent 30°C to be maintained, with the room thermostat cycling the light bulbs on and off as required, even when the workshop temperature dropped much lower than this in wintertime. This meant that I didn't have to keep the whole workshop at up to 15–20°C just to ensure that the resin cured in a reasonable time, which undoubtedly saved a lot of money. Alternative and possibly more efficient heat sources would include the tubular oil-filled heaters used for warming greenhouses, provided you buy ones with a reasonable power output. Adding some form of insulation to the outside of such a box would reduce the power requirement to maintain temperature.

The size of the components you want to make will determine whether or not building a 'warm box' is a practical proposition, and if so, what size and shape it needs to be. If you wish to produce larger components that make it impractical to build a closed box, then sectioning off part of the workshop and heating that will be your only viable alternative. It could be kept at an equable laminating temperature whilst working on the component, and warmed up to 30°C just to cure it. Again, electrical heating, ideally thermostatically con-

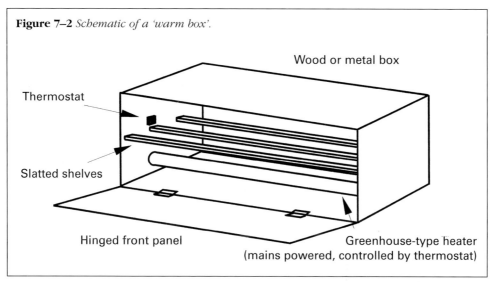

**Figure 7–2** *Schematic of a 'warm box'.*

Wood or metal box

Thermostat

Slatted shelves

Hinged front panel

Greenhouse-type heater
(mains powered, controlled by thermostat)

trolled, is preferred. Avoid paraffin- or gas-fuelled heaters, which not only have naked flames (an obvious safety hazard when working with flammable chemicals and resins, etc), but also produce water vapour as a by-product of their combustion. Once your warm area cools down, this may well condense and cause problems, possibly even damaging reinforcing fabrics. The electrical fan heater takes some beating, because it circulates the air and helps to provide an even temperature in your warm area. Convector heaters also work, as do sufficiently powerful oil-filled radiators, which are my preferred safe choice because the electrics are completely sealed. None of these heaters should be operated in such a confined space that they could overheat – take note of the supplier's guidelines. And no apologies for mentioning once again that you mustn't forget the importance of proper ventilation, to prevent the build-up of potentially harmful vapours.

Achieving temperatures of 50–80°C for post-curing operations requires more thought and planning, and some modified methods and components. It is possible to self-build an oven that can fulfil the requirement of attaining 80°C, but whereas a 'warm box' can be made from

wood, a metal casing such as sheet aluminium becomes a necessity for this higher maximum temperature. Double skins either side of insulation material will reduce the energy required to maintain the temperature, and polystyrene foam, glass wool and rock wool could all be used as suitable insulation, polystyrene having an upper working temperature of around 100°C before it starts to shrink. Providing the insulation is effective, the outer skin could be made in something like plywood or MDF if you can buy it at a lower price than aluminium.

The heat source could to be of an industrial type such as electrical radiant heaters, which are designed to operate in more demanding environments, or domestic cooking oven elements. The former are not hard to obtain, and suppliers are suggested in the appendix, while domestic cooker spares are easily found. The power required will depend on the size of oven you wish to build, but as a guide, the oven illustrated in the accompanying photograph – which is nearly 1.6m long by 0.5mm deep by 0.6m high internally – uses a 1200 watt domestic oven element.

In order to maintain temperature control, a suitable thermostat will be required

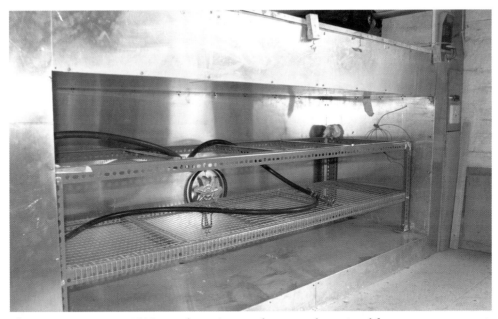

*This curing oven uses a 1200 watt domestic oven element and associated fan to cure components at 80°C.*

to switch the power to the heaters on and off once up to temperature. Again, a domestic oven controller will do the job. Some means of measuring and displaying the temperature is also required, and this is most likely going to be done with one or more 'thermocouples', which can be connected to a specially-made digital display that gives a direct readout of the temperature. It's important to be able to measure the temperature of the component itself so that the oven can be set to get it to the required temperature. And to achieve evenly distributed temperatures throughout the oven interior, a suitable oven fan to circulate the air is necessary. All of these items can be obtained from electrical and electronic component suppliers such as listed in the appendix.

It has also been suggested that this type of oven can be heated with a domestic electrical fan heater sited outside the oven box and positioned a few centimetres back from an orifice cut in the box walls, blowing heated air in through the orifice. Though I have no personal experience of it, I've no reason to doubt the functionality of this method. I wonder, however, if small industrial-type heaters might be better suited to the task.

Another way of obtaining an oven suitable for the purpose is to buy a second-hand laboratory oven – companies dealing in such equipment do exist. These ovens are constructed in sheet metal, are insulated and fan assisted, and come with temperature controllers already fitted. Larger ones are over a metre high and about 0.6m by 0.6m internally, and could certainly be used for smaller components. Turned on their sides, and fitted with modified shelving, reasonably long components could also be accommodated. Laboratory drying cabinets are another possibility worth consideration, and they're much cheaper than lab ovens.

It is important to highlight a few important points regarding the elevated temperature post-cure of moulded components. Firstly, it is vital to ensure that there are as few air bubbles in the laminate as possible. When a laminate is heated up, any bubbles trapped within it will also heat up, expanding and exerting stress on the surrounding material. If these bubbles exist near the surface, and especially just behind a gel coat finish, there is the risk that they will exert sufficient pressure to burst and damage the surface. So the emphasis on conscientious stippling and rolling in earlier chapters becomes still more important if elevated temperature treatment is to be used, and consideration should be given to placing a glass tissue layer behind the gel coat in all cases where it is appropriate, to reduce the risk of bubbles occurring adjacent to the gel coat. This advice applies just as much to moulds as to laminated components, if they are to be subjected to higher temperatures. Secondly, laminates using either polyester or epoxy resins should be left for a day or two at ambient temperature before being subjected to the elevated temperatures needed for post-curing. And finally, any elevated temperature treatments that are to be done in-mould require that the mould itself must have first been post-cured to at least this temperature.

## Vacuum consolidation

The first point to be made about vacuum consolidation is that although it can be used with polyester resin, this is frequently not recommended. The reason generally given is that the vacuum suction pulls the relatively volatile styrene out of the resin, and this reduction in styrene content inhibits the cure process. However, other authorities happily discuss vacuum moulding and polyester resin, whilst yet others are somewhat equivocal, and suggest that you need to be careful not to apply too much vacuum. I suspect that the latter advice is actually the best, and that experimentation is the order of the day. Polyester resin is usually supplied as a 'general purpose' type, but within that definition you can bet on variations in constituent content from batch to batch and, especially, supplier to supplier. So whilst vacuum cure may work well with one type, it may not with another. Read on, see how vacuum consolidation can be done, and decide whether you want to experiment with polyester, or go straight to epoxy resin for use with this technology. Arguably, it may not be justifiable to go to the expense of the equipment and consumables required to facilitate vacuum consolidation if you are going to carry on using polyester resin, whereas the increased gains in component quality from the combination of epoxy resin and cure under vacuum may well make the additional investment and running costs worthwhile. It all depends on what you are making, and what the component's requirements are.

So what is involved, and what extra equipment and consumables are needed? The basic principle of vacuum consolidation is that prior to resin cure commencing, a component and its mould are sealed in a plastic bag from which the air is then removed. This has the effect of squeezing the laminate onto the mould with a theoretical maximum possible pressure of one atmosphere, or roughly one bar (about 14lb/sq in). The advantages to be gained from doing this include the ability to ensure void-free (or virtually void-free) components, even where component shape is quite complex; gains in inter-laminar bond strength; and improved laminate consolidation. In short, the benefits are improved quality and mechanical properties.

The equipment and consumable requirements obviously centre on a vacuum pump, connections, piping, and suitable materials in which to bag the component. Depending on the scale of projects you are going to be working on, the type of vacuum pump needed is one which is capable of pulling at least 0.7 bar (about 10 lb/sq in) and preferably up to 0.8 bar of vacuum, and which can move somewhere around 150–200 litres (5–7 cubic feet) of air per minute. This may require a motor of perhaps 0.5 horsepower (about 350 watts). Or do what I did and get a refrigeration engineer friend to provide you with an old fridge compressor plumbed to suck instead of blow – you get good vacuum, if slightly slow air movement. A cheap and functional solution. Suitable rubber tubing capable of not collapsing under vacuum will also be needed, to connect the pump to the bag.

As well as a vacuum bag there are also various other materials needed to facilitate proper vacuum consolidation. In the order that you would apply them on the back of the lamination, these are known as peel ply (optional), release film, breather or bleeder fabric, and bagging film.

Peel ply is a lightweight woven material made of nylon, polyester, or PTFE-coated glass, which, as its name suggests, is designed to peel easily from the back of the laminate following cure to leave a clean, contaminant-free surface which is ready for any secondary bonding or lamination processes. Peel ply does not have to be used, but is helpful in cases where subsequent operations are planned, and it leaves a neat 'fine weave' embossed finish behind. It does not have to be removed until you are ready for those later operations. Peel ply can absorb a small amount of resin, and it needs to be used carefully where the resin ratio is already low, since it may adversely affect surface finish. This is unlikely to present any difficulties with a wet lay-up moulding, where the usual problem is having a little too much resin around. A rough guide price for peel ply in small quantities is around £2.50–£3.00 per square metre, and it is not re-useable.

Release film is a thin, non-stick plastic film used to separate the laminate from the stack of vacuum materials after curing. It can be obtained in perforated and non-perforated forms, the latter allowing the bleed-through of resin. The choice of film will depend on the resin system you are using and the job in hand, so ask your supplier for advice.

*Release film being placed on the back of a carbon laminate.*

With wet lay-up you will probably choose the perforated variety so as to remove some of the likely excess of resin during the cure cycle. Small quantities of release film cost about £3.00 per square metre, and with care it can sometimes be re-used.

Breather, or bleeder fabric is a felt-like, non-woven material made of polyester, nylon or glass, which serves two main purposes, as alluded to by its alternative names. Firstly, it ensures that air in the vacuum bag can be removed easily, by providing a pathway along which the air may flow, through the open structure of the fabric, perpendicularly through its thickness as well as along the plane of the material itself. The removal of air doesn't pertain just to applying the initial vacuum, but also to any trapped air or volatiles that need to escape during the cure process. Secondly, the material acts as an absorbent layer for excess resin when used with a perforated release film. One or more layers of breather fabric can

be used. It is relatively cheap at about £1.00 per square metre for small quantities, and it can be re-used provided it has not had to soak up resin.

The vacuum bagging material is usually a nylon film which has very low gas permeability and accordingly maintains a good vacuum, even if the vacuum pump is disconnected, provided there are no leaks in the bag construction. Bagging film usually comes in tube form, on rolls of various widths and in various thicknesses. You can also buy silicone rubber vacuum bags which will endure many uses, and which may be more cost-effective if you anticipate making a lot of repeat items that use a specific bag size. But nylon bagging film can also be re-used if care is taken, and offers more flexibility of shape and design – an important point if you are making lots of different-sized one-offs for a specific project. It is also possible to use ordinary commercial polythene sheet as bagging material, but being more gas permeable

*Breather or bleeder fabric.*

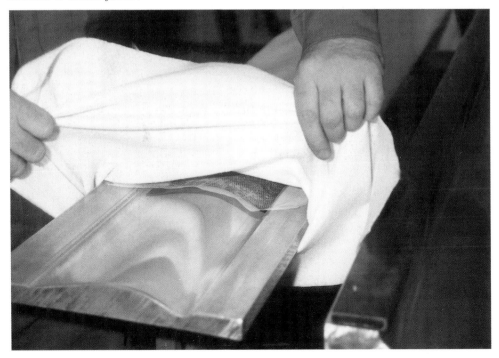

than nylon it is necessary to keep the vacuum pump on throughout the cure cycle, or at least until the component has hardened (and cooled down again, if ele- vated temperature cure is used). Bagging material will set you back about £1.75–£2.00 per square metre in small amounts.

*The tubular vacuum bag material has here been made into an envelope, closed with sealant tape at each end.*

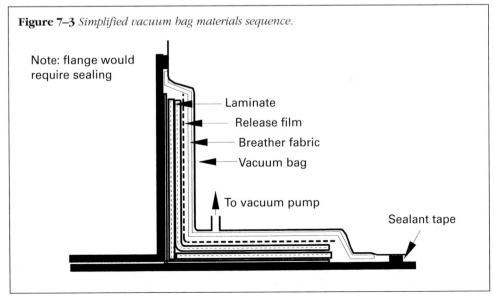

**Figure 7–3** *Simplified vacuum bag materials sequence.*

Note: flange would require sealing

— Laminate
— Release film
— Breather fabric
— Vacuum bag

To vacuum pump

Sealant tape

Bagging film is made into actual bags with the aid of sealing tape, or 'tacky tape'. This rubber-based adhesive tape, roughly 3mm (1/8in) thick, is adhesive-coated on both sides with a removable backing paper on one face. It can therefore be placed onto a mould flange or onto one side of the bagging material, and once in position the backing paper can be removed and the (other side of the) bag material can be stuck to it. If you are going to indulge in elevated temperature cure as well as vacuum consolidation, you will need to buy a made-for-purpose form of sealing tape, but if you are staying with ambient temperature cure for now, the variety you can buy at your DIY store for sealing double-glazed windows will do the job. The high temperature form of sealant tape costs about 50–60p per linear metre for small quantities, and only a little less for large quantities.

Finally, in order to connect the pipe from your vacuum pump to the vacuum bag, you need a suitable 'through-bag connector'. At its most simple, this can be the vacuum pipe itself or a length of metal pipe which fits into the vacuum pipe, with a ring of sealing tape wrapped around it, which is then stuck to the sealing tape somewhere on the periphery of the bag. The bag material then has to be tucked tightly around the pipe to form a good seal. Clearly this type of connection will only maintain vacuum as long as the pump is running, and it is important to disconnect the pipe should you turn the pump off so that the vacuum in the bag doesn't suck oil in from your pump. A better form of through-bag connector is the type which incorporates a quick-release mechanism and an internal non-return valve. Pushed through a small hole made in the bag, from the inside, this is held in place with a threaded sealing ring which clamps a gasket onto the outside of the bag. This type of connector holds a vacuum even when the pump is turned off.

*A through-bag vacuum connector.*

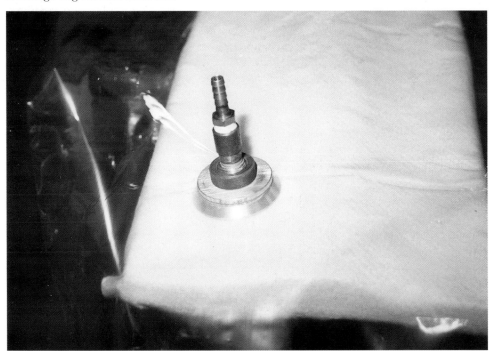

So that's the equipment and materials. Clearly there are consumables here that will increase the cost of your components, but using the technique that is about to be described will provide improved component quality. Only you can decide whether it is worth adopting it for your projects.

Before commencing lamination, make sure that the mould is free from any sharp corners or spikes of reinforcing fibre that may puncture or damage the vacuum bag. It is useful, too, to have a mould that the bag is going to be able to fully conform to on both the laminate side and the reverse side. Wide mould flanges are useful for sticking sealant tape and vacuum bags to, but if your mould doesn't have these you'll have to make your vacuum bag the 'envelope' type.

The time that you take to make your laminate is important insofar as you need to be able to apply the final vacuum before the resin starts to gel. So, figure out how long it will take to laminate the job, and also to get the component bagged up and under vacuum. As with all other aspects of composite moulding, good preparation is the key to a good job, and you need to ensure that all the bagging materials are to hand before you start laminating.

The actual laminating process is no different to those previously described. But as soon as you have put the finishing touches to your component, the next job is to apply peel ply to the back of the laminate, or relevant areas of the laminate, if you intend to carry out any bonding or lamination on the back of this first laminate. Next, you apply the release film. This material is thin and flexible, but does not stretch; it is therefore happy to follow single curvatures, but not complex ones. To cope with the latter you need to cut out pieces of release film and cover the whole of the back of the laminate with overlapping pieces. Make sure you get release film right into tight corners, and that no bridging occurs. Extend the release film 20 to 30mm (about an inch) beyond the edges of the mould, though not onto flanges to which you will subsequently need to stick sealant tape.

*Ensuring release film is pushed fully into the corners.*

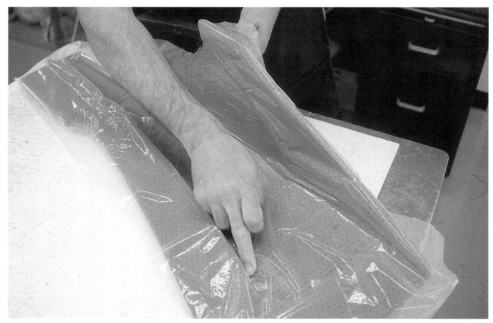

You then need to apply breather fabric. In some cases this will just be laid on the back of the release film, but when you are inserting the whole mould into an envelope-type bag you need to wrap the whole mould in a couple of layers of breather fabric, making sure it overlaps everywhere.

You are now ready to bag up the mould. Make sure that the work surface you do this on is clean and free of any sharp objects that might damage the bag. A piece of carpet offcut on the bench top forms a good surface on which to do this job. To make the vacuum bag itself, you can either stick sealant tape around the mould flanges and stick bagging material to the flanges, if that is appropriate, or you'll need to make an envelope-type bag in which to insert the mould. In the former case, your mould must be able to hold a vacuum. In either case, you have to allow for the fact that bagging film does not stretch, and so the bag must be made oversize, with the slack taken up as tucks and creases. Consequently you have to work out how big to make the bag in

the first place, and you do this by taking the length and width of the component, adding twice the depth to each measurement, and then adding a generous margin of about 20–25 per cent for good measure. To make an actual bag, you will need two pieces this size, stuck together with sealant tape. Alternatively you could buy the bag material in tube form at a width that will accommodate the mould with adequate slack. To take up the slack around the edges of the mould, tucks can be put into the sealant tape along flanges, and the bag film is stuck to these tucks. The more complex the component shape, the more tucks will be needed to accommodate the slack.

Before finally sealing the bag, you need to install one or more (for bigger components) vacuum outlets of whichever type you have elected to use. If you are using the simple pipe through the sealant tape connector, then attach a piece of rolled up breather fabric to the end of the pipe inside the bag to form an extension a few centimetres long, so that the bag doesn't just seal the end of the

*The component fully wrapped in breather fabric.*

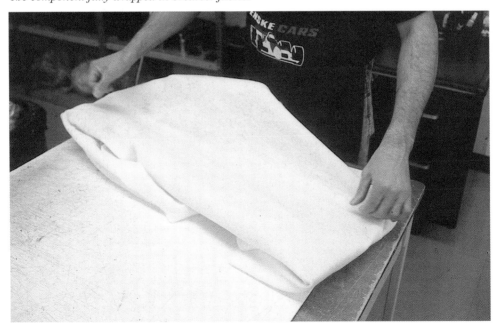

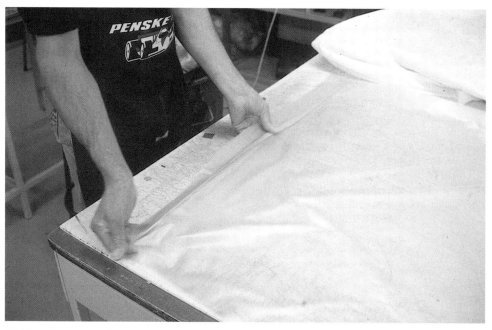

*Making the vacuum bag up.*

pipe when the vacuum pump is turned on. With any vacuum connection, put at least two extra layers of breather fabric beneath the connection itself and on top of the main breather cloth wrapping, to prevent any possibility of sucking resin

*Fitting the through-bag vacuum connector – notice how bulky the bag appears to be.*

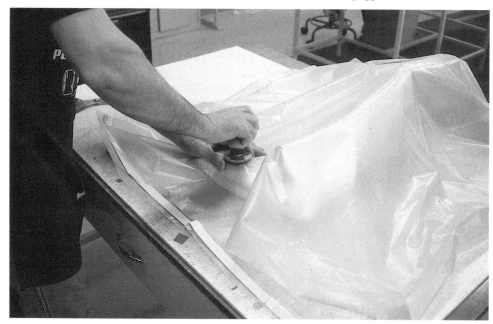

into the vacuum pipe. The consequences of such a misfortune hardly need to be spelled out!

Make sure the bag is tucked tightly into all the corners, and that there are no bridges anywhere. Then turn on the vacuum pump and watch the bag start to move and contract as the air is sucked out. Tucks and creases can be positioned as required at this point, and if necessary the pump can be turned off and the vacuum pressure partially released to reposition the bag or ease it into corners. Once all looks well, turn off the pump and see if a good vacuum is being held. It should not be possible to pull the bag away from the back of the laminate at all. You could use a vacuum gauge – connected earlier via another through-bag connector – to actually monitor the vacuum sustained, and make sure it doesn't decline too rapidly. Leaks can sometimes be picked up by listening for quiet hissing sounds, and can be stopped by pressing on the offending portion of sealant tape or, if in the bag itself, by

pressing a piece of sealant tape over the hole.

The component is then left to cure. This is likely to take several hours at ambient temperature, less if slightly elevated temperature is being used as discussed earlier in this chapter. Keep the vacuum pump running until you are certain that cure is well advanced. As an indicator of what stage the cure process has reached, you could make a small check sample to the same lay-up as the component and put it in the same environment. Remember, once you have turned off the vacuum pump disconnect it, so that the vacuum in the bag doesn't suck oil in from the pump.

Once cure is complete, carefully remove the vacuum bag so that it can be used again, then remove the breather fabric and release film and discard these. Leave any peel ply in place until you actually need to remove it. The beautifully consolidated, void-free product can now be trimmed and finished like any other composite component.

*Vacuum is applied, and creases and bridges in the vacuum bag materials are removed – the second through-bag connector enables a vacuum gauge to be connected.*

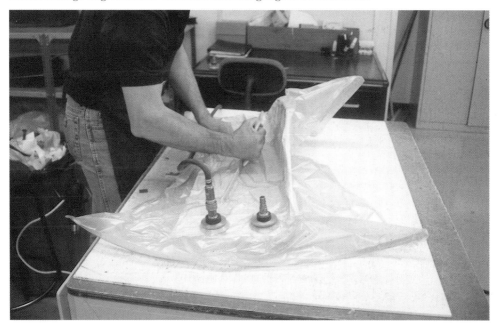

The extra cost involved in making composite mouldings using vacuum consolidation has to be weighed up against the benefits of improved quality and mechanically more efficient components. There is also extra time involved in the bagging up process, though once again, given the better likelihood of obtaining defect-free components, there is probably an overall net gain here, because you may waste much less time rectifying imperfections. As with all things, it's a case of horses for courses. You might consider that simple, essentially flat-shaped mouldings can be laminated well enough by simple contact pressure, but that more intricate components, perhaps with a deeper shape and tight internal radii, would justify the bagging process to ensure proper contact between laminate and mould. Once more, only you can evaluate the options in the light of your application and available budget.

**Elevated temperature and vacuum**

A couple of brief references were made in the previous section to using elevated temperature cure with vacuum consolidation. This would enable you to get the best out of wet lay-up composite components, combining well-consolidated laminates with relatively short cure times. With a suitable medium temperature post-cure, the mechanical properties would be about as good as you can get from wet lay-up too. You would need to modify your 'warm box' to enable vacuum pipes to pass through the wall somewhere, and be connected to the mould once inside the box. The quick release through-bag connectors are very useful here, so that you can apply the vacuum with the mould on your work bench, making sure the bag is fully sealed, and then disconnect the mould for transfer to the 'warm box' before re-connecting it for vacuum application during cure.

# Chapter 8

# Pre-pregs

MAKE NO MISTAKE, some very good results can be achieved using wet lay-up technology, both by contact moulding and, more especially, by vacuum consolidation, and possibly the application of moderate heat as well. Some people have even used these techniques to produce structural components like monocoque chassis for single-seater racecars, though if you intend to do this some pretty extensive materials proof-testing would seem to be a necessity before putting your faith, and your life, in the hands of such constructions. We tend, perhaps, to take it for granted that such components can be made in composites because professional racecar constructors have been doing so for some time, but, as we shall see in the next chapter, they don't put anything into use until it has been properly tested.

One of the difficulties with wet lay-up technique, as we have seen along the way, is that controlling the resin to fabric ratio, or the fibre fraction, is difficult because of the problem of obtaining totally uniform resin distribution throughout each ply of a laminate. This makes it more difficult to predict the performance of a laminate, because variations in fibre fraction create variations in mechanical properties. This is where pre-pregs provide a significant advantage.

Pre-pregs, or pre-impregnated fabrics, are supplied already impregnated with a resin system which cures with the application of heat – rather more heat than we have thus far considered. This pre-impregnation is performed as a precisely-controlled industrial process, either by a solvent dip method, where the dry fabric is dipped in a bath of resin and solvent prior to drying in an oven to drive out the solvent, or by a hot-melt technique, where the fabric is coated with a controlled weight of melted resin per unit area, and rollers then squeeze the resin into the fabric. Either method can provide the user with a wide choice of fibres and fabric types and styles, with an optimum quantity per unit area of resin. You no longer have to calculate resin requirements or carefully brush out a measured amount of resin in the hope of getting as close as possible to the optimum resin to fabric ratio. Rolling and stippling become redundant techniques because the fibres are already pretty well impregnated, and the ensuing heating and vacuum application ensure thorough wetting of the fibres and consolidation prior to cure. The pre-impregnation processes also enable the use of very tough and strong resins that would be far too viscous to laminate by wet lay-up by virtue of their chemical and consequent physical properties. For our purposes we are only going to consider epoxy resin-based pre-pregs. Others, such as phenolic resin systems, are available but will be regarded as outside our scope here. There is a wide enough range of epoxy systems alone to cater for the majority of applications likely to be required in the home workshop.

## Pre-preg properties

As stated above, pre-pregs require elevated temperatures in order to cure. Depending on the resin system, the required temperature can be anything from about 50°C to 200°C. As with most chemical reactions, further heat speeds up the reaction, and the converse of this is that at room temperature the cure is very slow indeed. This allows the material to be handled at room temperature with no fear (in most cases) of cure occurring prematurely. (It is possible to obtain low temperature-cure pre-pregs that do cure at ambient temperature, but these are specialised materials.)

Prior to use, pre-pregs are kept in a freezer to inhibit cure and provide extended storage time, or shelf-life, of a matter of several months and maybe up to a year. The typical temperature of a domestic freezer cabinet, -18°C, is fine for storing pre-pregs. The material should be removed from the freezer well before use to allow it to equilibrate at workshop temperature before any handling is attempted. There are two reasons for this; first, leaving the material sealed in its wrapping as it equilibrates prevents condensation from forming on its surface; and second, the material is prone to being very stiff when just removed from the freezer, and is thus rather brittle. Consequently you should not subject a cold pre-preg to handling or unrolling until the material is up to workshop temperature.

The time that pre-preg can be left at ambient temperature before its properties are affected is known as its 'out-life'. The longer a pre-preg's out-life, the more time you have available to laminate the component. It is possible to obtain pre-pregs that benefit from an out-life amounting to many days, even weeks, which can be handy in the case of an extremely complex component that takes a lot of time to lay up.

The actual cure process is interesting, especially when compared with that of wet lay-up resin systems, and it helps to look at it very generally to understand how pre-pregs work. At ambient temperature a pre-preg resin has a high viscosity that makes it seem as if it is almost solid, and it feels tacky but, to all intents and purposes, dry. As heat is applied, the viscosity of the resin drops markedly, allowing it to flow all around the reinforcing fibres within the laminate. The pre-preg fabric also becomes flexible and compliant and is able to conform with the contours and shape of the mould, with vacuum pressure now squeezing it against the mould. As the temperature continues to rise to the 'activation point', the catalyst in the resin system begins to react, and cross-linking between the molecules begins. This gradual polymerisation causes the viscosity to rise again, until eventually the resin is no longer capable of flowing at all. Finally, the cross-linking is completed and the resin becomes fully cured.

Once it is at ambient temperature the material usually feels slightly tacky. This tackiness is actually designed in to aid the lamination process – it helps the fabric to stick lightly to the mould during lay-up, and makes life a whole lot easier. As soon as you get hold of even a small sample of pre-preg you realise how much more stable and easy to handle it is than dry fabric. You can cut shapes from it, and the fabric stays that shape as long as you don't mishandle it. The weave orientation can be maintained, keeping the bundles of fibres as straight lines, which helps structurally and aesthetically. The edges are clean and tidy where you make your cuts, usually with a very sharp knife. It is possible to tailor very accurately to a mould shape. And the whole process is generally a lot less messy, particularly as the material is supplied with a backing film applied that enables you to do all of your cutting without actually exposing the pre-preg to contamination.

The resin viscosities can actually be tailored to suit particular applications as well. A 'high flow' type becomes less viscous when heated, and would be used with a heavier weight fabric in thicker

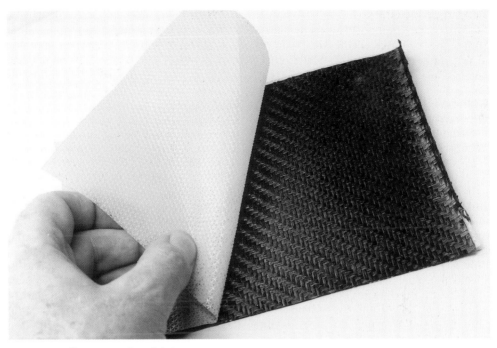

*Pre-preg twill weave carbon fabric.*

laminates to ensure the resin fully encapsulates the fibres, or perhaps in a thinner laminate where a good surface finish was required.

Some pre-pregs are also made to permit higher service temperatures, that is, a greater tolerance to high temperatures when the component is put to use. This might be relevant if you are making a component that is located near an engine exhaust, such as parts of the bodywork, or perhaps the outer can of an exhaust silencer. These pre-pregs are likely to have higher cure temperatures too, but I have seen a data sheet for a 130°C three-hour cure pre-preg that had a claimed upper working temperature in excess of 180°C.

Pre-pregs can be specified with respect to fibre type (glass, aramid, carbon, or hybrid); fabric type (plain, twill, satin weave, or, of course, uni-directional); resin type, which defines the cure regime as well as, to some extent, the end-product's properties; and resin content. This last point is a useful parameter to be able

to change in some circumstances. For example, for thicker laminates you could specify a lower resin content than with thin laminates; or if you are going to bond a core material to the skins using the impregnated resin only, you would specify a higher resin ratio. You might also specify a higher resin ratio for the outer layer of your component to further help towards achieving a good surface finish. Values of resin content typically fall in the range of 30 per cent at the low end to between about 40 and 45 per cent at the upper end. Most suppliers carry a range of high sales-volume materials in stock, and if you can choose from this range it usually means faster delivery, and lower prices too!

## Influences on mould design

Whatever moulding process you use, the mould must be capable of withstanding the manufacturing process over the envisaged number of uses. Thus, a mould intended for use with pre-pregs must primarily be capable of tolerating the elevated temperatures that it will encounter not just once, but possibly many times. Some pre-pregs have cure temperatures in the range 60°C to 80°C, whilst others need considerably more heat to cure them. Your mould has to be able to cope with these temperatures, and so, depending on what it will be made from, it must undergo at least one post-cure at the intended cure temperature.

If you are intending to use pre-pregs that cure at up to about 80°C, or maybe a little more, it is possible to use a suitable wet lay-up polyester resin for your moulds. Some of these polyester resins can be pushed to 90°C or even 100°C, but perhaps 90°C is a sensible maximum for a polyester-based mould. Such a mould would therefore need a post-cure at this temperature to ensure that it is stable when used to cure a component. Furthermore, as with any wet lay-up mould that is to be used at elevated temperature, great care must be exercised when it is laid up, in order to remove any entrapped air from within the laminate that could otherwise cause damage when the mould was subsequently heated.

If the dimensional tolerances of your components are really critical, then it is usually best to make the mould from the same material that you are going to use for the component. Glass components would therefore require a glass mould, and carbon components would require a carbon mould. This is because of differences in the expansion of the different materials when subjected to heat. Matching the thermal expansion of the mould and the component within it will ensure that the latter is the size and shape you intended when it is released from the mould.

If extra strength and durability is required from the mould, then it may be necessary to make it from pre-preg. The obvious problem with this is that, given the elevated temperature cure needed with pre-pregs, you now need a pattern that is capable of withstanding high tem-

peratures. However, there are some specialist pre-pregs available which, as mentioned earlier, actually cure at ambient temperature, and which are then post-cured at the temperature the mould is required to work at. However, for the kind of jobs you'll most likely be wanting to tackle in the home workshop, vacuum consolidated wet lay-up moulds in glass or carbon, subjected to a post-cure, will be satisfactory.

There is another method of making moulds for pre-preg curing which can be applicable in certain circumstances, and that is where the mould can be machined directly from a solid that will withstand the cure temperatures. For example, moulds can be machined from solid aluminium, which after polishing and suitable release treatment can produce mirror finish components. And a material the top race teams use is epoxy tooling block, which though intended as a pattern material could, after suitable surface finishing, be used to make a mould directly. Both these cases require access to, or knowing somebody with access to, a suitable machining centre capable of cutting the shape of the mould you want. This invariably means that you, or a suitably-equipped and located pal, has to produce a computer-aided drawing (CAD) which may then need to be turned into a three-dimensional drawing, before being used to create a tool path for a computer-controlled, or CNC, machining centre. This isn't as exotic as it might sound nowadays, and by making friends with a local machinist you might be able to have moulds made this way. But be warned, solid aluminium billet or block is not cheap; and cheap is definitely not a word to be used in the same sentence as epoxy tooling block.

One of the problems you'll encounter if you use aluminium block is to do with its thermal mass. Although it is a pretty good conductor of heat, a sizeable chunk of aluminium takes a while to heat up, and you need to be aware of this when timing a component's cure time. You

*Release agent being applied to a pre-preg carbon mould.*

therefore need to at least have some method of measuring the component's temperature (so that you know when it has reached the required cure temperature), if not some means of controlling your oven's heat input through this. If the block that your mould is machined from ends up with variable thickness, such as in a female mould for a lower aerofoil half (which would probably be considerably thinner around the centre of the wing than at the front or the back edges), then the thinner areas would heat up faster than the thicker areas, which further complicates matters. In such a case you would need to place a thermocouple on the laminate above the thickest part of the mould, and time the cure cycle from the point at which this reached cure temperature. This should ensure that every part of the component is subjected to the minimum cure time, and the job should turn out satisfactorily.

A point worth reiterating here concerns mould stability. Not only must a mould to be used with pre-pregs be thermally stable, it must also remain physically stable and not alter shape when sub-

jected to elevated temperature and vacuum.

Finally, if you intend to cure your mould on the pattern at a significantly elevated temperature, obtain your supplier's advice about the best release agent to use, or at least carry out some trials using similar materials to your pattern and mould, and your existing release agent. Wax release agents that work at ambient or slightly elevated temperatures may not cope with higher temperatures.

**The oven**

The designs of oven discussed in the previous chapter will be good enough to achieve a temperature suitable for use with the lower end of the elevated temperature cure pre-preg range, up to around 80°C. You can produce excellent results at this temperature, with the right materials of course. If you want to contemplate speeding things up, or using higher temperature cure materials, and you begin to think in terms of 120°C or so, you can still build an oven that will do the job, but you might want to think about speaking to an electrician or a

*If you've got around £30,000 to spare you could get a little autoclave like this one – notice its big brother on the left of picture...*

heating engineer to get a feel for the type of heat source to use. He could also help out with choosing and wiring heaters, controllers, fans, and thermocouples. Speaking to one heating engineer convinced me that obtaining proper advice and help from your local friendly expert is the way to go here, unless you are already conversant with the type of equipment needed. If you are intending to make small components, then the previously mentioned fan-assisted laboratory ovens might be a viable choice, given that some of these reach up to 300°C.

In very general terms, you still need to heat and circulate air in your oven, and a design which has a heating element contained within external ducting, that re-circulated the air into the oven with a fan, would be efficient. I have used an electric cooker element, which is designed to get very hot, as a heat source, and its associated circulating fan. The other components needed to achieve the requisite conditions and good temperature

control are relatively inexpensive, easy to obtain and well worth having. Beyond that, it wouldn't be right to advise here – where mains electricity is involved it is always prudent to obtain proper, expert advice – but hopefully these few notes will get your creative juices flowing. Some composite supply companies will also provide you with a ready-made oven if you are willing to part with sufficient cash.

### Handling and working with pre-pregs

Amongst the most important basics of handling pre-pregs is the fact that contact with moisture must be avoided, because epoxy resins are hygroscopic, meaning they absorb moisture, and the bond strength is reduced in the presence of water. In addition you must always wear gloves when handling pre-pregs, not so much for your own well-being as to prevent skin oils, which also impair bond strength, from getting onto the surface of the materials. And most importantly, you should keep release agents well away from your pre-preg handling area, and preferably in a different area altogether. This might prove difficult if you operate in the garden shed, in which case you must just be as scrupulous and thorough as you can in keeping release agent away from your pre-preg materials. The reason for stressing this is obviously to do with bond strength again, since getting release agent on pre-preg fabric does not so much impair its bond strength as make it disappear altogether. So use a different pair of gloves for applying release agent; don't put them, or the cloths you use for applying release agent, down on your fabric-cutting surface; keep the container of release agent well away from any fabrics; and so on – all basic, good workshop practices.

The 'out-life' of pre-pregs has already been mentioned. Although the catalysts in pre-preg resin systems are designed to remain, in effect, dormant until heat is applied, these materials do actually start to cure very slowly at ambient temperature, and over a period of time they gradually stiffen, lose their tackiness, and generally become less workable. Furthermore, they may not 're-flow' fully when they are raised to the appropriate cure temperature, which means that the resin will not flow properly amongst the fibres of the fabric, leading to a weaker laminate that is not internally bonded as well as it should be. This change in properties happens over a time-span ranging from perhaps two weeks up to maybe four months, depending on the resin characteristics. The supplier's technical data on a given pre-preg will tell you what its out-life is.

It is interesting to note that out-life is a cumulative effect, so that even if you put your roll of pre-preg back in the freezer as soon as you have cut the required amount of material from it, it will have been at ambient temperature for at least some hours equilibrating to workshop temperature. And each time the roll is out

*Always wear gloves when handling pre-pregs – the health risk may be fairly small, but the risk of ruining bond strength with skin oils is significant.*

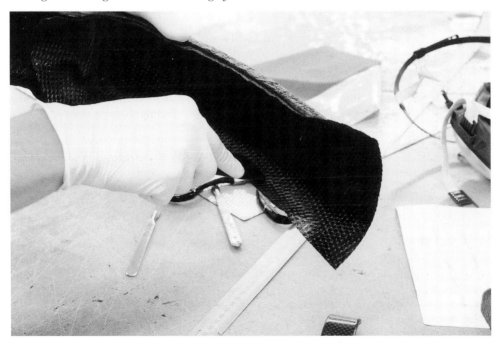

of the freezer it will use up some more of its out-life. This means that, in time, you will reach the specified out-life, and the material is likely to degrade from there on. Consequently, to avoid wasted effort and sub-standard components, keep a reasonably accurate running record of how long any given roll of pre-preg fabric has been at ambient temperature, and you will then know when you have used up the available out-life and the time has come to replace the material. It is therefore also a good idea, obviously, to only order as much pre-preg as you can use within a reasonable length of time. If you anticipate a high turnover of components and materials, that won't be a problem, but if you only make occasional one-offs, it's something to keep in mind so that you don't over-order. And if the material you choose has a short out-life, ask the supplier to send it by a 'next day' despatch system – you don't want it kicking around a transport depot for days!

The suppliers will always quote you a minimum cure temperature and a minimum cure time, so that you know what temperature is needed to cure your pre-preg, and how long it must remain at that temperature. But, as was stated earlier, raising the temperature shortens cure times, and the data below illustrates this for one example of a particular pre-preg resin system. Other pre-pregs will have different properties, but these figures illustrate the general principles.

| Out-life | up to eight weeks at 23°C |
| Storage life at −18°C | up to one year |
| Cure temperatures | 80°C to 120°C |

Impregnated into various fabrics, including unidirectional carbon, woven carbons, hybrid aramid/carbons, E-glass woven rovings

| Minimum cure temperature | 80°C |
| Minimum cure time @ 80°C | 12 hours |
| Cure time @ 90°C | 6 hours |
| Cure time @ 100°C | 3 hours |
| Cure time @ 110°C | 1½ hours |
| Cure time @ 120°C | 45 minutes |

As you can see, each 10°C increase in heat halves the curing time, and this can be significant in terms of productivity.

Onto practical matters, then. As mentioned previously, don't forget to take your pre-preg out of the freezer the day before you want to use it, so that it comes up to workshop temperature. Meanwhile, you can spend time making templates for cutting the pieces you need. To start with, make your templates out of paper so that you can curve and tailor it to the contours of your mould. For one-off or infrequently made components you could leave it at that, but if you are likely to make regular repeat items it could be worth transferring these paper shapes to something more durable. Thick card or plywood last pretty well, but it is useful to cut regularly used templates from aluminium sheet of around 1/16in (1.6mm) thickness. These can then be used as cutting guides with little risk of lumps being shaved off them. It is quite possible that you may need different templates for successive plies within a laminate, the reasons for which will be apparent as we get into laminate design. This might seem as though it is making heavy weather of the process, but it is just part of the systematic way in which you need to work with pre-pregs. And if you think having different-shaped templates for a laminate that may consist of just a few plies is hard work, spare a thought for the production people in the aerospace industry, who, when making a component like a helicopter rotor blade, for example, have to deal not just with tens but with hundreds of plies, each with its own specific part number.

The basic lay-up considerations of fibre type, weave type, fabric weight, and number of plies have to be established before you start, and are worked out in much the same way as for wet lay-ups, which is to say, using the best knowledge and experience you have available to you. You may already have a component that you are going to replace, whose lay-up, weight, and mechanical properties

*Cutting pre-preg with the aid of a template.*

are known to you. By making some test samples in pre-preg to various lay-ups you will quickly develop a feel for what is going to be possible, and how it will improve on the existing part. But as with the exercises in Chapters 5 and 6, where we looked at relative material properties in order to estimate what component lay-ups should be, you must have a starting point to work from, be it an existing component, or some knowledge – gleaned from a fellow competitor, perhaps – of the numbers of plies in component lay-ups, core type used, and so forth. In the absence of any of this, there is no substitute for making sufficient test samples that you can use to provide yourself with the requisite information.

A point that we haven't dwelt too much on so far is that a woven fabric that typically has fibres running in two directions at right angles to each other, has its essential mechanical properties aligned with these fibres. Thus, the optimum tensile strength and stiffness values will be found in directions parallel to these fibres. In components which are going to

be utilised for any structural requirement, it is necessary to take the orientation of the fibres into account at the design stage so that, if necessary, loads can be fed into the component along the fibre directions rather than across them.

In the case of non-structural components, you may want to make the part so that it has physical properties that are as even as possible in all directions. To achieve this you will need to laminate some of the plies at different angles. For example, using the standard notation that the warp threads run at 0°, then for reasonably uniform stiffness in a two-ply laminate you might use one ply at 0° and another at + or – 45°, that is, orientated north–east/south–west or north–west/south–east, so to speak. For equal stiffness north-south and east-west, you would lay up one ply at 0° and the other at 90°. This makes allowance for the fact that weft threads can have more curl in a woven fabric, and so are not as stiff as warp threads when laminated. This aspect of the lay-up may not be crucial to you, but it is important to be aware of the

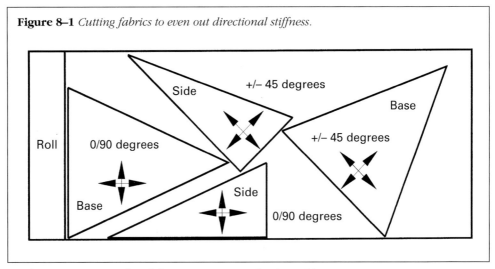

**Figure 8–1** *Cutting fabrics to even out directional stiffness.*

implications, especially if the component is load-carrying.

Another aspect of the lay-up of woven fabrics is laminate 'balance'. Why is this important? Because an unbalanced laminate can distort upon curing. So what is laminate balance, and what can be done to achieve it? There are two factors that contribute to a balanced laminate, and both relate to the orientation of the fibres in the plies and in the laminate as a whole. Firstly, a plain weave fabric has a similar appearance on both faces, and therefore contributes pretty even properties whichever way up it is laminated. However, satin weaves appear very different on each face of the material, one side having a predominance of warp threads, the other a predominance of weft threads. If, say, a two-ply lay-up was laminated with both the plies the same way up, the laminate would be unbalanced. However, by turning one ply the other way up, a balance is obtained. (Note: you would need to turn your template the other way up when cutting a piece of material that orientates that way.) For multi-layer laminates, the object would be to aim for symmetry about the centre of the laminate, with equal numbers of plies each way up, symmetrically distributed throughout the laminate.

The second aspect of balance goes back to fibre orientation once more. In a multi-layer laminate, a balance can be achieved by symmetrically distributing fibre orientation about the centre of the laminate. This means that in a four-layer laminate, for example, the two outer plies would have their 0° direction – that is, their warp fibres – aligned with the long-axis of the component (assuming, for the sake of this example, that it has one), and the two inner plies would have the 0° direction aligned across the long-axis. If more plies and mixed +/–45° plies were used, the same principle would apply, and the aim would be to achieve symmetry of lay-up either side of the laminate centre plane. To ensure that you laminate your plies in the correct sequence, number them on the backing paper as you cut them so that you know in which order they should be laid-up in the mould.

You are now ready to start working out your ply shapes. When allowing for overlaps, which should be about 15–20mm (0.6–0.8in), it is important that they should be staggered from layer to layer, otherwise if you place them all in line you end up with a considerably thicker strip in the laminate. Now you can see the reason why you might need different templates for each ply.

When cutting material that will go into

tight corners, it is conventional to go around the corner with the first ply, and butt and overlap subsequent plies. In the case of very tight radius corners, however, it may be safer to cut thin strips that you butt into the corner, and which are then overlapped by the first main ply. Strips will need to be cut to build flanges up to the required thickness, and to help in any other tight corners, joggles, steps, or other rapid changes of contour around small details.

If your component is simple, such as a conventional aerofoil shape, for example, then for the main part of the moulding you will only need to cut material to the correct dimensions, allowing for any inverted plies you decide are necessary to balance the laminate. 45° plies may not be necessary in an aerofoil because the shape of the finished component might

well provide adequate torsional stiffness, and if the 0° fibre orientation is aligned along the span, or width, of the wing, the greatest strength and stiffness will be where it needs to be. Such a component may also have sub-assemblies, such as transverse spars and fore and aft ribs. The spars will be fairly simple [ -section mouldings which will not require any special shapes to be cut, though they may benefit from being made from uni-directional fabric, given that they exist to provide strength and stiffness across the span of the wing. Ribs may be more complex, and require small details to be tailored into the material plies in order that the pre-preg will conform to the mould shape and be held in place by the vacuum process later on. The application of local heat with a hot-air gun will probably be necessary to

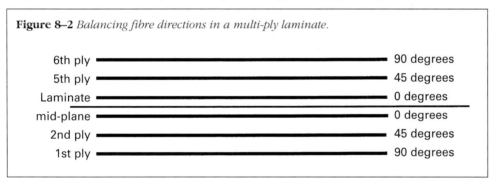

**Figure 8–2** *Balancing fibre directions in a multi-ply laminate.*

| 6th ply | 90 degrees |
|---|---|
| 5th ply | 45 degrees |
| Laminate | 0 degrees |
| mid-plane | 0 degrees |
| 2nd ply | 45 degrees |
| 1st ply | 90 degrees |

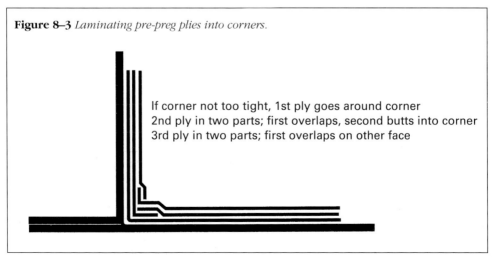

**Figure 8–3** *Laminating pre-preg plies into corners.*

If corner not too tight, 1st ply goes around corner
2nd ply in two parts; first overlaps, second butts into corner
3rd ply in two parts; first overlaps on other face

soften the resin matrix and get pre-pregs to conform readily to racecar aerofoil ribs, and other similar small, detailed components.

Cutting pre-pregs is best done with a sharp knife such as a scalpel, using something like vinyl flooring offcuts as a cutting board. This will need fairly frequent replacement, but provides a resilient backing that allows the scalpel blade to cut through the pre-preg without blunting the blade too rapidly. If you are using paper or card templates, you'll need to place a steel rule along the edges of the template to act as a blade guide when making each cut. If you are using plywood templates, then you can, with care, use the edges of these to guide your blade; however, avoiding little wood shavings falling onto the pre-preg material is not easy. As we have already said, sheet aluminium templates are the best choice for cutting. Incidentally, remember that scalpel blades are *extremely* sharp – I don't need to say any more, do I?

In general, preparing pre-preg materials for laminating is not a great deal different to tailoring dry fabrics prior to wet lay-up, but it is easier to do with control and accuracy, and that should be your aim.

## Laminating with pre-pregs

The general procedure that follows assumes that you already have available the mould or moulds needed to make your component, and that they are post-cured and ready to use at the relevant curing temperature for the pre-preg you have selected. It will also be assumed, for the purposes of this exercise, that no gel coat is to be used. So, the first step is to degrease the mould surface by wiping it over thoroughly and carefully with acetone, and you then need to leave it to air dry for a few minutes in your suitably ventilated workshop. Next you need to apply the supplier's recommended release agent. This will probably be a liquid, and needs applying with a clean, dry, non-linting cloth like mutton cloth.

This job must be done as diligently as with any other resin system, and ideally you should apply two or three coats, with time to dry between coats, followed by a light rub over with a clean cloth once the final coat is fully dry. Don't forget, if you can do this job well away from the area in which you are going to handle your pre-pregs then do so. If you have no alternative but to use the same work area, at least make every effort to avoid contaminating the pre-preg handling surfaces, equipment and tools with release agent.

Once you are sure that your preparation area is clean, you can prepare the tools and materials you need for laminating. You will need all the cut pieces of pre-preg to hand, obviously, plus a blunt plastic spatula of some description, maybe a plastic roller, a thinner (but not sharp-edged) spatula, and quite possibly a hot-air gun.

Lay-up can commence virtually anywhere you want. There are no strict rules to be observed, so begin wherever you think it is logical to. It might be prudent to start by applying strips to tight corners, if that is relevant on your component – if it is, then you will want these to go down before the main plies. Then the first main ply, or section, might be laid-up to an edge or flange. Peel the backing paper off one face of the pre-preg, pulling it back parallel with the surface so as not to distort the material. Hold the pre-preg carefully too – warmth and pressure even from gloved finger tips can cause weave distortions.

Lay the ply onto the mould, perhaps starting at an edge or flange as suggested, and press it – gently at first – onto the mould surface, just using your gloved hand for now. Once you are sure the ply has gone down in the right place, without creases, or bridges over tighter radii, start pressing it into place more firmly. Make sure it gets pushed into any tight corners, carefully using your sharper-edged spatula to squeeze it in and to ensure that it doesn't form bridges. Then

*Laminating the first ply into the mould.*

switch to your blunt plastic spatula and exert firm pressure all over the ply, to get it to stick to the whole mould surface. Don't be tempted to use any sharp-edged tools to push it into tight corners. If you do you're likely to cut or break the fibres, which will weaken the component.

If the mould has complex curvature, it

*Pressing the first ply onto the mould with a blunt plastic spatula.*

will very likely be necessary to use your hot-air gun to warm and soften the resin matrix, allowing you to utilise the drapeability inherent in your chosen fabric to press it into full and continuous contact with the mould surface. If there is a fair degree of complex curvature involved, hopefully you will have selected at least a twill weave fabric, and possibly a satin weave, so that you have increased drapeability on your side. You must make sure that the fabric is in full contact with the mould over its entire surface, and this may be achieved by a combination of blunt spatula over flat areas, and gloved fingers – perhaps with a piece of backing paper over your fingertips to protect your gloves from excessive abrasion – where there is more complex curvature or detail.

Once the first ply is satisfactorily laminated in place, peel off the backing film by carefully pulling it back parallel with the pre-preg material. (If you try pulling it away at an angle the force exerted may be sufficient to lift your carefully laid ply right off the mould.) Now you are ready for the second ply, which may well be in more than one piece, with overlaps between pieces. It may also be differently orientated with respect to fibre direction, but you will have dealt with this when you cut the ply earlier. You need to position the first piece so that its edge places the overlap where you intended, and in the case of a tight corner you'll probably finish it just past the corner, making sure to press it fully into the corner itself. The second piece would then be butted into the corner to give a neat overlap and a full strength laminate in the corner. On a simple component shape, such as a flat sheet or perhaps something like an aerofoil half, the second ply would just be laminated in place over the first, no joins or overlaps being necessary. Now you can apply firm pressure to the second ply to ensure it is in full contact with the first, using the same techniques as are described above.

The lamination process continues in this way, with staggered overlaps and joins, until all the plies have been put down. However, in a thick multi-layer laminate it is usual to carry out a vacuum consolidation about once every four or five plies. This process, known as 'debulking', is designed to ensure that the plies laid up thus far are fully consolidated before you proceed with the next few layers. Basically the procedure for vacuum bagging as outlined in Chapter 7 is followed, whereby the laminate is covered with a release film, then wrapped in a breather fabric, and finally enclosed in a vacuum bag (which need only be polythene rather than more expensive bagging film, since no high temperatures are involved). After suitable through-bag connections are installed, a vacuum is applied and maintained for around 20 minutes, usually at room temperature. Sometimes moderate heat is used in debulking, which helps to soften the resin matrix and facilitates improved consolidation. This would be carried out in your curing oven, but it is important that the temperature is kept well below the cure temperature to avoid a partial cure being accidentally initiated. If this happened, it would impair the tackiness that helps to hold the subsequent layer to the last one you put down.

After de-bulking is completed, the vacuum can be released, the component can be removed from the vacuum bag, and the breather fabric and release film carefully removed. Peel the release film away as you would the backing film from the pre-preg, so as not to lift it off the mould. Now continue laminating until all plies are put down, debulking again every few layers if necessary. Once this operation is complete you are ready to bag up the component for curing.

Bagging-up and curing again follow the procedures laid out in Chapter 7, which, in brief, are as follows. Apply peel ply to areas where subsequent lamination or bonding processes are planned, then place a layer of release film on the back of the laminate. Follow this with a couple of layers of breather fabric, which may involve wrapping the whole mould, including the component, and then place it into a suitably over-sized vacuum bag, which this time will probably be made from pukka vacuum bag film. Press home the sealant tape all around the edges of the bag using tucks to take up slack as required. Install the through-bag vacuum connection, and (possibly) another for a vacuum gauge. Apply vacuum, ensuring the bag pulls down evenly everywhere without too much creasing, and with no bridging occurring anywhere. Once full vacuum is achieved, turn off the pump and check for leaks. Larger leaks will be evidenced by hissing, whilst smaller leaks will only be apparent if the vacuum drops over the course of a few minutes. If all is well, turn on the vacuum pump again, and put the mould and component in the oven. Using high temperature 'flash tape' stick your thermocouples (for your temperature readout and your controller, if you are using one) to the back of vacuum

bag where it is in intimate contact with the laminate.

Turn on the oven, and follow the pre-preg supplier's instructions with regard to the cure cycle. This will specify a 'temperature ramp rate', or a rate of rise of temperature, in degrees per minute, and this should not be exceeded or there may be a risk of an exotherm occurring. The instructions will also specify the cure temperature and cure time you need to apply. As we saw earlier, there may be options for different times at different temperatures, and usually you would pick the temperature you can achieve in your oven with effective control, and use at least the cure time that this dictates. The temperature of the laminate is what matters here, and it is possible that you may need to set the oven a little higher than the required temperature, especially if it is not that well insulated. It is also important to start timing the cure cycle only when the component has reached the required temperature – the oven thermostat or controller may tell you that the oven is up to tem-

*Applying vacuum to the bagged-up component at DJ Racecars.*

perature, but the laminate itself will almost certainly take a little while longer to get there. The vacuum pump should be left on for the whole cure cycle.

Once the cure cycle is complete, turn off the oven, allow the component to cool to at least half the cure temperature, then turn off the vacuum pump, and release the vacuum from the vacuum bag. You can now remove the component and mould from the vacuum bag, peel off the breather material and release film (these will almost certainly be scrap), but leave any peel ply in place for now. You can then inspect your pre-preg component, and perform any trimming or finishing operations.

If you have progressed through the various technologies outlined in this book, you will notice how different your components are when made from pre-preg as compared to wet lay-up methods. They are thinner, stiffer, stronger, lighter, more consistent, and altogether more 'efficient' – much better suited to competition cars! But further improvements are possible with the aid of honeycomb cores, as outlined in the next section.

**Using honeycombs with pre-pregs**
We have seen several times throughout this book that core materials enable light, stiff and strong composite components to be made, and this is certainly true with pre-pregs, where the laminates themselves are as good as you can get (without going to vast additional expense on equipment, that is – see the next chapter). By combining pre-pregs with efficient core materials, you get the ultimate performance that's available. You can use pretty well all the core materials already discussed, including foams, plywood, and balsa wood, but to get the best in lightweight, stiff and strong sandwich materials, honeycombs take a lot of beating.

Both types of honeycomb – aluminium and Nomex (aramid paper) – are suitable for use with pre-pregs, and both have pluses and minuses, as discussed in earlier chapters. The choice will probably come down to cost, availability, and ease of use for your particular application. Both types are available in a range of thicknesses, and as we have also already seen, strength and stiffness go up markedly with increased sandwich panel thickness, and for very little extra weight. But thick panels are not always practical, because of clearance to the components beneath, for example, or maybe because of the increased difficulty of incorporating thick panels on smaller components. Alternative types of honeycomb to the simple hexagonal cell variety are also available, including 'extended' or 'expanded' cell honeycomb, in which the cells are stretched in one direction to make a core that is more compliant in the direction at right angles to the longer cell dimension. And there is also Flex-core, which is made up of cells with curved sides, which can adopt very tight curvature in a mould. The choice is yours.

With regard to the practicalities of combining honeycombs with pre-pregs, there are two lamination options. The cheapest, and possibly the simplest, option is to go for the single-shot curing process, where the outer skin, honeycomb, and inner skin are all laminated together, and the curing and bonding process takes place in one cure cycle. This uses one cure-cycle's worth of energy and one lot of vacuum-bagging consumables. The second option is to cure the outer skin first, then laminate the honeycomb and inner skin and cure these in a second cycle. This obviously uses twice the energy and probably twice the bagging consumables, but does have the potential advantage of giving a better surface finish. Let's look at these options in a little more detail.

In the one-shot process, the outer skin laminate – of one or more plies depending on the demands your component has to meet – is laid down first, and then the honeycomb is placed on the back of the outer skin. Your hot-air gun may be used to soften the outer skin pre-preg to increase its tackiness locally, which will help to hold the honeycomb in place.

*Warming film adhesive using a hot-air gun.*

You will need to check with your supplier that it is feasible to get a decent bond between the particular pre-preg you are using and the honeycomb – some pre-pregs work satisfactorily in this way, whilst other do not, and in the latter case you need to provide an additional material, known as film adhesive, to get a good bond.

Film adhesive, which looks like plastic

*Honeycomb being pressed into place on the now tacky film adhesive.*

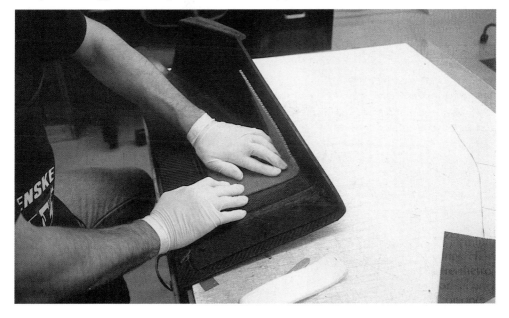

sheet, is available in a range of weights, and the suppliers will be happy to advise on what's best for you. Like the resin system within a pre-preg, it cures at elevated temperature, so obviously it has to have a cure cycle which is compatible with your chosen pre-preg. You cut out sections of film adhesive just slightly larger than your honeycomb sections to ensure that the honeycomb is fully bonded up to its edges, and lay them directly on the back of the outer laminate skin. Then you put the honeycomb down on the film adhesive, using the hot-air gun on the film adhesive to generate some local tackiness to hold the honeycomb in place. Another layer of film adhesive would then go over the honeycomb, followed finally by the inner skin laminate of however many layers are needed (usually the same as the outer skin). Once all the layers are in place, release film and breather fabric are applied as usual, then the component is bagged up, vacuumed, and cured.

Even with the use of film adhesive, if you are using a low resin-content pre-preg it is sometimes possible to get small,

resin-starved spots in the outer surface of your component where the honeycomb has drawn some excess resin onto its surfaces by capillary action. This is not a major defect, but it does slightly impair the visual quality of the component. If this still occurs with film adhesive, you might consider using a pre-preg with a higher resin content for the outer layer, or one with a greater resin flow characteristic. Alternatively, you could use the two-shot process.

In the two-shot process, the outer laminate skin is laid up, peel ply is placed in the areas to which honeycomb will subsequently be bonded, release film and breather fabric are applied, and then the laminate is vacuum-bagged and cured. Following cure and cooling, the consumables are removed, and the peel ply is stripped off to reveal a nice clean area on which to bond the honeycomb. Film adhesive obviously has to be used for this, since the outer skin is now fully cured. Then the honeycomb is put in place, the outer adhesive film (if needed) is placed next, and finally the inner skin laminate is laid down. The whole thing is

*Laminating the second ply over the honeycomb.*

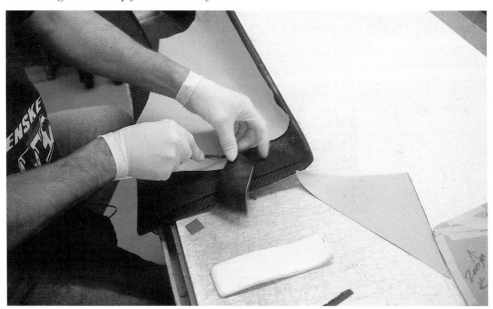

bagged up again and put through a second cure cycle.

Bear in mind, when laminating the inner skins onto the back, that if the honeycomb does not extend right to the edges of the component there is the possibility that the step from the honeycomb edge down onto the outer skin will create a void, which will be a line of weakness where there is effectively only one laminate's thickness. To help overcome this you can either laminate increasingly narrow strips of pre-preg in a stack at the edge of the honeycomb, to provide a 'ramp', or fillet, that the inner laminate may then adhere to, or alternatively, if

using aluminium honeycomb, you could use a blunt tool to gently crush the edge in order to chamfer it slightly, thus fulfilling the same purpose. An even neater method, perhaps, is to hold your honeycomb firmly onto the edge of something like a piece of smooth board with double-sided tape, and use a sander to put a shallow chamfer of about 30° onto the honeycomb edge. This works with aluminium or Nomex honeycomb.

If bolts are required to pass through a honeycomb sandwich panel, it is necessary to put 'hard points' into the sandwich which will not crush, as honeycomb would, when the bolt is tightened. Hard

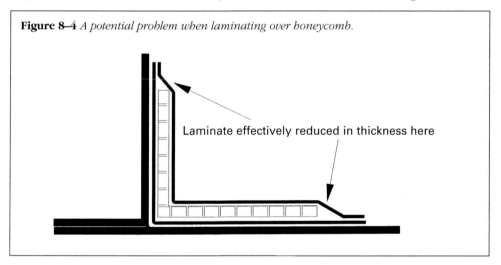

**Figure 8–4** *A potential problem when laminating over honeycomb.*

Laminate effectively reduced in thickness here

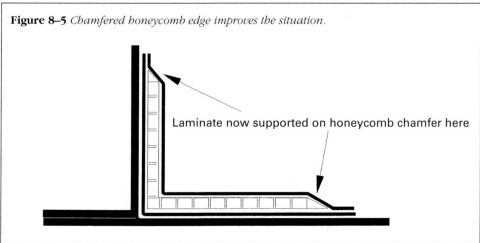

**Figure 8–5** *Chamfered honeycomb edge improves the situation.*

Laminate now supported on honeycomb chamfer here

points can be made of pre-cured carbon laminate, machined aluminium, steel washers, or even pieces of plywood, depending on what is appropriate to your application. Prior to placement onto the back of the outer skin laminate, the hard point should be thoroughly abraded and de-greased so that a good bond is formed. If it is to be inserted into the honeycomb, then a hole should be cut as accurately as possible for position and fit, and the insert, wrapped in film adhesive, should be placed in the hole prior to lamination of the inner plies. Alternatively a 'foaming epoxy adhesive', which expands to fill any voids in the honeycomb, can be used around the hard point. The hard point should be as close to the thickness of the honeycomb as possible, so that the inner laminate lies flush across the back.

You can also add inserts after cure, by carefully routing out the inner skin and honeycomb but leaving the outer skin untouched, then bonding the hard point in place in the hole with an epoxy adhesive. Finally, some plies of wet lay-up resin-impregnated fabric could be laminated over the back of the insert to regain full strength.

Flat panels of honeycomb core sandwich may have exposed honeycomb at their edges. These edges need to be sealed to make the panel weather proof and to look reasonable. To do this, push the honeycomb a little way back from the edges with an appropriate blunt tool, apply filler to the gap, and sand flush with the laminate edges. To maintain the

light weight of the honeycomb panel, use a lightweight filler such as an epoxy version based on 'microballoons', or glass bubbles. These air-filled bulking agents create a very low density filler, and the material is so light that when you pick up a tub of the stuff you think that the supplier has sold you an empty one. You can buy these low density bulking agents separately and add them to your own resin, but first check with the supplier that your resin is compatible.

Honeycombs, especially aluminium, can be difficult to handle, cut, and lay in place on a mould, and a little patience and perseverance are generally required. However, the results can be excellent, and the advantages in superior mechanical properties and weight-saving significant.

In common with other chapters, we should examine the approximate material costs involved in using pre-pregs. Table 8–1 has been assembled on the same basis as earlier costings tables, and it has been assumed that we are now making our hypothetical nosecone from two plies of 280gsm pre-preg carbon to replace the two plies of dry 280gsm carbon used previously, with honeycomb stiffeners replacing the Coremat used in earlier models. Carbon may not be the wisest choice for a nosecone, aramid or hybrid carbon/aramid probably both being better, but the comparison is only intended to be illustrative.

Prices are based on those available in 1999 for small quantities. Buying in bulk

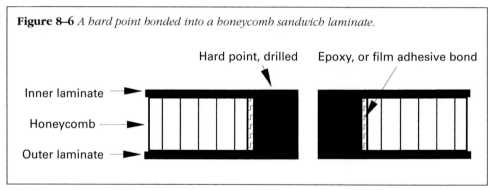

**Figure 8–6** *A hard point bonded into a honeycomb sandwich laminate.*

Hard point, drilled          Epoxy, or film adhesive bond

Inner laminate

Honeycomb

Outer laminate

**Table 8–1 Cost estimates for a hypothetical nosecone in pre-preg carbon fibre**

| | Quantity | Unit cost | Cost |
|---|---|---|---|
| Pre-preg carbon | 2.3sq m | £30.00 | £69.00 |
| Honeycomb | 0.0185sq m | £15.00 | £0.28 |
| Release film | 0.9sq m | £3.90 | £3.51 |
| Breather fabric | ~2sq m | £1.62 | £3.24 |
| Vacuum bag | ~3sq m | £3.74 | £11.22 |
| Sealant tape | ~4m | £0.55 | £2.20 |
| Sundries | Release agent etc | Estimated | £2.00 |
| | | **Total cost of materials** | **£91.45** |

would make substantial savings on the cost of the consumables in particular, and would show something in the order of a 10 per cent reduction on the carbon.

In Chapter 6 some values of relative stiffness and strength were given, based on some rather rudimentary workshop tests on real samples of material. It is interesting to compare the values obtained for pre-preg carbon cured under vacuum and at elevated temperature over 3mm thick aluminium honeycomb, as shown in Table 8–2.

**Table 8–2 Comparisons of relative specific stiffness and strength**

| Material | Specific stiffness | Specific strength |
|---|---|---|
| CSM/Polyester | 1.00 | 1.00 |
| Carbon/Polyester | 1.77 | 1.04 |
| Carbon/Epoxy | 1.98 | 2.12 |
| Pre-preg carbon over aluminium honeycomb | 79.05 | 3.23 |

Clearly the pre-preg sandwich material completely outclasses any of the wet lay-

*Using heat, vacuum, and pre-preg materials, results can be excellent, as with this DJ Racecars aerofoil.*

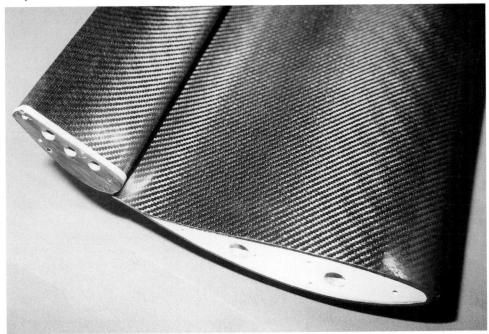

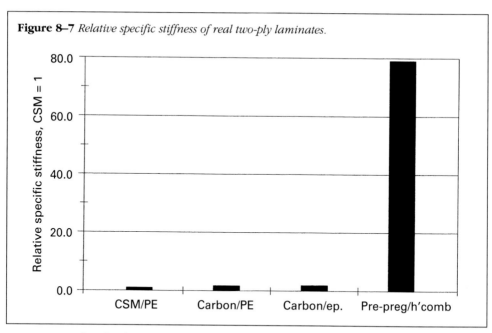

**Figure 8–7** *Relative specific stiffness of real two-ply laminates.*

up non-sandwich laminates when it comes to relative stiffness, while the improved strength comes by way of the better inter-laminar bond strength of the pre-preg. Obviously, wet lay-up sandwich components would also yield good stiffness values, but this vivid comparison puts the apparent high cost of pre-preg sandwiches into some kind of perspective.

Though making components from pre-pregs is not cheap, the costing in Table 8–1 doesn't work out a lot more expensive than the wet lay-up carbon-epoxy example in Chapter 6 (Table 6–6). And, as mentioned above, savings could be made if you were to purchase materials in larger quantities. So once you are equipped with your vacuum pump and oven, the unit cost of pre-preg components need not work out vastly more expensive than with wet lay-up. This probably could not have been said even as recently as a couple of years ago, when pre-pregs were quite a bit more expensive than they are now and the weight of fabric costed in Table 8–1 was over £50 per square metre instead of about £30. So there has probably never been a better time to get into pre-pregs, and start exploiting the materials which have been benefiting professional constructors for quite a while.

# Chapter 9

# The professionals

IT IS NOT so long ago that even the top racecar constructors in Formula 1 and Indycar were using vacuum-consolidated pre-pregs cured in an oven, much as described in the previous chapter, but with the influx of ever-bigger budgets into top level racing, techniques and technologies have now moved on. Composite component production is still based on the use of pre-pregs, but vacuum consolidation has now been supplemented with pressure, and quite high curing temperatures are also used.

Nor is it just production techniques that have progressed. The whole process of making and exploiting composite parts – from design, through production, quality assurance, and research and development – has developed to the extent that these days there is far more science and engineering involved than there is black art. Having said that, it was most heartening to be told recently by one leading Formula 1 designer that a lot of the design work for composites is still empirical, based on previous experience and knowledge, as opposed to computerised mathematical analysis of structures. Furthermore, it was equally cheering to see wet lay-up techniques in use whilst walking around another F1 composites facility, so we need not feel left behind when using the basic techniques available in our home workshops. But let's take a brief look at some of the facilities available to the leading constructors, in the expectation that not only can we learn something from the way in which they do things, but also in the hope that some of their facilities and methods will filter through and in time become more accessible to the rest of us.

## Component design

In common with all other design work in the top teams, components that are to be made in composite materials are drawn using three-dimensional computer-aided drafting (3D CAD) facilities. Though no doubt taken for granted by those who use it, this amazing technique allows designers to visualise their components from every angle by rotating the 'virtual parts' on their computer screens, enabling them to refine them and get them just right. They can also check their fit, and any possible interference with other components on the car long before anything is actually manufactured, so that there is no excuse for a component not fitting when it is finally made and assembled. This just has to be better than two-dimensional drawings on a piece of paper, and a distinct improvement on the back of a cigarette packet or old envelope, though that's not to say that these aren't good places for first concept sketches!

With designs stored in electronic format as computer files, they can then be transferred to computer-aided manufacturing (CAM) equipment for the production of patterns. Again, it is cheering to note that even in the top F1 teams, as many patterns are made by hand from

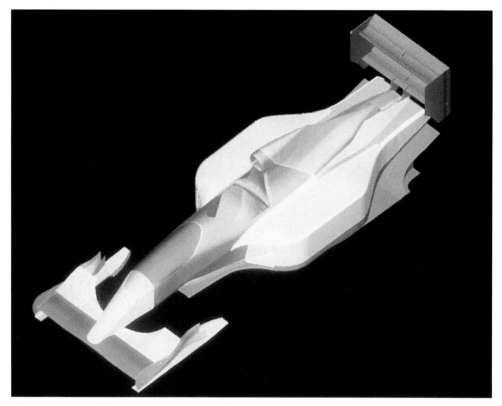

*CAD image of a Williams Formula 1 car.* (Brian O'Rourke)

timber and such-like as are manufactured by computer-controlled machining centres; but for the components where precision really matters, such as all those items that have been defined by months of wind tunnel testing, the ability to convert CAD drawings into the faithful, solid reproductions that are the patterns is invaluable. Drawings are therefore transferred to large, multi-axis milling machines capable of machining something as large as a monocoque chassis pattern out of epoxy tooling block. The pattern that emerges will be exactly the same shape and dimensions as are specified in the drawing, needing only surface finishing to be ready for mould manufacture. The tooling block used in the manufacture of patterns can withstand elevated temperatures, which enables moulds to be manufactured in pre-preg.

**Production facilities**

With so many parts on top-level racecars being made from composites nowadays (see Chapter 10), quite a substantial proportion of factory space – and, indeed, personnel – is utilised in the composite production areas. And the various activities are separated in order to maintain good working conditions, and control of items through the production process. Pattern production is in one, or possibly two, dedicated areas, with what you might call 'traditional' pattern making in one workshop; and the multi-axis machining centres are invariably in an area of their own (if only because they are relatively recent acquisitions that wouldn't fit into the original pattern shop!).

A totally separate workshop is set aside for the application of release agents to patterns and moulds, well away from pre-

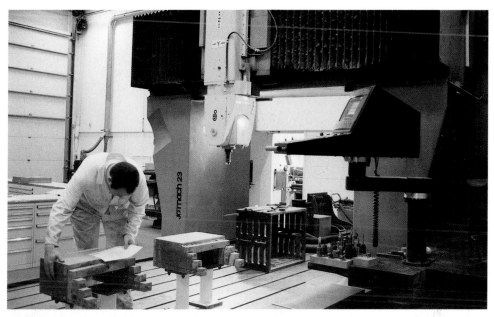

*A five-axis CNC machining centre at Benetton Formula.*

preg handling areas. One F1 team I have visited has located these areas diametrically opposite each other within the composites section of the factory, in order to separate the two by as great a distance as possible.

The lamination shops seem to occupy the most space, with multiple, spacious workbenches for the laminators. Laminating rooms are variously categorised as 'controlled areas', with positive pressure air supplies through filtration

*The lamination clean room at Williams F1.* (Brian O'Rourke)

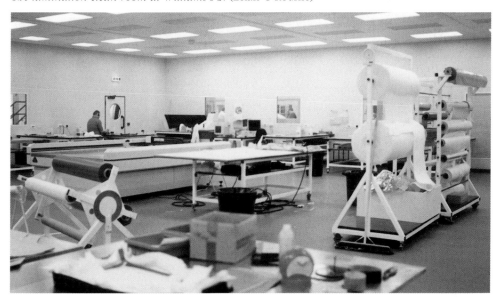

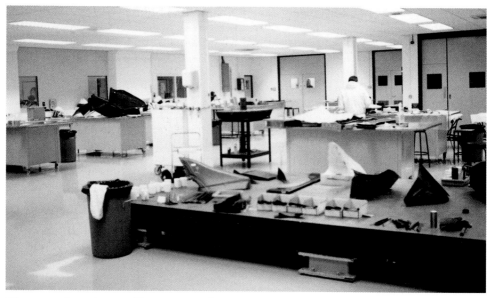

*The composites sub-assembly room at Williams F1.* (Brian O'Rourke)

systems, or 'clean rooms', with higher standards of filtration and a requirement that staff wear full-body coveralls, masks, and head coverings. The latter is the type of clean room you would previously have seen only in an aerospace environment, and suggests how seriously some composite production is regarded. Other senior teams are happy operating at the slightly lower standard of control in this

*CNC fabric cutter/plotter at DPS Composites.*

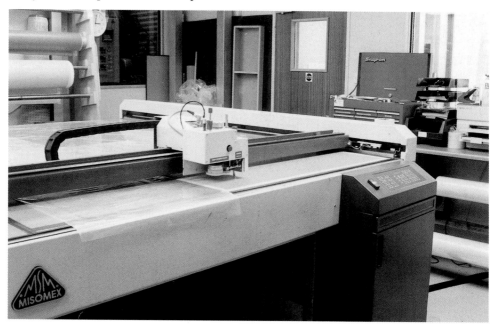

regard, and without mentioning any names, there wouldn't appear to be any direct correlation between a particularly high standard of cleanliness of production area and success on the track... Not in every case, anyway!

An asset in any professional laminating room is a CNC fabric cutter/plotter, which is basically a computer-controlled machine that cuts out and, if required, numbers the pieces of pre-preg to CAD drawings of the relevant shapes, and does so with great accuracy, speed, and lack of waste.

The trimming and fitting of components is again well segregated from other areas, and point-of-use dust extractors, and dust masks, prevent production personnel from inhaling the by-product of their labours. Finally, sub-assembly of components that need to be bonded together is generally carried out in yet another part of the factory, with fitting carried out in or adjacent to the car build area.

### Autoclaves

One of the biggest advantages that the pros have over the rest of us is the use of autoclaves. These are pressure vessels which can also be heated, and the ability to put components under pressure as well as vacuum during elevated temperature cure permits much improved consolidation, leading to the best attainable laminate quality currently available.

Vacuum consolidation enables a theoretical maximum of one bar, or one atmosphere of pressure, to be exerted onto components during cure, and because of the limitations on the level of vacuum practically attainable, it is more likely that a maximum of around 0.8 to 0.85 bar is actually achieved. However, with the benefit of an autoclave pressures of up to 7 bar are available. This is enough to persuade the most reluctant pre-preg to flow into the tightest of corners, to expel any entrapped air or volatiles, and even to force any excess resin out of the laminate, if that has been allowed to occur. It also enables thicker plies to be properly consolidated, and will ensure that fabrics are in full contact with even complex mould shapes.

*Autoclaves and their control units at Benetton Formula.*

So whilst vacuum consolidation is fine for non- or semi-structural components like bodywork, ducting, and even aerofoils in low stress applications, for highly stressed components such as the monocoque chassis of the world's fastest racecars, high downforce aerofoils, and suspension parts, the consistency, consolidation and confidence provided by autoclave curing is a must. Having said that, autoclave pressure is no guarantee of a perfect, void-free composite component – the laminators still have to be highly skilled at their job and diligent in their lay-up techniques to achieve top quality components, and it is not unknown for parts to occasionally be rejected. But if you are dealing with safety critical components like suspension links, and aerofoil mounts, then quality standards have to be set very high.

## Materials

Although the pros employ many similar materials to those we can use in our home workshops, they also exploit some more specialised materials. Uni-directional fabrics and ultra-high modulus (UHM) carbon fibre fabric are utilised, for example. Uni-directional fabric allows the fibres to be laid in exactly the orientation required by the component, so that loads can be fed along the lengths of the fibres within a laminate. Composites are unique materials in this regard, having properties that can be made directional at the time of manufacture. UD fabrics require careful handling during lamination because of the ease with which the fibres can be spread and separated if misused, leading to a significant loss of the sought-after directional strength and stiffness.

UHM carbon offers the ability to engineer very high stiffness values into laminates, but great care needs to be taken in its use since it can also yield very brittle components. There have apparently been instances in the past of the over-zealous use of UHM carbon in racecar components that needed a little more toughness and 'forgiveness', but which failed rather dramatically when put to the severest test. There is a much greater understanding nowadays, however, of how and when this highly specialised material is appropriate.

It is more likely that the pros would use a mix of fibres and fabrics to produce the desired properties in a laminate. It would be quite common, for example, for uni-directional carbon to be mixed with woven carbon for directional strength and stiffness coupled with good all round performance, and possibly aramid fabric as a 'fail-safe' that resists fracture, or as an anti-abrasion layer in an exposed component.

Honeycomb cores are extensively used in the production of stressed and unstressed components, monocoque chassis, for example, being typically made from carbon-skinned aluminium honeycomb. One of this honeycomb's useful properties is its propensity to crush gradually if subjected to an impact severe enough to fracture a component. This makes it a good choice for use in the 'impact structures' on racecar chassis, providing progressive energy absorption and less severe deceleration values for the driver if he should crash into something solid.

This is an area that the FIA, the governing body of world motorsport, and CART, the regulatory body that controls the USA's premier racecar category, are keeping under continuous review, with ever-improving standards of impact absorption and loading capacity. This gives race teams' structural composite designers a renewed headache at the start of every design cycle, but at least it helps improve the racecars' ability to withstand crash damage whilst protecting the drivers from certain types of impact. However, there is a counter-argument which says that the impact structures will only do any good at certain, very specific impact angles, and that more needs to be done to develop the all round impact strength of today's racecars. That these arguments exist is a good thing, because they will force the respective parties to seek still better solutions. These words were written just a few days after Michael Schumacher suffered a broken leg when his Ferrari apparently suffered rear brake failure before a corner on the first lap of the 1999 British Grand Prix, and plunged across a gravel trap and into a tyre barrier pretty well head on. Reactions in the media ranged from 'he would have been killed in the same accident a few years ago' to 'he shouldn't have been injured in that accident'. It's hard to argue rationally with either contention. What really matters is that the push for improvements continues, and that there is no complacency.

## Testing

In the quest for increased knowledge that, they hope, will enable improved competitiveness, the top teams have invested in a great deal of equipment to subject their composite materials and components to various mechanical and structural tests. This equipment ranges from electro-mechanical test machines that can perform relatively simple static load tests in tensile, flexural or compressive mode, and servo-hydraulic machines that can do these tests dynamically and at up to high frequency, through to rigs that are capable of putting a complete 'corner' of a competition car, including a gearbox casing, under dynamic and cycled loads. There are even whole-car rigs that can simulate and play back real load data logged on track. Whilst the latter machine is used more for chassis set-up purposes in motorsport, it can, in principle, also be used for component durability testing. But we get a little ahead of ourselves.

The electro-mechanical test machines are able to carry out tensile, compressive, flexural, shear, peel, and tear tests on materials like composites. They consist of, in essence, two sets of clamping jaws or other sample attachments, one of which remains static whilst the other is, in this case, electro-mechanically driven away from or towards the first. The upper

*Measuring the compressive strength of a honeycomb sandwich material on an electro-mechanical testing machine.* (Instron)

clamp is physically connected to a load measuring cell, and thence electronically to some form of output, either graphical or, more likely, computerised data capture. With appropriate sample attachment, pieces of composite material may be subjected to the aforementioned types

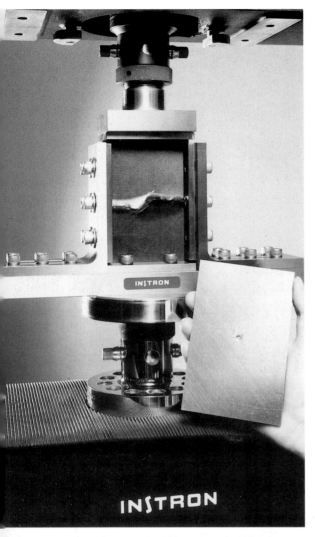

*Assessing compression properties after impact.*
(Instron)

cycling. This enables a given material – or component, even – to be subjected to a high number of repeated loadings to establish its durability, and even its fatigue life. If appropriate, these tests can also be done in an environmental chamber which can put the samples in a high temperature environment, for example, allowing competition car components that have to function in hot areas to be evaluated in realistic circumstances.

Evaluations can either be of the 'proof test' type, where a material or component simply has to pass a pre-determined limit in a given test, and may then be put into service, or maybe of the 'ultimate tensile strength' type, where the sample is tested to its failure point. An example of a component which could be put to either type of test is a composite suspension 'pushrod' link with a bonded metallic joint in each end. Such parts are quite commonplace on Formula 1 cars these days, and have required some pretty specialised adhesives to be developed that enable as much faith to be placed in them as is put in a welded joint. Using specially-made sample attachment points, either type of test machine can subject such a component to a tensile load, either to a pre-set 'proof test' limit, after which the component is put into stock for use, or until the component fails, and a measure of its ultimate tensile strength is made. Such is the efficacy of the structural adhesives now in use that it is not usually expected that the bond will fail in this type of test. This suggests that it is either the composite or the metal part of the link which fails. But part of it is bound to fail at some point – the aim is to ensure that it isn't stressed to breaking point in normal use. Other composite suspension components, such as wishbones and steering track rods, can also be tested on these machines, either for quality assurance or as an aid to development.

Corner test rigs are designed to put loadings onto complete suspension sub-assemblies, including the attachment

of load test, for research and development or quality assurance purposes. For example, as a routine quality test 'coupons' of laminate to the same lay-up as a component will be cured at the same time as the component itself, and specified tests can then be performed on the coupons to establish that the component will perform to the requisite standard.

The servo-hydraulic type of machine is capable of performing the same types of test, but can also carry out dynamic

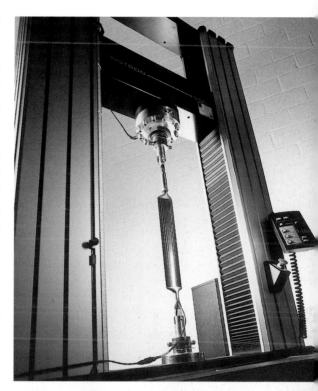

points on a competition car. In the case of a conventional mid-engined formula car, this would usually involve the gearbox casing, to which the suspension is normally attached; in other installations, a section of dummy chassis would be used, the main purpose being to assess the rigidity and strength of the suspension components. Servo-hydraulic actuators can input vertical, lateral, longitudinal, and braking loads, and with the relevant control software attached to such a test rig it is possible to replay data logged from laps around real circuits using strain gauges on wishbones and pushrods, and suspension displacement measurement devices. The suspension corner is then subjected to repeated load cycles, or logged laps, for the assessment of component durability. There are obvious advantages to being able to do this type of testing in the laboratory as opposed to on-track: it is much safer, since it doesn't require a driver to put himself, or a fairly valuable car, at risk; it is not susceptible to bad weather; it is entirely repeatable; and it is possible to stop at any point in time to inspect or test components. And in today's highly competitive environment, tests can be carried out in total secrecy, without any new parts leaving a team's premises until they have been laboratory proven under pretty realistic conditions.

Other tests that can be carried out either as quality assurance or as post-impact inspection methods include ultrasonic testing of composite laminates. Ultrasound can be used to detect flaws like contaminant inclusions, voids, and delamination, and hence can be effective in checking basic laminate quality as well as likely damage resulting from an

*Setting up to perform durability testing of a carbon composite Formula 1 suspension wishbone by means of a servo-hydraulic testing machine.* (Instron)

impact. It's a little more advanced than the old test of tapping the laminate with the edge of a coin, and listening for a sharp tap (good) as compared to a dull thud (bad), though this rather more rudimentary test probably still has its place for the DIY composite tester!

In addition to this type of materials and components testing that teams themselves carry out routinely, there is also the thorny topic of static load and impact tests carried out under the supervision of the regulatory bodies each year on the primary structure of Formula 1 cars (and others, now including Formula 3). In these tests, examples of full composite monocoques are strapped to sleds, and launched at a fixed barrier at a predefined speed. For example, the new F3

tests introduced by the FIA in 1999 require that after an impact at 10m per second (about 22mph), damage to the front part of the 'survival cell' shall be confined to the area of the frontal impact structure ahead of the front axle. In the case of Formula 1, the impact speed specified for tests in 1999 was raised from 12m to 13m per second (about 29mph). If these speeds sound hopelessly unrealistic, keep in mind that the tests require ramming the chassis into a barrier which is completely immovable. Even in a worst case on track, where a car hits an armco barrier head on, the barrier is designed to flex and absorb some impact energy. But each year the FIA gets tougher on these and the other static load tests it imposes, and each year the composite designers

*Frontal impact testing of a Formula 3 Ralt nose structure – this is before... (MIRA)*

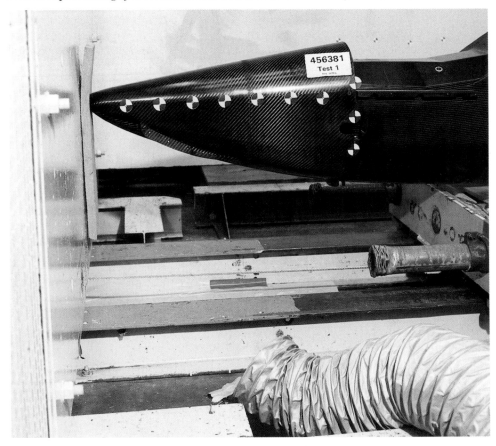

*… And this is after.* (MIRA)

*Ready to undertake a roll-hoop impact test on the Ralt Formula 3 chassis.* (MIRA)

*Carbon composite details on a 1997 McLaren Formula 1 car. Just three years on, and all the front suspension links are now in carbon composite.*

*This OMS hillclimber has a carbon composite chassis – an example of how the technology developed by the top level teams eventually becomes more widely available.*

grow a few more grey hairs as they re-engineer their cars to meet the criteria.

The professionals are clearly able to do quite a few things for which the home constructor does not usually have the facilities. But our ability to use composites in the home workshop at all is down to the gradual filtering down of techniques and technologies developed previously in the upper echelons of motorsport, as well as the resultant wider availability of the materials. The first all-composite Formula 1 chassis was the McLaren MP4/1, raced in the 1981 season by John Watson and Andrea de Cesaris, and a few years later all-carbon chassis appeared in Formula 3000 and Formula 3. A number of categories then legislated against the use of carbon chassis on the basis of high cost, although the use of the materials continued to flourish on periph-eral components like bodywork and aerofoils. But during the 1990s a number of cars built for a category with more liberal rules – the UK's Speed Hillclimb and Sprint scene – were made from composites, including the Scott Megapin 5, the Brytec, and the OMS CF34/94. The first two were home-constructed specials, whilst the last is a production racer, but all three reflect the wider availability of composite technology that has slowly seeped down from motorsport's top levels.

As DIY enthusiasts we should take heart from this, knowing that the methods and technologies currently in use by the professionals will, in time, become available for use in the home workshop. What price a cut down autoclave designed to fit the average shed or lock-up garage?

# Chapter 10

# Motorsport applications

THE CAN BE very few motorsport categories in which composites are not employed in one way or another,

*Jedi hillclimber with a carbon dash panel and GFRP bodywork.*

whether in the form of good old, value-for-money glass fibre reinforced plastic, or one of its more sophisticated cousins. In this final chapter we'll take a brief tour around some different motorsport disciplines to see not only how the designers and builders of their respective cars have exploited composites, but also to get a feel for the appropriate application of materials within the various categories. But a word of warning – before you decide to make any new components in composite materials for any car, in any category, do make sure you are totally familiar with the technical regulations, especially as they apply to permitted materials. It would be a real shame to make new lightweight bodywork for your car, only to turn up at a meeting and be informed by the scrutineers that the carbon fibre, or whatever, that you've used is specifically banned in your class. My previous book, *Competition Car Preparation* (Haynes, 1999), provides the sources of information you'll need to get you on top of this situation.

## Hillclimb and sprint cars

This branch of motorsport incorporates a wide range of machinery built to equally widely ranging budgets, and includes saloons, sports cars, sports racing cars and racing cars, with each category subdivided into a number of engine capacity classes. As such the use of composite materials is largely dictated by budget, because there is a fair degree of technical freedom in the rules, with no restrictions on the types of composites that can be employed.

At the lower-cost end of the category is the Jedi single-seater, a production racer that comes with GFRP bodywork as standard. The cars are already incredibly lightweight, but in all probability the odd kilo or two could be saved with a carbon body kit. Indeed, company principal John Corbyn admits that his customers 'love a bit of carbon fibre', a testimony to the aesthetic appeal of the stuff, so he fits a carbon dash panel; carbon wing end-plates are an option too. These are nice, if unnecessary touches, that are there simply for visual appeal. And why not? The Jedi seat is moulded GFRP, which again could be made a few ounces lighter if carbon, or carbon/aramid hybrid, was used, though the cost would naturally increase a little.

The particular hillclimb Mallock Mk 20 shown here sports a body kit designed and made by the author in 1991. The biggest change from the original Mallock design was the switch to the narrow nose configuration that accepted front two-element aerofoils to give more, and tuneable, downforce. The nosecone pattern was made from MDF, polyurethane foam block, and body filler, which was painted and rubbed down before the GFRP mould was taken from it. The nosecone itself was made in glass (CSM) and woven carbon, with local stiffeners.

The body top was reshaped over the engine, and was split at a transverse vertical flange just ahead of the dashboard bulkhead. The original top was a one-piece affair that stretched from the back of the nosecone right to the back of the car, and was an unwieldy, floppy affair. The new kit separated at the dash, so that the engine cover could be lifted off easily and the rear cover could be left in place. These two sections were also made in CSM and carbon, and achieved a

*Mallock Mk 20 hillclimber with a modified body kit in carbon and glass, and carbon front aerofoils – all the author's own work.*

respectable weight saving as well as a gain in stiffness over the original panels. A NACA duct was made and bonded in to the rear cover at a later stage to feed cooling air to the rear-mounted radiator. The front wings were made from carbon skins over a carbon and glass sub-structure of ribs and spars. This wing construction has since been improved by the use of core materials to enhance skin and wing rigidity. Polyester resin was used throughout this kit.

One of the latest designs to emerge from the Pilbeam Racing Designs stable is the MP82 single-seater. Pilbeam is a name synonymous with hillclimbing for over 20 years, and the company's cars are always amongst the lightest in their classes. Mike Pilbeam is a great advocate of the merits of aluminium-skinned aluminium honeycomb as a chassis construction material, and this is, substantially, the material used for the monocoque of the MP82. However, the forward, upper section of the chassis is of bonded and riveted, pre-moulded carbon fibre in epoxy resin over

honeycomb, which not only enhances the stiffness of the front of the chassis but also blends in with the lines of the bodywork forward to the nosecone. The bodywork itself can be specified in either lightweight GFRP or carbon. Interestingly, the MP86 – a new design that made a brief competition debut in 1999 before its engine was destroyed – is Pilbeam's first all-carbon monocoque, made in response to the success of the Gould-Ralt hillclimber.

The Gould-Ralt is a design based on the 1993 Formula 3 Ralt RT37, which, though not a successful car on the circuits, had achieved great success on the hills following the fitting of a variety of ex-Formula 1 3.5-litre V8 engines, in particular the DFR. It won the British Hillclimb Championship in 1998, and was on course for a repeat in 1999 even as this chapter was being written. Gould Engineering modified the car with their own suspension and aerodynamic packages, as well as installing the V8 engine and appropriate driveline, but the RT37

*Carbon chassis top on the Pilbeam MP82.*

*The Gould-Ralt hillclimber is based on the Ralt RT37 carbon chassis.*

base was chosen because of the strength and rigidity of its carbon over aluminium honeycomb monocoque. It also uses carbon over thin Nomex honeycomb for its body panels, and the aerofoils, too, are in carbon fibre. Note in addition the

*Carbon silencer cans look good and sound quieter.*

carbon silencer cans – not only do these look smart, but they tend to deaden sound more effectively than aluminium or steel cans.

## Drag racing

Another branch of motorsport with numerous categories and classes, each with its own technical definitions, drag racing permits the use of glass fibre, carbon, and aramids in the construction of body panels and aerofoils. The Top Fuel dragster pictured runs to a minimum weight limit, and as such doesn't necessarily have to use the lightest bodywork possible. But doing so allows the designers to put weight where they want it to go, perhaps at the rear of the chassis to benefit crucial start-line traction. The front aerofoil in the photograph is obviously made from carbon fibre, and rear wings are often made from the same material. The loadings that rear wings on the fastest dragsters have to withstand are considerable – downforce in excess of 5,000lb (2,270kg), and possibly up to

7,000lb (3,180kg) at the 300mph-plus terminal speeds being achieved these days. A wing would need to be thoroughly tested to ensure it could withstand such loads before a driver is asked to use it!

## Rally cars

The two principal rally categories, World Rally Car/Group A and Formula 2 'Kit Car', are very much based on production cars, and, as such, on production shells, which means their primary structures are made in steel, reinforced and strengthened with sturdy tubular steel roll cages, primarily for safety reasons. However, the leading teams use composites fairly extensively where they can to make lightweight panelling. The categories have minimum weight limits, but given the pounding these cars have to contend with, a lot of their major components have to be engineered principally for durability. So in order to save weight, what you might call the peripheral components such as inner door skins, footwells, and some under-bonnet pan-

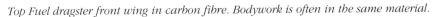

*Top Fuel dragster front wing in carbon fibre. Bodywork is often in the same material.*

*This VW Golf GTi Formula 2 rally car displays wide use of carbon composite under the bonnet.*

*The Golf turbo-diesel rally car shows hybrid fabrics in the seats and footwell, as well as using carbon for the dash and door linings.*

elling and components and so forth are often made in composite materials.

Take the F2 VW Golf GTi 'Kit Car' pictured here. The induction system airbox and associated trunking has been made in carbon, for strength with low weight. The GTi's sister car, the remarkable turbo-diesel TDi, shows how the Golfs use carbon for the dashboard binnacle and the door linings, whilst for toughness and lightness the footwell heel pads are in carbon/aramid hybrid, as, in this instance, are the seats.

The Group A Mitsubishi Lancer which won the 1998 World Rally Championship for Manufacturers in Evo 5 trim, and also took Tommi Makinen to his third successive World Drivers' Championship (and at the time of writing looked a good bet, in

*The front end of the Mitsubishi Evo 6 Group A rally car has various carbon panels and ducts.*

Evo 6 guise, for the 1999 Drivers' title too), exploits composites in similar ways. There are carbon panels around the intercooler at the front of the engine bay, and the airbox – again on the right-hand side (as pictured) of the engine bay – is also carbon. Carbon once more abounds in the cockpit, in the dash binnacles, the

*The Mitsubishi's interior favours carbon seats and footwell to match the dash and door panels.*

*The cooling duct on the tarmac-specification brake system on the Mitsubishi Group A rally car is of hybrid aramid/carbon construction.*

door linings, and the footwells and seats.

The brakes fitted to the Mitsubishi for use on tarmac rallies are fearsome devices, with eight piston, four pad, water-cooled callipers clamping big ventilated iron discs. Further cooling is provided via carbon/aramid ducts that feed air into the centre of the discs.

## Circuit racers
### Formula 750

F750 is the UK's premier low-cost circuit-racing category, and operates within a strict framework of rules established by the 750 Motor Club to keep the costs of building cars, and competing in them, as low as possible. Having said that, the category also encourages innovation and ingenuity, and may well still be a breeding ground for future Colin Chapmans, Eric Broadleys, and Gordon Murrays, each of whom passed through F750 on their way to motorsport's dizziest heights.

With the emphasis on low cost in F750, it is hardly the place for the more expensive fibres – indeed, carbon and

aramid fibres are expressly forbidden – but as we have seen throughout this book, that leaves plenty of scope for creating effective glass fibre components without the need to spend large sums of money. Clever use of the less expensive core materials for stiffening, and woven fabric to replace at least some chopped strand matt, can enable lightweight laminates to be made at sensible cost.

At a more basic level, using moulded composite components enables the designer, builder, or modifier to build sleek, curvaceous, aesthetically pleasing and aerodynamically effective bodywork that only a master craftsman could hope to achieve in, say, aluminium. It is much simpler to create good-looking shapes with complex curvature using the methods of pattern construction outlined in these pages, followed by a mould and then your components, than it is to clad a car in sheet metal. The resultant panels are also much tougher, durable, and easier to replicate should they get damaged.

*The Formula 750 Darvi Mk 6 has nicely crafted GFRP bodywork.*

The cars pictured here illustrate what excellent results can be achieved with patience and hard work. Car 42A is a Darvi Mk 6, and has adopted the front-engined 'clubman's' configuration, with a nicely shaped narrow nosecone, engine

*The PC Special F750 car has skilfully moulded sidepods.*

cover, and sidepods crafted in GFRP. The front wings are aluminium rather than GFRP, even though the former is more likely to be dented by stones, clumsy feet in the paddock, and the occasional dropped spanner, which would compromise their aerodynamic effectiveness. Although making wing patterns and moulds is time consuming, once you've made them reproducing wing sets is relatively rapid, and you get exact replicas every time. The same would apply to ducting within the sidepods, to direct air away from the radiators.

The builder of Car 17B, a PC Special, has gone to considerable lengths to make the patterns, moulds, and sidepods. The design is similar in concept to the 'twin floor' tried by Ferrari on one of their Formula 1 cars a few years ago, with a deep scallop under the main part of the sidepod and a flat floor beneath that. The sidepod is also elegantly curved in plan view, and is aesthetically pleasing. However, bearing in mind Ferrari's fairly rapid abandonment of its own twin floor concept, one hopes the PC Special's aerodynamic treatment was more successful. But on a practical note, imagine trying to make a shape like this in aluminium sheet. It just couldn't be done. The only realistic option for making complex, or even quite simple curved shapes is to go the moulded composite route, via pattern and mould.

### Radical Clubsports

The Radical was also designed as a low-cost sports racer, and now runs in its own one-make championship under the aegis of the 750 MC. Given the cost constraints, bodywork is made in a pretty durable GFRP, although some components, notably the engine airbox, the rear chain cover, and the front and side 'splitters', are made in carbon, possibly for no more than cosmetic reasons. The seat is also a moulded GFRP item. Clearly the more extensive use of carbon or aramid fibres in the bodywork would produce a lighter but also a more expensive car, not just to

*Low cost is also the watchword of the Radical Clubsports, which uses durable GFRP body panels, but with a few carbon components for that professional-look.*

purchase but to maintain in the event of body damage. Given that the championship is a one-make series, there is little point in making the cars artificially expensive, so GFRP is a sound choice in this instance. The touches of carbon add an aesthetic professional look.

### Formula 3

Formula 3 cars have been referred to as scaled-down Formula 1 cars, and in the exploitation of composites they are scarcely any less sophisticated than their older brothers. The chassis are constructed from carbon fibre over aluminium honeycomb to form strong and stiff 'survival cells', which, as described in the previous chapter, now have to undergo impact and static load testing before a design can be used in production. The front nosebox is an impact-absorbing structure likewise made in carbon over aluminium honeycomb, which also serves to carry the loads fed in from the front aerofoil. All the body-work panels, including the aerofoils, 'bargeboards', and rear diffuser, are made in carbon fibre over honeycomb to produce light yet rigid components. Although the Italian Dallara, as pictured here, is numerically the dominant force in British and European F3, the Ralt marque – which was itself dominant from the late 1970s to the late 1980s – has been attempting to re-establish itself in 1999 with its F399. Here the Advanced Composites Group-manufactured monocoque can be seen in close up. This car also features carbon over honeycomb body panels, rear diffuser and aerofoils.

### Sports Racing World Cup

Formerly known as the International Sports Racing Series, this category of sports racers is divided into two classes, SR1 and SR2, the former using turbocharged engines, the latter using normally aspirated power plants of maximum 3-litres capacity. Chassis are not permitted to be made in carbon composite, and the

*The Dallara currently dominates Formula 3 in the UK and Europe. Chassis, bodywork, and aerofoils are all in carbon composite material.*

*The Ralt F399 also has a carbon monocoque.*

Pilbeam MP84 SR2 car – that company's first foray into an international racing category which has already yielded a class win during 1999 – uses aluminium-skinned aluminium honeycomb for its primary structure. However, to keep to the weight limit, composites are employed extensively elsewhere. The carbon front splitter, with NACA ducts let in to increase downforce and feed air to the brakes and

*The Pilbeam MP84 SR2 sports car may not have a composite chassis, but the body panels are carbon composite.*

*The Pilbeam's front splitter is carbon.*

the radiators, is made in carbon so as to be rigid enough not to distort at speed, yet reasonably lightweight.

The body sections are made in carbon over polyurethane core panels, a core material which costs a lot less than honey-

*The main body panels are carbon over polyurethane foam sandwich construction.*

*The rear wing of the MP84 is carbon composite.*

comb – useful when a formula also has a fixed price ceiling, as this one does. The rear wing is also in carbon over honeycomb, with carbon-clad sandwich construction end plates.

### Indycar

The regulators of Indycar racing in the USA go further than most motorsport ruling bodies in that they actually specify the lay-up that manufacturers must use in

*The monocoque of this Penske Indycar is a very sturdy carbon composite component designed to cope with severe impacts.*

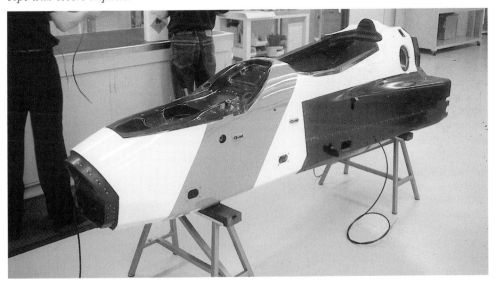

*The nose and front wings of a Penske Indycar in 'high speed oval' trim.*

the construction of the carbon composite chassis. The reason behind this is safety, and CART, the ruling body, has a philosophy that differs somewhat from the FIA's in this respect. Not that the FIA is not concerned with safety, but CART has been able to bring the Indycar designers into the rule-making fold and, somehow or other, has persuaded them to put their individual and their team's vested interests aside in the furtherance of sensible rules. The result is chassis that are considerably heavier than their F1 cousins, but which have been designed with the possibility in mind of (usually) oblique collisions with the solid concrete walls that circle high speed ovals.

Extensive use of composites, usually carbon-fibre based, is made elsewhere in Indycars, including all the bodywork, underbodies, and aerofoils. The category permits the generation of downforce by profiled underbodies beneath the sidepods, which are subject to fairly substantial forces and which obviously benefit from the strength and stiffness of carbon

fibre reinforcement. Aerofoils come in different, mandated configurations for the different disciplines that Indycars have to tackle, namely the ovals, road courses, and street circuits. The high-speed oval front wing and extremely sturdy monocoque of a Penske Indycar are pictured here.

### Formula 1

Not without good reason is F1 considered to be the technological pinnacle of motorsport. This also applies to the exploitation of composites on its cars, more components being made from composites than in any other motorsport category. Not only are body panels made from carbon and/or aramid over honeycomb, and chassis made from carbon over aluminium honeycomb, but the majority of suspension links are also constructed from carbon fibre these days. Even the wind tunnel models come in for composite application, as on this Benetton example.

The Jordan 199 pictured here shows

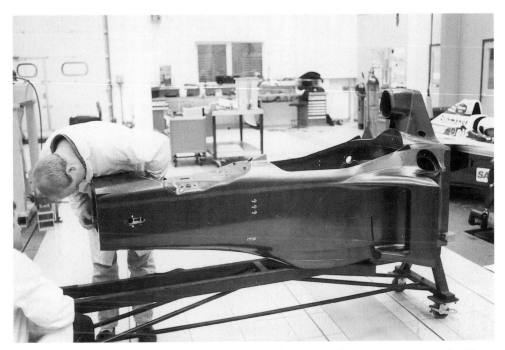

*The Williams FW19 monocoque is made in carbon over aluminium honeycomb.* (Brian O'Rourke)

*This scale model of a Benetton Formula 1 car used for wind tunnel testing is beautifully crafted in carbon fibre, although the aerofoils are machined from solid aluminium.*

*The rear of the Jordan 199 F1 car shows extensive use of carbon composite in the aerofoil elements, some of the rear suspension, the brake cooling duct, and the rear impact structure, which also forms the rear wing mount.*

the upper rear suspension links made in carbon, although in common with other teams the lower rear links are still made in steel because of the heat output from the engine exhausts, which could adversely affect structural composite parts. It is evident that the aerofoil elements, brake cooling ducts, and rear impact

*The front suspension links on the Jordan 199 are all made from carbon composite, as, of course, is the bodywork.*

*The earlier Jordan 197 front end shows some interesting carbon details.*

structure to which the aerofoil attaches are made in carbon reinforced composite too. This car also has the rear section of its transmission casing made in carbon from the driveshaft axis backwards, the front part being cast magnesium. Other F1 constructors have made complete trans-mission casings in carbon, but only Arrows is persevering in 1999, Stewart having switched back to an all-magne-sium casing after experimenting with an all-carbon one in 1998. Seemingly the team had problems with oil seepage, aris-ing from the different rates of thermal

*Rear wings have to contend with high loadings, preferably without flexing!*

*The Tyrrell 024 shows some superb carbon composite detailing, especially in the central rear 'diffuser', rear impact structure, and the rear wing and its end-plate mounting structure.*

expansion of composite and metal components, affecting resin bonds.

Aerofoils are also manufactured in carbon, as shown in the picture of an earlier Jordan. The brake cooling duct and curved 'bargeboard' behind the front wing are also in carbon. Rear wings, as shown on the Ferrari, have to contend with loads from some unexpected directions, as well as downforce and drag! The start of both the 1998 and 1999 F1 seasons saw spates of rear wing mounting failures, variously attributed to vibrations arising from changes in the natural frequency of the mountings, to heat from engine exhausts, and bizarrely, in 1999, to apparently deliberate efforts to make the mountings flex backwards at high speed, allowing the aerofoils to adopt a lower angle of attack and thus reduce drag. This quite clearly contravened the rule that says aerodynamic devices shall not be moveable, and before long the FIA stepped in with a static load deflection test to stamp out the practice. It's

hard to imagine why designers put their drivers at risk like that, and almost as hard to figure out why the drivers accept such a risk – assuming that they knew these devices were being tried.

Undertrays and diffusers are also made in carbon over honeycomb, as are all manner of other detailed components, including airboxes feeding the engine induction systems, the inlet trumpets that sit atop the inlet manifolds, ducting feeding radiators, and even teams' pitboards, briefcases, and clipboards!

Clearly, the types of composite you use, and the applications that you put them to, will ultimately depend on the regulations for your particular category of motorsport, and the budget available to you. Hopefully this book has shown you how to exploit pretty well all the available materials and most of the available techniques and enable you to make composite components for your own competition car.

Happy laminating!

# Appendix 1

# Useful contacts

*Advanced Composites Group*, Sinclair Close, Heanor Gate Industrial Estate, Heanor, Derbyshire, DE7 7SW; Tel 01773 763441/534599.

*Amber Composites Ltd*, 94 Station Road, Langley Mill, Nottingham, NG16 4BP; Tel 01773 530899.

*Carr Reinforcements*, Unit 1a, Heap Riding Business Park, Ford Street, Chestergate, Stockport, SK3 0BT; Tel 0161 429 9380.

*Cellbond Composites Ltd*, 5 Stukeley Business Centre, Blackstone Road, Huntingdon, Cambridgeshire, PE18 6EF; Tel 01480 435302; website www.cellbond.co.uk.

*DJ Engineering*, Unit 10a, Britannia Trading Centre, Buxworth, High Peak, Derbyshire, SK23 7NF; Tel 01663 734518.

*DPS Composites Ltd*, 18–21 Bookham Industrial Park, Church Road, Great Bookham, Surrey, KT23 3EU; Tel 01372 459666; website www.dpscomposites.com.

*Duroy Composites*, Unit 1, Mercury Yacht Harbour, Satchell Lane, Hamble, Southampton, Hampshire, SO31 4HQ; Tel 02380 453781.

*GRP Materials Supplies Ltd*, Alchorne Place, Burrfields, Portsmouth, Hampshire, PO3 5QU; Tel 02392 697444.

*Hexcel Composites Ltd*, Duxford, Cambridge, CB2 4QD; Tel 01223 833141.

*Multi-Sport Composites Ltd*, Unit 2, 8 Kirkhall Lane, Bolton, Lancashire, BL1 4AT; Tel 01204 494184.

*PBS Glass Fibre Supplies*, Unit 3, Marshland's Spur, Deacon Trading Estate, Farlington, Portsmouth, Hampshire, PO6 1ST; Tel 02392 380816.

*Plastic Reinforcement Fabrics Ltd*, 20 Hankinson Road, Bournemouth, Dorset, BH9 1HJ; Tel 01202 680022.

*RS*, PO Box 99, Corby, Northamptonshire, NN17 9RS; Tel 01536 210210; website http://rswww.com. Electrical components, heaters, controllers etc.

*Scott Bader Co Ltd*, Wollaston, Wellingborough, Northamptonshire, NN29 7RL; Tel 01933 663100.

*Severn Sales*, Olveston Road, Horfield, Bristol, BS7 9PB; Tel 0117 935 4125. Used laboratory equipment.

*Structural Polymer Systems*, Love Lane, Cowes, Isle of Wight, PO31 7EU; Tel 01983 284000; website www.spsystems.com. Also produce an excellent composite materials handbook on CD-ROM.

# Appendix 2

# Further reading

Aird, F., *Racer's Encyclopedia of Metals, Fibers and Materials*, Motorbooks International, 1994.

Aird, F., *Fiberglass and Composite Materials*, HP Books, 1996.

Foy, D., *Automotive Glassfibre*, Motor Racing Publications, 2nd edn, 1995.

McBeath, S., *Competition Car Downforce*, G.T. Foulis, 1998.

McBeath, S., *Competition Car Preparation*, Haynes, 1999.

Multi-Sport Composites, *A Practical Guide to Composites*, Multi-Sport Composites Ltd, 1995.

Newey, C., and Weaver, G. (ed), *Materials Principles and Practice*, Butterworth Scientific, 1990.

Noakes, K., *Build to Win*, Osprey, 1988.

Noakes, K., *Successful Composite Techniques*, Osprey, 1989.

Noakes, K., *The Fibreglass Manual*, Windrow & Greene, 1998.

Scott Bader Co Ltd, *Polyester Handbook*, Scott Bader, 1994.

SP Systems, *Composite Materials Handbook* CD-ROM, SP Systems, 1998.

Staniforth, A., *Race and Rally Car Source Book*, G.T. Foulis, 4th edn, 1997.

Weidman, G., Lewis, P., and Reid, N. (ed), *Structural Materials*, Butterworth-Heinemann, 1990, reprinted 1994.

Wiley, J., *Working with Fiberglass: Techniques and Projects*, Tab Books, 1986.

Wills, J.A., *Glass Fiber Auto Body Construction Simplified*, Dan R. Post Publications, revised edn, 1976.

# Glossary of terms and abbreviations

WORDS IN *ITALICS* have their own individual entries elsewhere in the glossary.

**Aramid** Aromatic polyamide reinforcing fibres used to achieve a *laminate* of high strength and reasonably high stiffness. Trade names are *Kevlar* and Twaron.

**Autoclave** A vessel used to cure *laminates* under pressure and elevated temperature.

**Binder** A chemical applied to *glass fibre chopped strand mat* to hold the fibres together prior to laminating.

**Bleeder cloth** Usually a felt-like, *non-woven* material used in *vacuum moulding* that soaks up excess resin during cure. Also allows removal of air during application of vacuum (see *breather fabric*).

**Breather fabric** Like *bleeder cloth*, a *non-woven* material that allows air to be removed from a vacuum bag, and which may soak up excess *resin*.

**Bridging** Refers to reinforcing *fabric* which has not properly compacted into a corner of a mould, but instead forms a 'bridge' across the corner.

**CAD** Computer-aided drawing or draughting.

**Carbon fibre** A reinforcing fibre used to achieve a *laminate* of high strength, high *stiffness*, and low weight.

**Catalyst** A compound which accelerates a chemical reaction without itself forming a part of the reaction. In *composites* moulding, small amounts of catalyst are added to *resin* to initiate the *cure*.

**CFRP** *Carbon fibre* reinforced plastic.

**Chopped strand mat** A *non-woven* form of *glass fibre fabric* consisting of randomly orientated chopped fibres held together with a *binder*. Available in various lengths, widths, and masses per unit area.

**CNC** Computer numerically controlled, referring to machines that work to computerised instructions, enabling computer-aided drawings (CAD) to be turned directly into accurately manufactured components.

**Composite** A material created by combining a fibre *reinforcement* with a *resin* matrix.

**Compressive strength** A fibre or material's ability to resist a crushing force.

**Consolidation** The compressing of fibre and matrix to expel entrapped air voids, and press plies of a *laminate* together.

**Contact moulding** A moulding process in which fibre *reinforcement* and *resin* are placed in or on a mould, and are cured at ambient or elevated temperature with no additional pressure.

**Core** The middle layer in a *sandwich construction*, to which outer *laminates* are bonded.

**CSM** *Chopped strand mat.*

**Cure** The process which changes a *resin* into a hard and variously tough substance, and which causes it to adhere to reinforcing fibres.

**Curing temperature** The temperature at which a *resin* impregnated *reinforcement* is intended to be cured.

**Curing time** The period of time that a moulded component is required to be cured prior to removal from the mould.

**De-bulking** The application of a temporary vacuum to consolidate a *pre-preg lay-up*.

**Denier** Unit of imperial measurement of a *glass fibre yarn* or *roving*, being the weight in pounds of 10,000 yards of material.

**Drape** The ability or propensity of a *fabric* to conform to complex three-dimensional shapes.

**Dry lay-up** The manufacture of a laminated component with *pre-preg* material.

**E-glass** The most common form of glass used in *glass fibre* reinforced plastics.

**Exotherm** The liberation of chemically generated heat during a reaction. Also slang for the version of this effect in which the heat liberation runs out of control, creating sufficient heat to damage or destroy a *laminate* and even cause a fire.

**Fabric** A material made by intertwining *yarns*, fibres or filaments into a flat, flexible sheet.

**Fatigue** The failure or degradation of the mechanical properties of a material after the repeated application of load or stress.

**Fibre reinforced plastic** A cured plastic (*resin*) whose mechanical properties are greatly enhanced by the presence of reinforcing fibres embedded in the *resin*.

**Fibre volume fraction** The ratio of the volume of fibre in a *laminate* to the total volume of fibre plus *resin*.

**Fibre weight fraction** The ratio of the weight of fibre in a *laminate* to the total weight of fibre plus *resin*.

**Film adhesive** A thin, dry film of adhesive which cures at elevated temperature, used to bond *core* materials to *laminate* skins.

**Flexural rigidity** The rigidity of a fibre or material when resisting bending forces.

**Flexural strength** The resistance of a fibre or material to bending forces; the ultimate strength of a material at the point of failure when subjected to bending forces.

**Flow** The fluid movement of *resin* which allows it to fill all parts of a mould.

**FRP** *Fibre-reinforced plastic.*

**Gel** The point at which a *resin* begins to thicken to a jelly-like semi-solid state during the initial *cure* phase.

**Gel time** The time between mixing *catalyst* or *hardener* with *resin*, and *gel* formation.

**Gel coat** A viscous form of *resin* applied to the surface of a mould, which becomes the outer finished layer of the laminated component.

**GFRP** *Glass fibre-reinforced plastic.*

**Glass fibre** Filaments of glass made by extruding fibres from molten bulk glass; generic term for *non-woven* and woven *glass fibre fabric*, and products thereof.

**GPa** Giga Pascal, or one million million Pascals; see *Pa*.

**Graphitisation** A high-temperature process that converts carbon into its graphitic (layered crystalline) form.

**GRP** Glass reinforced plastic, a shortened form of *GFRP*.

**Hand lay-up** The process of manually placing successive plies of fibre *reinforcement* into a mould.

**Hardener** A chemical added to a *resin* to promote or control the *cure* process by actually forming part of the reaction.

**HM** High modulus, applied to *carbon fibres* with a *tensile modulus* over 325GPa and up to 440GPa.

**Honeycomb** Sheet material composed of aramid paper (*Nomex*), aluminium foil, etc, which is formed into hexagonal-shaped cells and is used as a lightweight *core* material of various thicknesses.

**HS** High strength, the name given to what might be regarded as 'general purpose' *carbon fibre*, also known as standard modulus, with a *tensile modulus* of up to 270GPa.

**Hybrid fabric** A *fabric* composed of two or more reinforcement fibres, such as *carbon* and *aramid*, woven together.

**Hygroscopic** Able to absorb atmospheric moisture vapour.

**IM** Intermediate modulus; applied to *carbon fibre* with a *tensile modulus* over 270GPa and up to 325GPa.

**Impact strength** The ability of a material to withstand a high-stress shock load; the work done in fracturing a material under a specified shock load.

**Impregnate** *Wet out* the *reinforcement fabric* with *resin*.

**Inter-laminar shear strength** The strength with which layers within a *laminate* resist internal shear forces; a measure of how well layers are bonded together.

**Isotropic** Having the same physical properties in all directions.

**Joggle** A joint between two separate sections of a component in which one section overlaps a recessed lip on the other.

**Kevlar** Trade name for *aramid* fibre.

**Laminate** A composite material comprising one or more layers of fabric *reinforcement* impregnated with *resin* and cured; the process of making a laminate.

**Lay-up** The *reinforcement* material and *resin* positioned in a mould; the process of positioning *reinforcement* material and *resin* in a mould; the *laminate*; the geometry of the *laminate* materials.

**Modulus of elasticity** The ratio of stress, or load per unit area, divided by *strain*, or elongation, in a material when it is elastically deformed; also known as *Young's Modulus*.

**Moulding** The process of shaping a *composite* material in or on a mould; the finished moulded component.

**MPa** Mega Pascal, or one million Pascals; see *Pa*.

**Nomex** In the composites context, a trade name for *aramid* paper, used for making a type of *honeycomb core*.

**Non-woven fabric** *Fabric* made by mechanically or chemically binding randomly-laid fibres together.

**Out-life** The length of time for which a *pre-preg* material retains its original properties and remains handleable after being removed from freezer storage.

**Pa** Pascals, or Newtons per square metre, a unit of force per unit area, or pressure; MPa = mega Pascal, or one million Pascals; GPa = giga Pascal, or one million million Pascals.

**Peel ply** A fine woven polyester or nylon *fabric* applied to the back of a *laminate* prior to curing, which leaves a clean, *resin-rich* surface ready for subsequent lamination or bonding operations.

**Plain weave** A weave pattern in which a *fabric* is formed by *warp* and *weft* threads alternating simply, each over the other.

**Polymerisation** A chemical process in which the molecules in a monomer link to form bigger molecules, creating a polymer. The polymer usually has very different physical properties to the monomer.

**Post cure** An elevated temperature process performed after the initial *cure* to complete the cure process, or to improve the physical properties of the cured *laminate*.

**Pot life** The period of time, also known as its 'working life', that a quantity of catalysed *resin* remains in workable liquid form before it *gels*.

**Pre-preg** *Fabric* pre-impregnated with partially-cured *resin*, supplied in a form requiring low temperature storage to inhibit further cure; it is laminated by the *dry lay-up* method, and usually cured at elevated temperature and at least vacuum pressure.

**Precursor** A material from which another is formed by a chemical reaction.

**Pressure moulding** A form of moulding requiring the use of matched male and female moulds, which are pressed together to apply pressure to a *laminate* during *cure*.

**Reinforcement** A fibre, or assemblage of fibres, embedded into and bonded by a cured plastic *resin* matrix, which

greatly enhances the mechanical properties of the matrix.

**Release agent** A chemical that is applied to the surface of a mould prior to laminating to prevent the *resin* in a *laminate* from bonding to the mould.

**Release film** A thin plastic film which is applied to the back of a *laminate* beneath the *breather fabric* prior to *vacuum bag moulding*.

**Resin** The chemical which is used to bind the *reinforcement fabric* together in a *laminate*, which is cured to a solid, plastic matrix by the addition of *catalyst* and/or heat.

**Resin content** The proportion of a *laminate*'s total weight that is *resin*.

**Resin-rich** An area of a *laminate* which is totally *resin*, and devoid of reinforcing fibres.

**Resin-poor** An area of a *laminate* which has insufficient *resin*, often seen as voids or loose fibres.

**Roving** A bundle of filaments or fibres, usually glass, without significant twist.

**S-glass** A form of *glass fibre* with high *tensile strength*.

**Sandwich construction** Materials comprising a *core* sandwiched between two outer skins, often of *fibre reinforced plastic*.

**Satin weave** A *weave* pattern in which a *fabric* is formed by *warp* threads passing over four or more *weft* threads, and vice versa, before looping beneath and then repeating.

**Stiffness** The resistance of a fibre or material to bending when under load; the ratio between stress and deformation.

**Strain** The deformation, or change in dimension, as the result of applied stress or load, expressed as a percentage of the original dimension.

**Tack** The stickiness of a material.

**Tensile modulus** The ratio of the *tensile stress* divided by the *strain* in a material over the range of load for which the value is constant, that is, before plastic deformation occurs.

**Tensile strength or stress** The maximum tensile load per unit area of a material when under test, immediately prior to failure.

**tex** Unit of metric measurement of a glass fibre *yarn* or *roving*, being the weight in grams of 1,000 metres of material.

**Thermoset** A plastic material which cures chemically into a more or less solid state. Examples include polyester and epoxy *resin*.

**Torsional rigidity** Resistance to twisting loads.

**Twill weave** A *weave* pattern in which a *fabric* is formed by one or more *warp* threads passing alternately over and under two or more *weft* threads in a repeating pattern that creates a characteristic straight or broken diagonal 'herringbone' appearance.

**U/D** *Unidirectional fabric.*

**UHM** Ultra-high *modulus*; applied to *carbon fibre* with a *tensile modulus* over 440GPa.

**Undercut** Where a component tapers in such a way that a split mould is necessary in order to release it.

**Unidirectional** A *fabric* in which the large majority of fibres run in only one direction.

**Vacuum bag moulding** A moulding process in which a sealable plastic bag is placed over or around a *laminate* in a mould, and a vacuum is applied to suck the air out of the bag, thus applying approximately one atmosphere of *consolidation* pressure to the *laminate* during *cure*.

**Viscosity** The resistance to flow, or 'stickiness', of a fluid or semi-solid.

**Warp** The *fabric* direction running along the length of a roll; threads running in that direction; distortion or change of dimensions of a cured *laminate* from its original moulded shape.

**Weave** The manner in which *warp* and *weft* threads are interlaced; the process of interlacing threads to make a *fabric*.

**Weft** The *fabric* direction running across the width of a roll; threads running in that direction; also known as 'woof' or 'fill'.

**Wet lay-up** The process in which liquid *resin* is applied to dry *reinforcement fabric* to make a *laminate*.

**Wet out** Process of ensuring that a *fabric* is fully impregnated with *resin*.

**Woven fabric** A *fabric* produced by weaving threads together, usually at right angles.

**Woven roving** A *fabric* produced by weaving *rovings*, usually of *glass fibre*.

**w/w** Weight for weight.

**Yarn** A bundle of twisted fibres or strands spun into a continuous length for weaving into a *fabric*.

**Young's Modulus** See *modulus of elasticity*.

# Index